Clive Oxenden

Christina Lath… …enig

…son

New ENGLISH FILE

Pre-intermediate
Student's Book

Paul Seligson and Clive Oxenden are the original co-authors of *English File 1* (pub. 1996) and *English File 2* (pub. 1997).

Contents

		Grammar	Vocabulary	Pronunciation
1				
4	**A Who's who?**	word order in questions	common verb phrases, classroom language	vowel sounds, the alphabet
6	**B Who knows you better?**	present simple	family, personality adjectives	third person and plural *-s*
8	**C At the Moulin Rouge**	present continuous	the body, prepositions of place	vowel sounds
10	**D The Devil's Dictionary**	defining relative clauses (*a person who…, a thing which…*)	expressions for paraphrasing: *like*, *for example*, etc.	pronunciation in a dictionary
12	**PRACTICAL ENGLISH**	At the airport		
13	**WRITING**	Describing yourself		
14	**REVISE & CHECK**	What do you remember? What can you do?		
2				
16	**A Right place, wrong time**	past simple regular and irregular verbs	holidays	*-ed* endings, irregular verbs
18	**B A moment in time**	past continuous	prepositions of time and place: *at, in, on*	/ə/
20	**C Fifty years of pop**	questions with and without auxiliaries	question words, pop music	/w/ and /h/
22	**D One October evening**	*so, because, but, although*	verb phrases	the letter *a*
24	**PRACTICAL ENGLISH**	At the conference hotel		
25	**WRITING**	The story behind a photo		
26	**REVISE & CHECK**	What do you remember? What can you do?		
3				
28	**A Where are you going?**	*going to*, present continuous (future arrangements)	*look* (*after*, *for*, etc.)	sentence stress
30	**B The pessimist's phrase book**	*will / won't* (predictions)	opposite verbs	contractions (*will / won't*), /ɒ/ and /əʊ/
32	**C I'll always love you**	*will / won't* (promises, offers, decisions)	verb + *back*	word stress: two-syllable words
34	**D I was only dreaming**	review of tenses: present, past, and future	verbs + prepositions	sentence stress
36	**PRACTICAL ENGLISH**	Restaurant problems		
37	**WRITING**	An informal letter		
38	**REVISE & CHECK**	What do you remember? What can you do?		
4				
40	**A From rags to riches**	present perfect (experience) + *ever*, *never*; present perfect or past simple?	clothes	vowel sounds
42	**B Family conflicts**	present perfect simple + *yet, just, already*	verb phrases	/h/, /j/, and /dʒ/
44	**C Faster, faster!**	comparatives, *as…as / less…than…*	time expressions: *spend time*, *waste time*, etc	sentence stress
46	**D The world's friendliest city**	superlatives (+ *ever* + present perfect)	opposite adjectives	word stress
48	**PRACTICAL ENGLISH**	Lost in San Francisco		
49	**WRITING**	Describing where you live		
50	**REVISE & CHECK**	What do you remember? What can you do?		
5				
52	**A Are you a party animal?**	uses of the infinitive (with *to*)	verbs + infinitive	word stress
54	**B What makes you feel good?**	verb + *-ing*	verbs followed by *-ing*	*-ing*
56	**C How much can you learn in a month?**	*have to, don't have to, must, mustn't*	modifiers: *a bit*, *really*, etc.	sentence stress
58	**D The name of the game**	expressing movement	prepositions of movement, sport	prepositions
60	**PRACTICAL ENGLISH**	At a department store		
61	**WRITING**	A formal e-mail		
62	**REVISE & CHECK**	What do you remember? What can you do?		

		Grammar	Vocabulary	Pronunciation
6				
64	**A If something bad can happen, it will**	*if* + present; *will* + infinitive (first conditional)	confusing verbs	long and short vowels
66	**B Never smile at a crocodile**	*if* + past; *would* + infinitive (second conditional)	animals	stress and rhythm
68	**C Decisions, decisions**	*may* / *might* (possibility)	word building: noun formation	sentence stress, *-ion* endings
70	**D What should I do?**	*should* / *shouldn't*	*get*	/ʊ/, sentence stress
72	**PRACTICAL ENGLISH** At the pharmacy			
73	**WRITING** Writing to a friend			
74	**REVISE & CHECK** What do you remember? What can you do?			
7				
76	**A Famous fears and phobias**	present perfect + *for* and *since*	words related to fear	/ɪ/, and /aɪ/, sentence stress
78	**B Born to direct**	present perfect or past simple?	biographies	word stress
80	**C I used to be a rebel**	*used to*	school subjects: *history*, *geography*, etc.	sentence stress; *used to* / *didn't use to*
82	**D The mothers of invention**	passive	verbs: *invent*, *discover*, etc.	*-ed*, sentence stress
84	**PRACTICAL ENGLISH** A boat trip			
85	**WRITING** Describing a building			
86	**REVISE & CHECK** What do you remember? What can you do?			
8				
88	**A I hate weekends!**	*something*, *anything*, *nothing*, etc.	adjectives ending in *-ed* and *-ing*	/e/, /əʊ/ , and /ʌ/
90	**B How old is your body?**	quantifiers, *too*, *not enough*,	health and lifestyle	/ʌ/, /uː/, /aɪ/, /e/; linking
92	**C Waking up is hard to do**	word order of phrasal verbs	phrasal verbs	/g/ and /dʒ/
94	**D 'I'm Jim.' 'So am I.'**	*so* / *neither* + auxiliaries	similarities	vowel and consonant sounds, sentence stress
96	**PRACTICAL ENGLISH** On the phone			
97	**WRITING** Giving your opinion			
98	**REVISE & CHECK** What do you remember? What can you do?			
9				
100	**A What a week!**	past perfect	adverbs: *suddenly*, *immediately*, etc.	revision of vowel sounds, sentence stress
102	**B Then he kissed me**	reported speech	*say*, *tell*, or *ask*?	rhyming verbs
104	**Grammar** Quick grammar check for each File			
106	**Vocabulary, Pronunciation** Quick check of vocabulary, sounds, and word stress			

108 **Communication**
118 **Listening**
126 **Grammar Bank**
144 **Vocabulary Bank**
156 **Sound Bank**

Look out for Study Link
This shows you where to find extra material for more practice and revision.

G word order in questions
V common verb phrases, classroom language
P vowel sounds, the alphabet

What do you do? Where do you live?

Who's who?

1 INTRODUCING YOURSELF

a Introduce yourself to all the other students. Try to remember their names.

Hello. I'm ___ .

Hi. I'm ___ . Nice to meet you.

b Can you remember? Does anybody in the class have…?

- a very long name
- a very short name
- a name that's difficult to spell
- an unusual name
- the same name as a famous person from your country
- a very traditional name
- the same name as another student

2 GETTING TO KNOW EACH OTHER

a Complete the groups of questions 1–5 below with a verb.

b 1.1 Listen and repeat the FREE TIME questions. Copy the rhythm.

c In pairs, ask and answer the questions.
Can you find two things you have in common?

We live in the city centre and we do yoga.

1 HOME AND FAMILY

Where ___ you from?
Where do you ___ ?
Do you ___ any brothers and sisters?

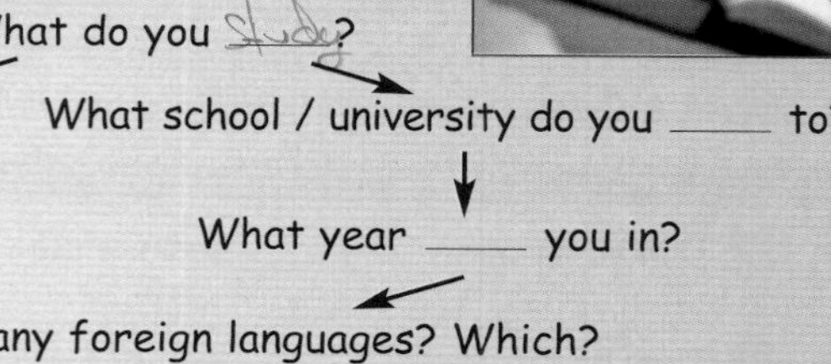

2 JOB / STUDIES

What do you ___ ?
Where do you ___ ?
Do you ___ your job?
What school / university do you ___ to?
What year ___ you in?
Do you ___ any foreign languages? Which?

3 FREE TIME

What kind of music do you ___ to?
Do you ___ a musical instrument? Which?
Do you ___ TV? What programmes?
Do you ___ any sport or exercise? What?
What books or magazines do you ___ ?

4 THE FUTURE

Where are you going to ___ after the class?
What are you going to ___ this weekend?

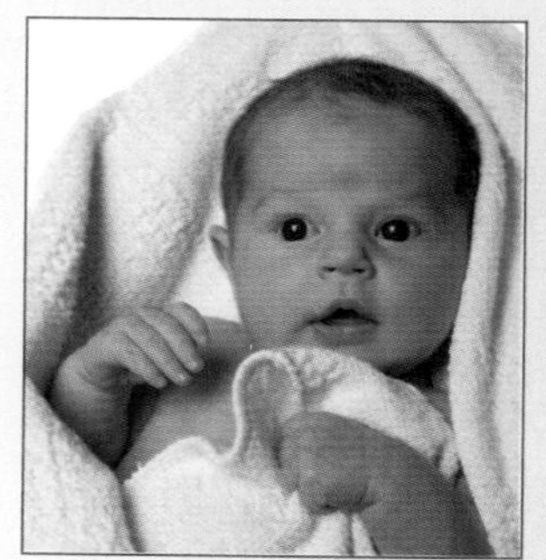

5 THE PAST

Where ___ you born?
Where did you ___ English before?
What did you ___ last summer?

3 GRAMMAR word order in questions

a Can you remember the questions? Re-order the words.

1 from are you where? where are you from
2 watch you do TV? what do you wacth TV?
3 to music you what kind of listen do?
4 English where you before did study?
5 are do what you weekend going this to?

b p.126 Grammar Bank 1A. Read the rules and do the exercises.

4 LISTENING & SPEAKING

a 1.2 Listen and choose a or b.

Days of the week

1 What day of the week is the exam?
a Tuesday **b** Thursday

2 What day is it today?
a Sunday **b** Monday

Telling the time

3 What's the time?
a 8.35 **b** 9.25

4 What time does the class start?
a 9.45 **b** 10.15

The date

5 When was the woman born?
a 21st August **b** 23rd August

6 What day does he want tickets for?
a 5th June **b** 5th July

Numbers

7 What number is the house?
a 117 **b** 170

8 How much are the flowers?
a €15 **b** €50

b In pairs, ask and answer the questions.

What day is it today?
What days do you have your English class?
What time does the class start and finish?
What's the time now?
When's your birthday?
What's the date today?
What's the number of your house or flat?

5 CLASSROOM LANGUAGE

a Complete the teacher's and student's phrases.

b p.144 Vocabulary Bank *Classroom language*.

6 PRONUNCIATION vowel sounds, the alphabet

a How do you pronounce the letters of the alphabet below? Use the sound pictures to help you.

b Complete the alphabet chart with these letters.

c Practise saying the letters of the alphabet.

d Listen to your teacher. Write the words.

e Play *What does it mean?*

1 B

G present simple
V family, personality adjectives
P third person and plural -*s*

He likes films.
He doesn't smoke.

Who knows you better?

1 VOCABULARY family and adjectives

a Can you remember these words? Do the puzzle in pairs.

1 The opposite of thin or slim is ...
2 Your brother's wife is your ...
3 Your sister's daughter is your ...
4 Your mother's brother is your ...
5 Your aunt's children are your ...
6 The opposite of fair is ...
7 The opposite of short is ...
8 Your brothers, sisters, cousins, etc. are your ...

b What's the 'mystery word'?

c p.145 Vocabulary Bank *Adjectives*. Do part 1.

2 READING

a Who do you think knows you better, your family or your friends? Why?

b Read the introduction to the article.

1 Who is Richard?
2 Who is Danny?
3 What do Richard's mum and Danny try to do?
4 What does Richard have to do?

c Now read what Richard says. Mark the sentences T (true) or F (false). Correct the false ones.

1 He sometimes travels with his job. *T*
2 He's friendly and extrovert.
3 He likes music and parties.
4 He prefers women who are shorter than him.
5 He likes women who talk a lot.
6 He doesn't talk to his family about girls.
7 His mother doesn't think he's good at choosing girlfriends.

d Guess the meaning of the highlighted words or phrases.

Who knows you better, your family or your friends?

In our weekly 'test' single people who are looking for a partner ask their mother and their best friend to help. Their mother chooses one partner and their best friend chooses another. The test is to see who can choose the best partner!

This week's single man is Richard Taylor, a 26-year-old musician from Southampton. His mother Meg chooses one girl, and his best friend Danny chooses another. Then Richard goes on a date with each girl. Which girl does he prefer? Who knows him better, his mother or his best friend? Who chooses the right girl for him?

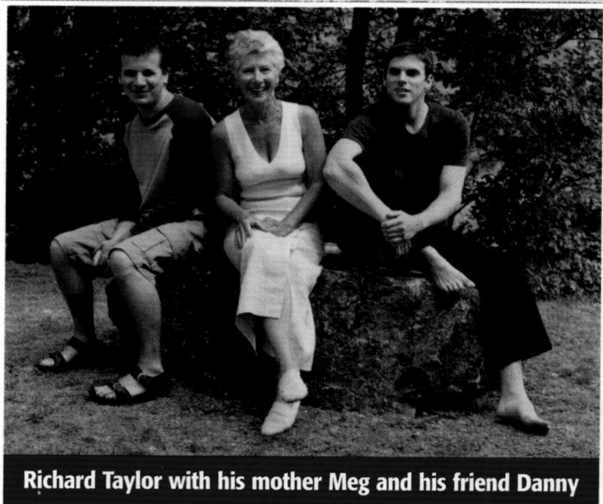

Richard Taylor with his mother Meg and his friend Danny

'I usually work in England but sometimes I work abroad too. When I'm not working I like going to the cinema and eating in nice restaurants. I'm not very sporty and I don't do any exercise, but at least I don't smoke.

I think I'm open and friendly – I get on well with most people – but I'm sometimes quite shy too. For example, I don't like going to parties. I prefer to meet friends individually or in small groups.

I like intelligent, funny women who make me laugh, and ideally who love music. Physically I prefer women with dark hair who are not taller than me. And I like women who are good listeners.

I'm sure that my friend Danny knows me better than my family because we often talk about girlfriends and the problems we have. I don't usually talk to my family about that kind of thing. My mum always says that I look for the wrong kind of girl but that's what mothers always say!'

3 GRAMMAR present simple

a Complete the questions about Richard.

Where *does he live* ?
In Southampton.

1 What ______________ do?
He's a musician.

2 Where ______________?
In England and abroad.

3 ______________ smoke?
No, he doesn't.

4 ______________ exercise?
No, he doesn't. He isn't very sporty.

5 What kind of women ______________?
Intelligent and funny ones.

6 ______________ to his mother about girls?
No, he doesn't.

b **p.126 Grammar Bank 1B.** Read the rules and do the exercises.

c Cover the text. In pairs, try to remember five things about Richard.

He lives in Southampton.

d Look at the photos of Claire and Nina.

HIS FRIEND'S CHOICE
Claire

HIS MOTHER'S CHOICE
Nina

Communication *Claire and Nina A p.108 B p.112.*
Who do you think is more Richard's type? Why?

4 LISTENING

a Listen to Richard talking about what happened when he met Claire and Nina. Does he like them? What are the problems?

1.3 **Claire** 1.4 **Nina**

b Now listen again and write down any adjectives or expressions that Richard uses to describe Claire and Nina.

Claire *Very friendly* **Nina** *Very attractive*

c Who knows Richard better, his mum or Danny? Are you surprised?

5 PRONUNCIATION -s

a 1.5 Listen and repeat.

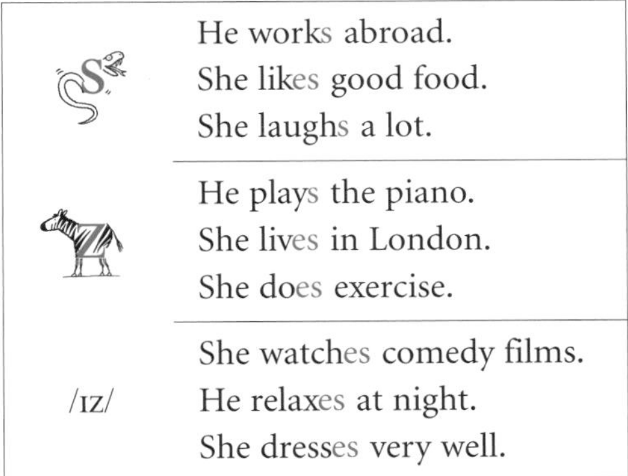

s	He works abroad. She likes good food. She laughs a lot.
z	He plays the piano. She lives in London. She does exercise.
/ɪz/	She watches comedy films. He relaxes at night. She dresses very well.

b How do you say the *he / she / it* form of these verbs?

choose cook go know stop teach

c How do you say the plural of these nouns?

book friend girl language niece parent party

d 1.6 Listen and repeat the verbs and nouns.

6 SPEAKING

a Work in pairs, A and B. Think of a person you know well, a family member or a friend, who is single. You are going to tell your partner about him / her. Look at the chart below and prepare what you are going to say.

- **NAME?**
- **AGE?**
- **JOB/STUDIES?**
- **LIVES IN?**
- **PHYSICAL APPEARANCE?**
- **PERSONALITY?**
- **SMOKES?**
- **LIKES?**
- **DOESN'T LIKE?**

b A describe your person to B.
B listen and ask for more information. Do you know anybody who would be a good partner for this person? Then swap roles.

1 C

G present continuous
V the body, prepositions of place
P vowel sounds

At the Moulin Rouge

The woman on the right is wearing a hat.

1 VOCABULARY the body

Portrait of Dora Maar **(1937) Pablo Picasso**

a Look at this painting. Do you like it? Why (not)?

b Label the woman's face with words from the box.

ear eyes hair lips mouth neck nose

c ➔ **p.146 Vocabulary Bank** *The body*.

d In pairs, how many words can you remember in two minutes?

2 PRONUNCIATION vowel sounds

a Look at the sound pictures. What are the words and sounds?

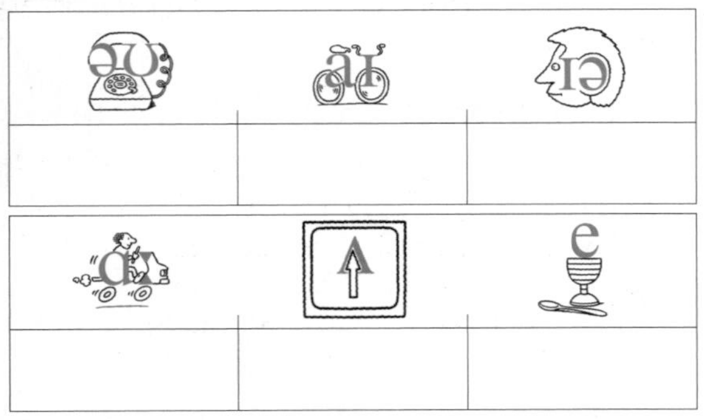

b 1.7 Put the words in the correct columns. Listen and check.

arms bite ears eyes head hear heart nose shoulders smell stomach touch

c ➔ **p.157 Sound Bank.** Look at the typical spellings for these sounds.

3 GRAMMAR present continuous

a Look at the painting *At the Moulin Rouge*. In pairs, ask and answer the questions.

1 What clothes are the people wearing?
2 What are the people at the table doing?
3 What are the two women at the back doing?
4 What are the two men at the back doing?
5 Describe the woman on the right. What do you think she's doing?
6 One of the people in the painting is the artist, Toulouse-Lautrec. Which person do you think he is?

I think the artist is the tall man who is sitting between the two women.

b Underline the correct form of the verb.

1 In the picture the men **wear / are wearing** hats.
2 In Britain women often **wear / are wearing** hats at weddings.
3 Karina usually **sits / is sitting** at the front of the class.
4 Today she **sits / is sitting** at the back.

c ➔ **p.126 Grammar Bank 1C.** Read the rules and do the exercises.

4 LISTENING

a 1.8 Listen to a guide in an art gallery talking about *At the Moulin Rouge*. Answer the questions.

1 What was the Moulin Rouge famous for?
2 Who did Toulouse-Lautrec include in his paintings and posters?
3 Which person is Toulouse-Lautrec?
4 Why do some people think he liked painting the dancers?

b Listen again. Write the numbers of the people next to their names.

Toulouse-Lautrec ☐
His cousin Gabriel ☐
His friend, a photographer ☐
Jane Avril, a dancer ☐
La Macarona, a dancer ☐
La Goulue, a singer ☐

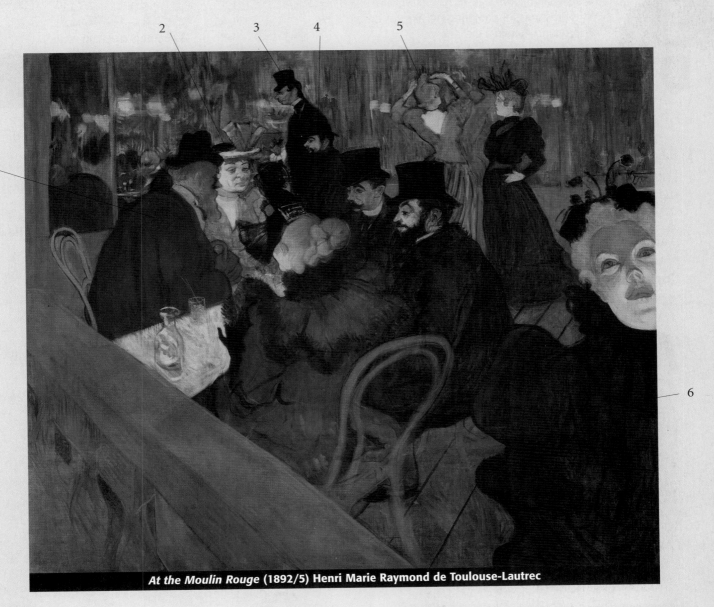

At the Moulin Rouge **(1892/5) Henri Marie Raymond de Toulouse-Lautrec**

5 SPEAKING

a Match the prepositions with the pictures.

behind between in in front of in the middle next to
on on the left on the right opposite under

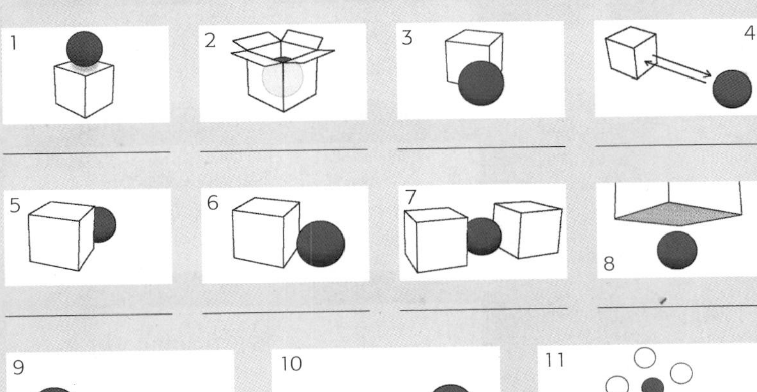

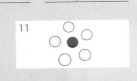

b **Communication** *Describe and draw A p.108 B p.112.* Describe your picture for your partner to draw.

c In small groups, ask and answer the questions.

1 Do you paint or draw? What kind of things?
2 Do you have a favourite painter? Who?
3 Do you have a favourite painting? What? Can you describe it?
4 What pictures or posters do you have on the wall in your bedroom or living room?

d Look again at the paintings in this lesson (here and on p.108 and p.112). Which one would you choose to have in your house or flat?

6 1.9 SONG ♫ *Ain't got no – I got life*

G defining relative clauses (*a person who…*, *a thing which…*)
V expressions for paraphrasing: *like*, *for example*, etc.
P pronunciation in a dictionary

The Devil's Dictionary

A dentist is a person who looks after your teeth.

1 READING

a Look at the dictionary definition. What do you think the missing word is?

_______ is a person who puts metal in your mouth and takes coins out of your pocket.

b Read the text once. Where is the definition from?

A *different* kind of dictionary

Ambrose Bierce was a 19th-century American author and journalist. His most popular book is probably the *Devil's Dictionary*, written between 1881 and 1887. Bierce's dictionary does not contain normal definitions – his definitions are funny and cynical. For example,

in a normal dictionary, the definition of dentist is 'a kind of doctor who looks after people's teeth'. But in the *Devil's Dictionary*, the definition of a dentist is 'a person who puts metal in your mouth and takes coins out of your pocket'. Today on the Internet you can find many websites with more modern versions of the *Devil's Dictionary*.

c Read the text again and answer the questions.

1 Who was Ambrose Bierce?
2 What is the normal definition of 'dentist'?
3 Where can you find modern versions of the *Devil's Dictionary*?

d In pairs, think of **normal** definitions for these words or phrases.

a bank   a boring person   the brain   a star   a friend   a secret

e Now match the words / phrases in **d** to these **cynical** definitions.

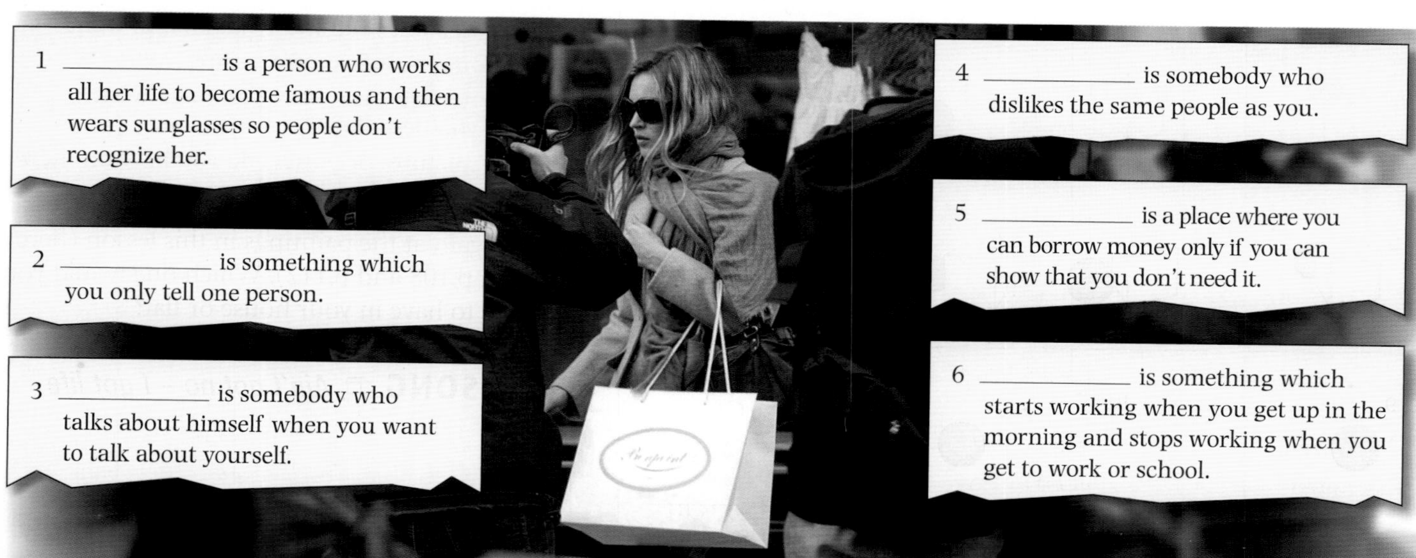

1 _____________ is a person who works all her life to become famous and then wears sunglasses so people don't recognize her.

2 _____________ is something which you only tell one person.

3 _____________ is somebody who talks about himself when you want to talk about yourself.

4 _____________ is somebody who dislikes the same people as you.

5 _____________ is a place where you can borrow money only if you can show that you don't need it.

6 _____________ is something which starts working when you get up in the morning and stops working when you get to work or school.

2 GRAMMAR defining relative clauses

a Read the definitions in **1e** again. When do we use *who*, *which*, and *where*?

b ➲ **p.126 Grammar Bank 1D.** Read the rules and do the exercises.

c Tell a partner about **three** of the things below. Say why.

- a person who is very important to you
- a famous person who you like a lot
- something which you couldn't live without
- a thing which you often lose
- a place where you'd like to go for a special evening
- a place where you were very happy when you were a child

3 LISTENING

a 1.10 Listen to the introduction to a TV game show, *What's the word?* How do you play the game?

b 1.11 Now listen to the show. Write down the six answers.

1 ________ 4 ________
2 ________ 5 ________
3 ________ 6 ________

c 1.12 Listen and check your answers.

4 VOCABULARY paraphrasing

a What's the best thing to do if you're talking to someone in English and you don't know a word that you need?

a Panic and stop talking.
b Try to mime the word.
c Try to explain what you mean using other words you know.

b 1.13 Complete the **useful expressions** with these words. Then listen and check.

example how kind like opposite person place similar somebody thing

Useful expressions
explaining a word that you don't know

1 It's ________ who works in a restaurant.
2 It's the ________ who takes the food from the kitchen to the tables.
3 It's a ________ where you go when you want to buy something.
4 It's a ________ which you use to talk.
5 It's a ________ of machine.
6 It's the ________ of fat.
7 It's ________ thin, but it means thin and attractive.
8 It's ________ to worried.
9 It's ________ you feel when you have a lot of things to do.
10 For ________, you do this with the TV.

c Complete the definitions for these words.

1 **a tourist** *It's somebody…*
2 **a sports centre** *It's a place…*
3 **a key** *It's a thing…*
4 **worried** *It's how you feel…*
5 **laugh** *You do this …*

5 SPEAKING

a Look at part of a crossword. Ask your teacher for a definition of **1 across** and **2 down**.

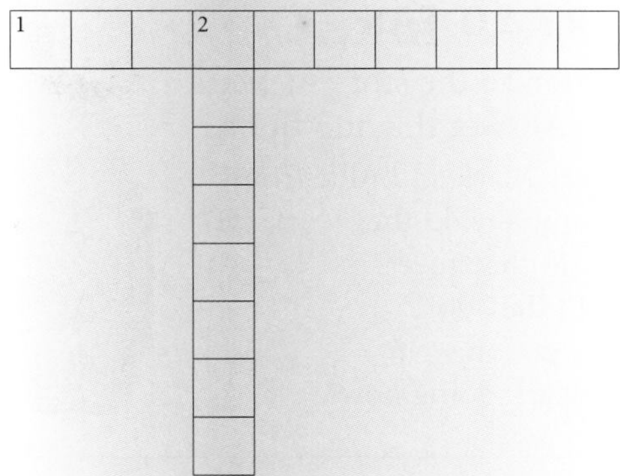

b **Communication** *Crossword A p.108 B p.112.* Give each other definitions to complete the missing words in the crossword.

6 PRONUNCIATION using a dictionary

a Look at the two dictionary extracts. How do you pronounce the words?

busy /ˈbɪzi/ adj *occupé*
guitar /gɪˈtɑː/ n a musical instrument with strings

The apostrophe(') shows stress. The stressed syllable is the one after the apostrophe.

b Look carefully at the pronunciation of the words below. Practise saying them correctly.

laugh /lɑːf/ **eyes** /aɪz/ **example** /ɪgˈzaːmpl/
keys /kiːz/ **kind** /kaɪnd/ **eighteen** /eɪˈtiːn/

The **Sound Bank** on p.156 can help you use your dictionary better.

THE STORY SO FAR

1.14 Listen to the story of Mark and Allie. Answer the questions.

1 Where are Mark and Allie from?
2 What company do they work for?
3 Where did they meet?
4 What did they do?
5 Did they get on well?
6 What's Mark doing now?

AT IMMIGRATION

a 1.15 Cover the dialogue and listen. How long is Allie going to stay in the United States?

YOU HEAR	YOU SAY
Good evening, *ma'am*.	Good evening.
_______ are you arriving from?	From London.
_______ the purpose of your visit?	Business. I'm here for a conference.
_______ long are you staying in the US?	A week.
_______ are you staying?	In San Francisco. At the Pacific View Hotel.
_______ you know anybody here?	Yes, Mark Ryder.
_______ he family or a friend?	He's a colleague – and a friend.
_______ you have his phone number?	Yes, his mobile is 405 655 7182.
_______ this your first visit to the US?	Yes, it is.
Enjoy your stay in San Francisco.	Thank you.

b Listen again. Complete the YOU HEAR phrases.

c 1.16 Listen and repeat the YOU SAY phrases. Copy the rhythm.

d In pairs, roleplay the dialogue. **A** (book open) you're the immigration officer, **B** (book closed) you're Allie. Swap roles.

SOCIAL ENGLISH Allie arrives

a 1.17 Listen. Answer the questions.

1 How long was Allie's flight?
2 Why couldn't she sleep?
3 What time is it…?
   a in San Francisco b in London
4 Where is Mark going to take her?
5 Where's Mark's car?

b Complete the USEFUL PHRASES. Listen again and check.

c 1.18 Listen and repeat the phrases. How do you say them in your language?

USEFUL PHRASES

M You look g_______!
M How was the f_______?
M You must be really t_______.
M I'm so p_______ you came!
A It's great to see you a_______.

US English	*parking lot*
UK English	*car park*

Describing yourself

a Read the e-mail. The computer has found ten mistakes. They are either grammar, punctuation, or spelling. Can you correct them?

From: Alessandra [alessandra@andes.com.ar]
To: Daniel [dani2199@yahoo.com]
Subject: Hi from Argentina

Hi Daniel,

My name's Alessandra. It's an italian name, because my grandmother was from Italy, but I'm Argentinian and I live in Mendoza, a big city in the west of the country. I live with my parents and my two brothers. I have 19 years old, and I'm at university. I'm studing computer science. I'm in my first year and I really like it.

I'm going to tell you about myself. As you can see from the foto, I have long hair – it's quite fair – and greens eyes. I wear glasses, but I want to get contact lenses soon.

I think I'm a positive person. I'm quite extrovert and frendly. My mother says I'm very talkative – I think she mean that I talk too much!

In my free time I love reading and going to the cinema. But I dont have much free time becuase I have classes every day, and a lot of work to do even at weekends. I also go to English classes on friday afternoon.

Please write soon and tell me about you and your life.

Best wishes

Alessandra

b Read the e-mail again from the beginning. Then cover it and answer the questions from memory.

1 Where's Alessandra from?
2 Why does she have an Italian name?
3 Where does she live?
4 Who does she live with?
5 What does she do?
6 What colour are her eyes?
7 Is she shy?
8 What are her favourite free time activities?
9 When does she go to English classes?

WRITE a similar e-mail about you. Write four paragraphs.

Paragraph 1 name, nationality, age, family, work / study
Paragraph 2 physical appearance
Paragraph 3 personality
Paragraph 4 hobbies and interests

CHECK the e-mail for mistakes (grammar , punctuation , and spelling).

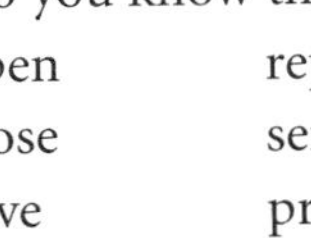

ⓘ
Do you know these 'e-mail' verbs?

open	reply
close	send
save	print
delete	

1 What do you remember?

GRAMMAR

Circle the correct answer, a, b, or c.

What's _____ name?

a yours (b) your c you

1 **A** What _____?
B I'm a student.
a you do
b do you do
c do you work

2 Where _____ from?
a your parents are
b is your parents
c are your parents

3 _____ David smoke?
a Does
b Is
c Do

4 Liz _____ at a primary school.
a teach
b teachs
c teaches

5 Sonia _____ a job.
a hasn't
b doesn't have
c don't have

6 _____ a picture in your bedroom?
a Is there
b Is it
c There is

7 The girl in the painting _____ a blue dress.
a wears
b wearing
c is wearing

8 You don't need an umbrella. It _____.
a isn't raining
b doesn't rain
c not raining

9 She's the woman _____ works in the office.
a what
b which
c who

10 I need a Workbook _____ has all the answers.
a what
b which
c who

10

VOCABULARY

a classroom language

Complete the sentences with one word.

Sit *down* and open your books.

1 _____ do you say 'coche' in English?
2 What does 'abroad' _____?
3 Go _____ page 78, please.
4 See you _____ Monday!
5 _____ a good weekend.

b word groups

Underline the word that is different.

third	seventh	eighteen	twentieth
1 uncle	grandfather	niece	husband
2 shy	tall	dark	slim
3 mean	unfriendly	lazy	generous
4 arms	ears	eyes	fingers
5 mouth	fair	head	nose

c definitions

Read the definitions. Write the word.

It's the place where you sleep. *bed*
1 It's the opposite of *lazy*. _____
2 It's a place where you can buy stamps. _____
3 It's a person who plays a musical instrument. _____
4 It's a verb. You do it when you're thirsty. _____
5 It's a kind of food, for example macaroni. _____

15

PRONUNCIATION

a Underline the letter or word with a different sound.

1	iː	B	E	J	T
2	ɔː	abroad	walk	board	work
3	ɜː	person	word	third	heart
4	eə	hair	parents	hear	there
5	aɪ	give	shy	quiet	eyes

b Underline the stressed syllable.

infor*ma*tion

address university extrovert stomach example

10

CAN YOU UNDERSTAND THIS TEXT?

a Read the article and match the headings with paragraphs A–D.

Space invaders ☐
Small children ☐
Conversation makers ☐
Nervous fliers ☐

b Tick (✓) the things the writer says.

1 You can't sleep if there are children next to you.
2 Children eat all your food.
3 Some people want to talk all through the flight.
4 'Space invaders' have long arms and legs.
5 Nervous fliers have a drink every five minutes.

c What do the highlighted words mean? Circle a or b.

1 a letting (toys) fall from your hand
  b putting (toys) somewhere
2 a say hello to
  b know and understand
3 a goes into the air
  b touches the ground
4 a try to do something
  b give the impression of doing something
5 a space
  b seat

Not next to me, please!

When you're travelling by plane or train, there are some passengers you just don't want to have next to you...

A ________

Perhaps you normally like them, but when you are sitting next to them on a plane it's a different thing. They usually spend all the flight moving around and [1] dropping their toys on the floor, and when they're drinking their orange juice it ends up on your trousers. Then they decide they want to play with you, so you can't have the little siesta that you were planning.

B ________

You [2] recognize this type as soon as you sit down. They immediately start talking about the plane, or the weather, or they ask you a personal question. It's very difficult not to talk to these people, and you'll probably have to continue talking until the plane [3] lands.

C ________

These are the people with white faces who sit down and immediately ask for a double whisky. Every five minutes they call a flight attendant to ask if there are any problems with the plane. They also tell you about air disasters (which you are not interested in!). The best thing to do is to buy them a few drinks or [4] pretend to sleep.

D ________

These people are not necessarily very big, but they have a terrible habit of taking up all their [5] room, and some of your room too. They usually sit so that you can't move, with their arms and legs in your space. They also have a lot of hand luggage which takes up all the room in the overhead locker.

Adapted from a travel website

CAN YOU UNDERSTAND THESE PEOPLE?

a 1.19 Listen to five short conversations. Circle the correct answer, a, b, or c.

1 Her party is on ________.
  a Wednesday the 6th b Saturday the 9th c Friday the 8th
2 How old is his mother?
  a 59 b 50 c 60
3 Mr Jarvis has a problem in ________.
  a his left leg b his right knee c his left knee
4 John doesn't like the painting of ________.
  a the woman b the boy c the guitar
5 The girl wants to buy ________.
  a a computer b a digital camera c a USB cable

b 1.20 Listen to Martha showing Jim some photos. Complete the sentences with a name.

Martin Alice Bill Serena Gary

1 ______ is at university.
2 ______ doesn't live in Britain.
3 ______ wears glasses.
4 ______ doesn't like sport.
5 ______ isn't very hard-working.

CAN YOU SAY THIS IN ENGLISH?

a Can you...? Yes (✓)

☐ give personal information about yourself
☐ talk about a person in your family
☐ describe a picture you have in your house
☐ give definitions for these words

journalist hospital guidebook aeroplane

b Complete the questions with *is*, *are*, *do*, or *does*.

1 What kind of books ______ you read?
2 ______ there an art gallery in your town? Where?
3 What ______ your friends usually do at weekends?
4 ______ your town have a local festival? When?
5 What do you think your parents ______ doing at the moment?

c Ask your partner the questions in **b**. Ask for more information.

G past simple regular and irregular verbs
V holidays
P *-ed* endings, irregular verbs

When did you go there?
I went when I was 17.

Right place, wrong time

1 VOCABULARY holidays

a In one minute, write down five things you like doing when you're on holiday.

b p.147 Vocabulary Bank *Holidays*.

The Holiday Magazine

In the **right** place... but at the **wrong** time!

Last week we asked you to tell us about a holiday when the destination was perfect but, for some reason, the time wasn't right... Here are some of your replies.

1 Tim, 20, student from Manchester

When I was a teenager I went on holiday with my parents to Brittany in France. My parents rented a lovely house on the beach, and the weather was great. But I was 17, and I didn't want to be on holiday with my mum and dad and my little brother. I wanted to be with my friends. We went to the beach every day and sunbathed and we went to a fantastic seafood restaurant for my birthday. But I was miserable and I hated every minute of it. I didn't smile once in two weeks. What really made me furious was that my parents let my older sister, who was 19, go to Spain with her friends.

2 Gabriela, 28, marketing manager from Rome

I'm from Rome and the summer here is really hot. So last year my husband and I decided to go to Sweden, to escape from the heat. We booked a 10-day holiday in Stockholm, where the temperature in the summer is normally about 20 degrees. But when we got to Stockholm there was a heatwave and it was 35 degrees every day. It was awful because there was no air-conditioning anywhere. We couldn't sleep at night – it was boiling in the hotel, and in the shops and museums too. We didn't want to go shopping or go sightseeing or do anything – we were too hot. We just sat in cafés and argued all day. We didn't need to go to Sweden to do that!

3 Kelly, 26, TV journalist from Belfast

Three years ago I broke up with my boyfriend and I decided to go on holiday on my own to the Seychelles. My travel agent told me that it was a wonderful place. But he didn't tell me that it was also a very popular place for people on their honeymoon. Everywhere I looked I saw couples holding hands and looking romantically into each other's eyes! The travel agent also said it was always sunny there – but the weather was terrible – it was cloudy and very windy. To pass the time I decided to do a diving course (one of my lifetime ambitions). But it was a complete disaster because the first time I went under the water I had a panic attack. I couldn't escape from the island so I spent an incredibly boring (and expensive) two weeks in 'paradise'.

2 READING

a Read the three letters to **The Holiday Magazine** and match them with the photos.

b Complete the sentences with Tim, Gabriela, or Kelly.

1 ______ wanted to go somewhere hot.
2 ______ wanted to go somewhere cool.
3 ______ had great food.
4 ______ wanted to forget somebody.
5 ______ had problems sleeping.
6 ______ wanted to go on holiday with different people.

c Find four adjectives in the article that mean *very good* and two that mean *very bad*. Underline the stressed syllable.

lovely (text 1)

3 GRAMMAR past simple regular and irregular

a What's the past simple of these verbs? Are they regular or irregular? Check your answers with text 1.

be ______ go ______ rent ______
want ______ sunbathe ______ make ______ let ______

b Now underline the other [+] past simple verbs in texts 2 and 3. What are the infinitives?

c Underline two negative past simple verbs in the magazine article. How do you make negatives and questions in the past simple...?

- with normal verbs
- with *was* / *were*
- with *could*

d **p.128 Grammar Bank 2A.** Read the rules and do the exercises.

4 PRONUNCIATION regular and irregular verbs

> Remember! There are three possible pronunciations of regular *-ed* verbs.

a 2.1 Listen and repeat the sentences. When do you pronounce the *e* in *-ed*?

t	d	/ɪd/
We booked a holiday. We walked to the hotel.	We sunbathed. We argued all day.	They rented a house. We decided to go to Sweden.

b How do you pronounce the past simple of these verbs?

ask hate need smile stay talk

c 2.2 Listen and check.

d Circle the irregular verb with the different vowel sound.

1 bought saw told caught
2 put spoke took could
3 paid said made came

5 LISTENING

a 2.3 Listen to the story about Sean's uncle and aunt. Why was the holiday a disaster?

1 Because the weather was awful.
2 Because the place was very noisy.
3 Because they argued a lot.

b Listen again. Correct the wrong information.

1 Sean went to Ibiza.
His aunt and uncle went to Ibiza.
2 They're about sixty.
3 They wanted an exciting holiday.
4 They usually spend their holidays abroad.
5 They knew it was 'The Party Island'.
6 They first went there in the 1950s.
7 They booked the holiday at a travel agent's.
8 The hotel was in a quiet part of town.
9 They're going to go abroad again next year.

6 SPEAKING

a Think about your answers to these questions.

Your last holiday

Where / go? When?
Who / go with?
How / get there?
Where / stay?
How long / be / there?
/ have good weather?
What / do during the day?
What / do at night?
/ have a good time?
/ have any problems?

b Work in pairs.

Ask a partner about his / her holiday.
Listen and ask for more information.

c Swap roles.

2B A moment in time

G past continuous
V prepositions of time and place: *at*, *in*, *on*
P /ə/

What was happening when he took the photo?

1 GRAMMAR past continuous

a Look at the photos. Where are they? What do you think is happening?

b Read the text and match paragraphs 1–3 with the photographs.

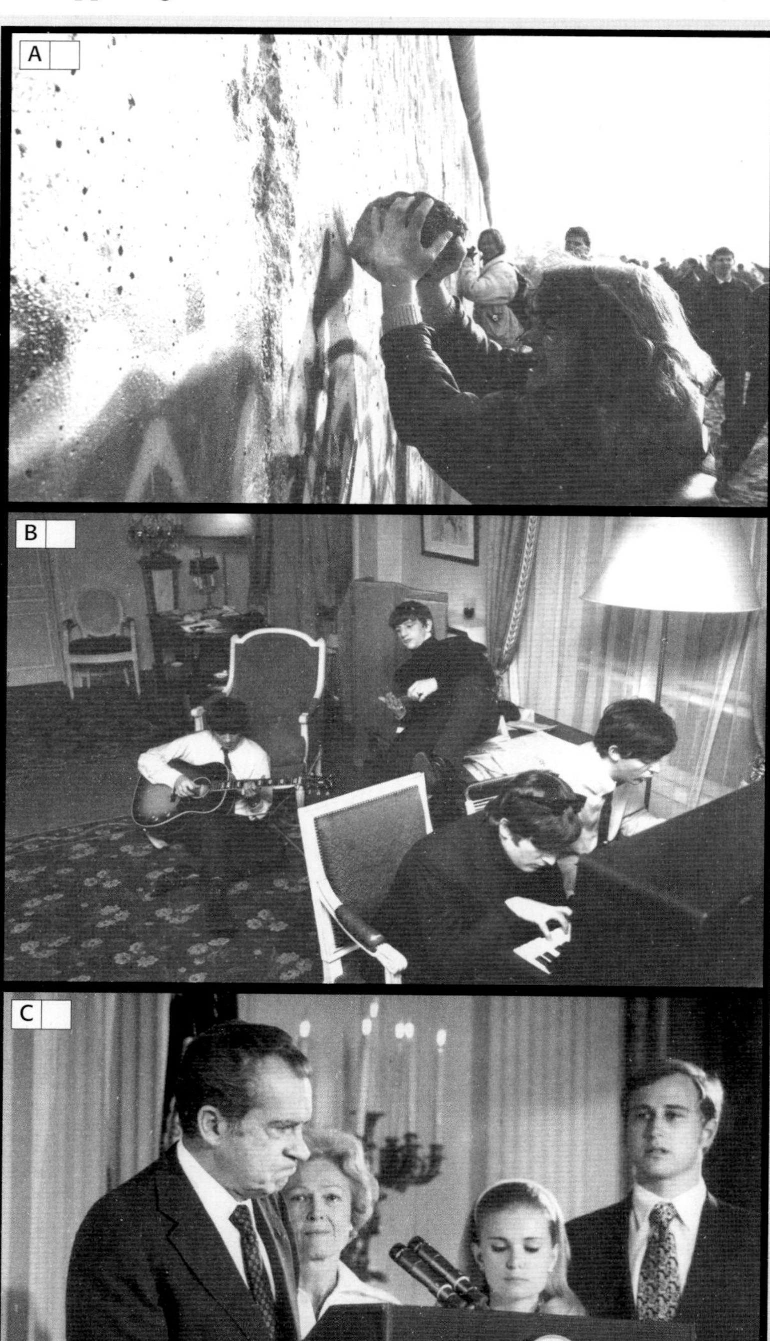

HARRY BENSON spent 50 years taking dramatic and memorable photographs for national newspapers and magazines. Here he talks about three of his best-known pictures.

1 I took this picture on August 9th 1974. He was saying goodbye to his cabinet and the White House staff after the 'Watergate' scandal. All his family were standing round him. You can see from their faces what they were feeling.

2 In 1989, I was working in London on a story when suddenly I heard the news that the Russians were planning to make Berlin an open city. So I got on a plane. When I arrived in Berlin many people, young and old, were attacking the wall with stones. The woman in the photo was shouting, 'I hate it, I hate it'.

3 When I took this photo we were in a hotel room in Paris in 1964. John and Paul were at the piano and at first nothing much was happening, but suddenly they became completely focused. First the melody came, and then the words. *'Baby's good to me you know, she's happy as can be you know…'*. They were composing their song *I feel fine*.

c Read the texts again. Cover them and try to remember. What was happening when he took the photos?

When he took the photo in Berlin, people were attacking the wall and a woman was shouting.

d Look at the highlighted verbs in paragraph 1. What tense are they? What's the difference?

e **p.128 Grammar Bank 2B.** Read the rules and do the exercises.

2 READING & LISTENING

a Look at the photo. What can you see? Where are they? What are they doing?

b Read what the photographer says and check your answers to a. What happened to the photo? What happened 30 years later?

c 2.4 Now listen to Marinette and Henri talking about their photo. Are they still in love?

d Listen again and mark the sentences T (true) or F (false).

1 They always knew that their photo was famous.
2 Marinette saw the book with their photo in a bookshop.
3 When the photographer took the photo they were laughing.
4 Marinette wanted Henri to stand near her.
5 They didn't know that the photographer was taking their photo.
6 Henri was trying to kiss Marinette.
7 Henri thinks they were arguing about their wedding.
8 They got married a year after the photo.
9 Marinette and Henri work together every day.
10 She says that she and Henri are very similar.

Willy Ronis talks about his most famous photo

'It was March 1957 and I was taking photographs in Paris. One afternoon I went up the Bastille and I saw two lovers on a balcony. They were standing very near each other. They were talking. I took just one photo and they didn't hear me. I called it *Lovers at the Bastille*. Luckily for me this photo became very popular in France. Soon posters and postcards with my picture of the two lovers were everywhere. But I never knew who the two young people were. They never contacted me.'

'30 years later I had an exhibition of my photos in Paris. I was talking to some friends when suddenly a man came up to me and said, "I know your two lovers. They live near here. I can take you there if you want." I immediately decided to go and meet them. This was their story.'

3 VOCABULARY *at, in, on*

a Complete the sentences with *at*, *in*, or *on*.

1 President Nixon left the White House _______ August 9th 1974.
2 The Beatles were _______ a hotel room _______ Paris _______ 1964.
3 Willy Ronis took the photo _______ the balcony _______ March 1957.
4 The young couple went up to the balcony _______ 3.00 in the afternoon.
5 Henri and Marinette see each other every day, _______ home and _______ work.

b **p.148 Vocabulary Bank** *Prepositions*. Do part 1.

4 PRONUNCIATION /ə/

⚠ /ə/ is the most common sound in English.

a 2.5 Listen and repeat the sound word and sound.

b 2.6 Listen to these words and underline the stressed syllable.

about exhibition photographer together balcony October

c Listen again and repeat the words. Practise making the /ə/ sound.

d 2.7 Listen and repeat the dialogue. Copy the rhythm.

A Where were you at six o'clock in the evening?
B I was at work.
A What were you doing?
B I was having a meeting with the boss.

e In pairs, take turns to answer the questions about yesterday.

Where were you at…? What were you doing?
6.00 p.m. 6.30 a.m. 3.00 p.m. 11.00 a.m. lunchtime 10 p.m.

5 SPEAKING

a **Communication** *Famous photos* *A p.109 B p.113*. Tell your partner about a famous photo.

b Talk to a partner. Ask more questions if you can.

Do you have a photo you really like? *Who took it? What was happening at the time?*
Do you have any photos in your bedroom or living room?
Do you like taking photos?
Who is good at taking photos in your family?
Do you like being in photos?

G questions with and without auxiliaries
V question words, pop music
P /w/ and /h/

Who wrote that song?

2C Fifty years of pop

1 VOCABULARY & SPEAKING

a In pairs or groups, answer the questions.

1. What music / song / album do you like listening to...?
   when you're happy — when you're in a car
   when you're sad — when you're studying
   when you're at a party — when you're in love
2. What's your favourite decade for pop music? (the 80s, 90s, etc.)
3. Who are your favourite bands / singers of all time?
4. Which was the last CD you bought?

b Complete the quiz questions with a question word.

How How many Where What How long
Which (x2) Why Who (x2) Whose When

c In pairs, answer the questions.

2 GRAMMAR questions with and without auxiliaries

a Cover the quiz and from memory complete the questions.

1. Which song ______ Robbie Williams ______ with Nicole Kidman?
2. Who ______ *I can't get you out of my head?*

b Answer these questions.

1. How is question 1 different from question 2?
2. What is the subject of the verb in question 1?
3. What is the subject of the verb in question 2?

c ➲ **p.128 Grammar Bank 2C** Read the rules and do the exercises.

1. ______ did Freddie Mercury, the lead singer of Queen, die? — **a** 1981 **b** 1991 **c** 2001
2. ______ did the Eagles stay in their 1976 song? — **a** Heartbreak Hotel **b** Hotel California **c** Hilton Hotel
3. ______ did the Beatles stay together? — **a** For eight years **b** For thirteen years **c** For seventeen years
4. ______ husband is the film director Guy Ritchie? — **a** Dido's **b** Barbra Streisand's **c** Madonna's
5. ______ happened to Mick Jagger in 2004? — **a** He left the Rolling Stones. **b** He became Sir Mick Jagger. **c** He divorced Jerry Hall.
6. ______ song did Robbie Williams sing with Nicole Kidman in 2002? — **a** Angels **b** Something Stupid **c** Let me entertain you
7. ______ sang *I can't get you out of my head*? — **a** Britney Spears **b** Kylie Minogue **c** Beyoncé
8. ______ did Nirvana stop playing in 1994? — **a** Because they argued. **b** Because Kurt Cobain left. **c** Because Kurt Cobain died
9. ______ band included Phil Collins and Peter Gabriel? — **a** Dire Straits **b** Genesis **c** Pink Floyd
10. ______ Spice Girls were there? — **a** four **b** five **c** six
11. ______ did Elvis Presley die? — **a** In a plane crash **b** He shot himself **c** An accidental drugs overdose.
12. ______ did Chris Martin, lead singer of Coldplay, marry in 2003? — **a** Gwyneth Paltrow **b** Kate Winslet **c** Drew Barrymore

3 PRONUNCIATION /w/, /h/

a Look at the two sound pictures. What are the words and sounds?

b Write the words in the box in the right column.

what who when where how which why whose

w	h

c 2.8 Listen and check. Practise saying the words.

d p.159 Sound Bank. Look at the typical spellings for these sounds.

e 2.9 Listen and write the questions. Say the questions. Copy the rhythm.

4 SPEAKING

Communication *Music quiz A p.109 B p.113.* First write the questions. Then ask them to your partner.

5 READING

a Read the article once and mark the sentences T (true) or F (false).

1 *Imagine* was a hit three times.
2 Yoko Ono helped to write *Imagine.*
3 Ono wrote poems for John Lennon.
4 Lennon never said that Yoko helped him with the song.
5 *Imagine* was written in two places.
6 John Lennon opened the new Liverpool Airport.

b Read the article again. Number the sentences in the order that things happened.

A John Lennon read Ono's poems. ☐
B John Lennon wrote *Imagine.* ☐
C Yoko Ono helped her little brother. 1
D John Lennon spoke about the song in an interview. ☐
E Liverpool Airport was renamed John Lennon Airport. ☐
F Yoko Ono spoke about the song on a TV programme. ☐
G The song became a hit again when Lennon died. ☐
H The song became popular again after September 11th 2001. ☐

6 2.10 SONG ♫ *Imagine*

Who wrote *Imagine*?

Imagine, John Lennon's most famous song, was recently voted 'Britain's favourite song of all time'. It's an idealistic song about peace and the hope for a better world. 'Imagine all the people living life in peace.' The song was a big hit in 1971, and again in 1980 when Lennon was murdered in New York. It became a hit for a third time after the terrorist attacks of September 11th 2001.

But who really wrote the song? Until recently the answer to this question was always John Lennon. But on a TV programme this week Lennon's wife, Yoko Ono, spoke for the first time about how she, in fact, helped to write the song.

Ono said that the idea and inspiration for *Imagine* came from some of her poems that John Lennon was reading at that time. The poems began with the word 'Imagine': 'Imagine a raindrop, Imagine a goldfish.' Ono said, 'When I was a child in Japan during the Second World War my brother and I were terribly hungry. I imagined delicious menus for him and he began to smile. If you think something is impossible, you can imagine it and make it happen.'

In an interview just before he died, Lennon admitted that Yoko deserved credit for *Imagine*. He said, 'A lot of it – the lyrics and the concept – came from her, from her book of poems, imagine this, imagine that.' Lennon said that he was 'too macho' to share the credit with her at the time.

Ono said that some of the song was written when they were flying across the Atlantic and the rest was written on the piano in their bedroom at their home in England. Ono said, 'The song speaks about John's dream for the world. It was something he really wanted to say.' *Imagine* became a popular song for peace activists everywhere.

In March 2002 the airport in his home town of Liverpool was re-named John Lennon Airport. A sign above the main entrance has a line from *Imagine*: 'Above us only sky'.

Adapted from a British newspaper

2D One October evening

G *so, because, but, although*
V verb phrases
P the letter *a*

She was going very fast because she was in a hurry.

1 READING

A [ ] Next day Jamie phoned Hannah and invited her to dinner. He took her to a very romantic French restaurant and they talked all evening. After that Jamie and Hannah saw each other every day. Every evening when Hannah finished work they met at 5.30 in a coffee bar in the High Street. They were madly in love.

B [ ] Suddenly, a man ran across the road. He was wearing a dark coat so Hannah didn't see him until it was too late. Although she tried to stop, she hit the man. Hannah panicked. She didn't stop and she drove to the coffee bar as fast as she could. But when she arrived Jamie wasn't there. She phoned him, but his mobile was turned off, so she waited for ten minutes and then went home.

C [*1*] **Hannah met Jamie in the summer of 2004**. It was Hannah's 21st birthday and she and her friends went to a club. They wanted to dance, but they didn't like the music so Hannah went to speak to the DJ. 'This music is awful,' she said. 'Could you play something else?' The DJ looked at her and said, 'Don't worry, I have the perfect song for you.'

D [ ] Two hours later a police car arrived at Hannah's house. A policewoman knocked at the door. 'Good evening, Madam,' she said. 'Are you Hannah Davis? I'd like to speak to you. Can I come in?'

E [ ] One evening in October, Hannah was at work. As usual she was going to meet Jamie at 5.30. It was dark and it was raining. She looked at her watch. It was 5.20! She was going to be late! She ran to her car and got in. At 5.25 she was driving along the High Street. She was going very fast because she was in a hurry.

F [ ] Two minutes later he said: 'The next song is by Coldplay. It's called *Yellow* and it's for a beautiful girl who's dancing over there.' Hannah knew that the song was for her because she was wearing a yellow dress. When Hannah and her friends left the club, the DJ was waiting at the door. 'Hi, I'm Jamie,' he said to Hannah. 'Can I see you again?' So Hannah gave him her phone number.

a 2.11 Read the story and order the paragraphs 1–6. Listen and check.

b Read the story again and answer the questions.

1. When did Hannah meet Jamie?
2. Why did Hannah go and speak to Jamie in the club?
3. Why did Jamie play *Yellow*?
4. What happened when Hannah left the club?
5. Where did they go on their first date?
6. Where did they go every evening?
7. What was the weather like that evening?
8. Why was Hannah driving fast?
9. Why didn't she see the man?
10. What did she do after the accident?
11. Was Jamie at the coffee bar?
12. What happened two hours later?

2 GRAMMAR *so, because, but, although*

a Complete these sentences from the story with *so*, *because*, *but*, or *although*.

1. She was going very fast ________ she was in a hurry.
2. ________ she tried to stop, she hit the man.
3. They wanted to dance, ________ they didn't like the music.
4. He was wearing a dark coat ________ Hannah didn't see him.

b **p.128 Grammar Bank 2D** Read the rules and do the exercises.

3 VOCABULARY verb phrases

a Make verb phrases with a verb from circle **1** and a phrase from circle **2**.

invite somebody to dinner

b Cover circle **1**. Try to remember the verb for each phrase.

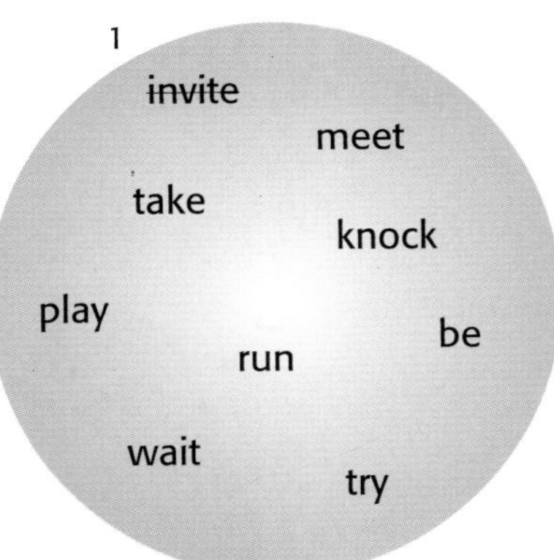

1
~~invite~~
meet
take
knock
play
be
run
wait
try

2

in a hurry
across the road
on the door
a song/CD
~~somebody to dinner~~
in a coffee bar
somebody to a restaurant
to stop
for somebody

4 PRONUNCIATION the letter *a*

Hannah met Jamie in the summer of 2004.

⚠ The letter *a* has different pronunciations.

a 2.12 Listen and repeat the sound words in the chart.

b 2.13 Put these words in the right columns. Listen and check.

again all although arrive dark
fast play ran romantic wait

æ	eɪ	ɔː	ɑː	ə
madly	later	saw	dance	along
panic	take	talk	bar	across
______	______	______	______	______
______	______	______	______	______

5 SPEAKING

a Read the story of Hannah and Jamie in **1** again.

b In pairs, use the pictures 1–6 to re-tell the story.

6 LISTENING

⚠ Remember! When people speak fast, they link words together.

a 2.14 That evening a policewoman went to Hannah's house. Listen to six extracts from their conversation. What are the missing words?

1 A policewoman ______ ______ the door.
2 Can ______ ______ ______?
3 Well, I'm afraid I have ______ ______ news for you.
4 It was a ______ ______ ______ ______ car.
5 Every police officer in the town ______ ______ ______ her.
6 Did you know your ______ ______ is broken?

b 2.15 Now listen to all the conversation. **When the teacher pauses the recording**, answer the questions.

1 What do you think the policewoman is going to say?
2 What do you think the bad news is?
3 Do you think Jamie is OK?
4 Who do you think was driving the car?
5 Why do you think the policewoman wants to see her car?

c Now close your books and listen again. Can you follow the story?

CHECKING IN

2.16 Listen to Allie checking in. Answer the questions.

1 Does the receptionist call Allie 'Ms Gray' or 'Mrs Gray'?
2 How many nights is Allie staying?
3 What's her room number?
4 What time's breakfast?
5 Which floor is the Pavilion Restaurant on?

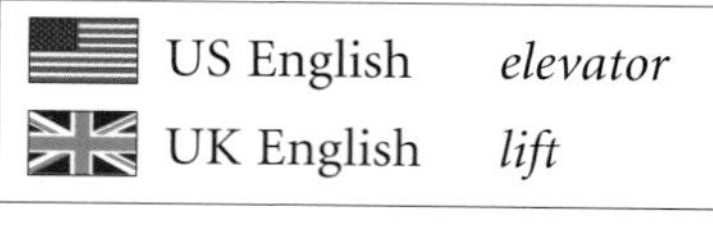

US English	*elevator*
UK English	*lift*

CALLING RECEPTION

a 2.17 Cover the dialogues and listen. Who does Allie phone? Why?

YOU HEAR	YOU SAY
Hello, reception.	Hello. This is room 419.
How can I help you?	I have a problem with the air-conditioning. It isn't working, and it's very hot in my room.
I'm sorry, ma'am. I'll ______ someone up to look at it right now.	Thank you.
______ service. Can I help you?	Hello. This is room 419. Can I have a tuna sandwich, please?
Whole wheat or ______ bread?	Whole wheat, please.
______ or without mayo?	Without.
With ______ ______ or salad?	Salad, please.
______ to drink?	Yes, a Diet Coke.
With ______ and lemon?	Just ice.
It'll be there in five minutes, ma'am.	Thank you.

b Listen again. Complete the YOU HEAR phrases.

c 2.18 Listen and repeat the YOU SAY phrases. Copy the rhythm.

d In pairs, roleplay the dialogues. **A** (book open) you're the receptionist / room service, **B** (book closed) you're Allie. Swap roles.

SOCIAL ENGLISH coffee before the conference

a 2.19 Listen and mark the sentences T (true) or F (false).

1 Mark is going to take Allie to dinner tonight.
2 The cocktail party is on Thursday.
3 Allie wants to see the bay and the Golden Gate Bridge.
4 Brad is from the San Francisco office.
5 Brad offers to take Allie sightseeing.

b Complete the USEFUL PHRASES. Listen again and check.

c 2.20 Listen and repeat the phrases. How do you say them in your language?

USEFUL PHRASES

A W______ done!
M Did you s______ well?
A How are t______? **M** They're fine.
A What are the p______ for the week?
M Allie, t______ is Brad Martin.
M It's t______ to go.

The story behind a photo

Every week we ask readers to send in a favourite photo, together with a short description of why the photo is important to them. This week's winner is Dominic, a graphic designer from London.

1 One of my favourite photos is of a man cooking fish.

2 I took the photo [1] *in* the summer of 1994 when I was [2]______ holiday in Africa.

3 We were [3]______ Zanzibar, and we were sailing round the islands. We caught some fish, and then landed [4]______ one of the islands, and our guide made a fire and cooked the fish.

4 Richie, the guide, was a wonderful person – he became a good friend. He was also a fantastic cook. I can't remember exactly what fish he was cooking in the photo, but it tasted delicious!

5 I keep this photo [5]______ the wall in my studio. [6]______ a grey, rainy day in London, I just have to look [7]______ it and then memories of a wonderful adventure come back, and I can imagine that I'm [8]______ sunny Africa again.

a Match the questions with paragraphs 1–5.

- What was happening when you took the photo? ☐
- Where do you keep it? Why do you like it? ☐
- What's your favourite photo? ☐
- Who took it? When? Where? ☐
- Tell me more about who or what is in the photo. ☐

ⓘ You can keep a photo…

in	an album. your wallet. your bedroom.
on	the wall. a table.
by	your bed.

b Complete the text with *at*, *in*, or *on*.

WRITE about your favourite photo. Answer the questions in **a** in the right order.

CHECK your description for mistakes (grammar , punctuation , and spelling). Attach a copy of the photo if you can.

2 What do you remember?

GRAMMAR

Circle the correct answer, a, b, or c.

What's ______ name?

a yours (b) your c you

1 Where ______ on holiday last year?
a you went
b did you go
c you did go

2 He didn't ______ to come to France with us.
a wanted
b wants
c want

3 We ______ to San Francisco last August.
a flown
b fly
c flew

4 When I took the photo you ______ looking at me.
a weren't
b wasn't
c didn't

5 What ______ doing when you phoned him?
a he was
b was he
c were he

6 Who ______ that song?
a did write
b wrote
c did wrote

7 When ______?
a he died
b died he
c did he die

8 She was driving fast ______ she was late.
a although
b because
c so

9 ______ the music was bad, we danced all night.
a But
b Although
c So

10 It was dark ______ she didn't see him.
a but
b so
c because

[ ] 10

VOCABULARY

a holiday verbs

Complete the phrases with a verb.

go shopping

1 ______ photos
2 ______ for a walk
3 ______ in a hotel
4 ______ two days in Paris / 1,000 euros
5 ______ a good time

b prepositions

Complete the sentences with *at*, *in*, or *on*.

I'm sitting *in* a taxi.

1 We met ______ a party.
2 The two lovers were talking ______ a balcony.
3 We were sitting ______ the garden.
4 There was a photo ______ the wall.
5 I was waiting ______ the bus stop.

c question words

Complete the questions with a question word.

What is Sting's real name?

1 ______ did The Police make their first record?
2 ______ wrote their songs?
3 ______ records did they sell?
4 ______ happened to them in the end?
5 ______ of their albums do you like best?

[ ] 15

PRONUNCIATION

a Underline the word with a different sound

1	 wore	wrote	thought	saw
2	 took	could	found	put
3	 shop	choose	exhibition	musician
4	 whose	how	who	when
5	 job	argue	jealous	manager

b Underline the stressed syllable.

information

incredible horrible photographer suddenly although

[ ] 10

CAN YOU UNDERSTAND THIS TEXT?

Mountain climbers rescued by text message

Two British climbers were rescued yesterday after sending an SOS text message to a friend in London.

Rachel Kelsey, 34, and her partner, Jeremy Colenso, 33, who are both experienced climbers, were on a climbing holiday last week in Switzerland. But on Saturday night, when they were 3,000 metres up in the mountains, there was a terrible storm. The wind was incredibly strong and the snow was two metres deep. They couldn't move and they had to spend the night on the mountain. Rachel had her mobile phone with her, so she sent a text message to five friends in the UK asking for help.

About four hours later, one of her friends, Avery Cunliffe in London, replied with a text message. Avery said, 'I don't usually have my mobile in the bedroom. At about 4 a.m. I woke up and saw Rachel's message. I found the number of the police in Switzerland and phoned them. They contacted the mountain rescue team.'

But the weather was so bad that the helicopter couldn't get to the two climbers. The rescue team sent a text message to Rachel and Jeremy telling them that they had to spend a second night on the mountain. The message said: 'So sorry Rachel. We tried. Wind too strong. Have to wait till morning. Take care. Be strong.' Rachel said, 'I thought we were going to die. It was freezing, –15ºC, and really windy on the mountain. We spent the night talking and planning a holiday in the sun!'

Next morning the storm passed and the helicopter arrived to take them off the mountain. Avery said, 'When I heard that Rachel and Jeremy were safe I was dancing around my flat.' Rachel said that she and Jeremy were now looking forward to a hot bath and a good meal. But first they were going to buy the rescue team a bottle of whisky!

Adapted from a British newspaper

a Read the article and mark the sentences T (true), F (false), or DS (doesn't say).

1 Rachel and Jeremy were climbing for the first time.
2 They couldn't go down the mountain because of bad weather.
3 Avery was sleeping when Rachel's message came.
4 He called the mountain rescue team in Switzerland.
5 Rachel's other four friends didn't reply.
6 The helicopter couldn't rescue them immediately.
7 Rachel and Jeremy spent three nights on the mountain.
8 They wanted to buy Avery a bottle of whisky.

b Underline and learn six new words or expressions from the article. Use your dictionary to check the meaning and pronunciation.

CAN YOU UNDERSTAND THESE PEOPLE?

a 2.21 Listen and circle the correct answer, a, b, or c.

1 Where did the woman go on holiday this year?
a Portugal b Scotland c Spain
2 What was the weather like in Italy?
a It rained. b It was hot. c It was sunny.
3 Where did the photographer take the photo of the actor?
a On the stairs. b In reception. c In the street.
4 What was the model doing when he took the photo?
a Talking b Reading c Walking on the 'catwalk'
5 What year did the pop group make their last album?
a 2001 b 2002 c 2003

b 2.22 Listen to the story and mark the sentences T (true) or F (false).

1 She was driving to work.
2 It was raining.
3 She saw a man in the road asking her to stop.
4 The two men drove away in her car.
5 She rang the police on her mobile.

CAN YOU SAY THIS IN ENGLISH?

a Can you...? Yes (✓)

☐ talk about your last holiday
☐ talk about your favourite photo
☐ talk about your favourite singer or band

b Complete the questions with *was*, *were*, *do*, *did*, or –.

1 What kind of books ______ you read?
2 Where ______ you at 9.00 this morning?
3 What ______ happening when you got home last night?
4 What ______ you doing on September 11th 2001?
5 How many people ______ came to class today?

c Ask your partner the questions in **b**. Ask for more information.

G *going to*, present continuous (future arrangements)
V *look* (*after*, *for*, etc.)
P sentence stress

When are you going?
When are you coming back?

Where are you going?

1 READING

a When was the last time you went to an airport (or station)? Were you meeting someone or going somewhere?

b Read the magazine article. Complete it with these questions.

A	*Do you know anybody here?*
B	*Are you going to stay for long?*
C *1*	*Is this your first visit?*
D	*What are you planning to do?*
E	*When are you leaving?*
F	*Does he know you're coming?*
G	*How are you going to get there?*
H	*How long are you going to stay?*
I	*Where are you staying in London?*

c Read the article again and write **R** (Rima), **J** (Jonathan), or **M** (Maki).

1 *M* is going to stay at a hotel.
2 ___ is going to stay at a friend's house.
3 ___ is going to visit a family member.
4 ___ is going to the theatre tomorrow.
5 ___ is only going to be in the UK for four weeks.
6 ___ is going to work.

2 GRAMMAR *going to*, present continuous

a In pairs, cover the text. Can you remember three of Rima's plans? Can you remember three of Jonathan's plans?

Rima's going to work.

b Look at the interview with Maki and Koji. Highlight six present continuous sentences. Do they refer to the **present** or the **future**?

c **p.130 Grammar Bank 3A.** Read the rules and do the exercises.

Airport Stories

Heathrow airport near London is the busiest international airport in the world. Every day thousands of travellers arrive at Heathrow from many different countries. Every one of them has a different story to tell. We spent an afternoon in the Arrivals Hall at Heathrow last week talking to travellers arriving from abroad. We asked them: Why are you here?

LOOKING FOR A JOB

Rima, 23, from Vilnius in Lithuania

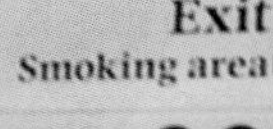

Why are you here?

I'm going to look for a job. Maybe as an au pair, looking after children. And I want to improve my English too, so I can get a better job when I go back home. I hope I can find some work quickly, because I don't have much money.

1 Is this your first visit?

Yes, it is. I'm really looking forward to living here, but I'm a bit nervous too.

2 ________________

Six months or a year. It depends how things go.

3 ________________

Yes, I have a friend who's working here in a restaurant. I'm going to stay with her for a few weeks until I can find my own flat.

Well, good luck!

A FAMILY REUNION

Jonathan, 35, just arrived from Melbourne, Australia

Why are you here?

I'm going to see my Dad in Wales. It's his seventieth birthday tomorrow.

4 ________________

No. It's going to be a big surprise for him. And it's going to be very emotional too. I moved to Australia in 1990, and the last time I saw my Dad was five years ago. It's too expensive to visit very often and my father can't fly – he had a heart operation last year.

5 ________________

By train. All the family are waiting at my parents' house. We're going to have a big party there tomorrow night.

6 ________________

Yes, for a month. It's too far to come for a short time – and I want to see all my old friends here as well as my family.

3 LISTENING

a 3.1 Listen to Rima talking six months later. Mark the sentences T (true) or F (false).

1 She's working in an Italian restaurant.
2 It was easy to find a job.
3 She isn't living with her friend now.
4 She isn't going to English classes.
5 She doesn't know if she's going to go back to Lithuania.
6 She's leaving the restaurant next month.
7 Her boyfriend is a waiter.
8 Her family are very happy that she's getting married.

b Listen again for more details. Correct the false sentences.

4 VOCABULARY *look*

a Look at Rima's interview on p.28 again. Find and underline three expressions with *look*. Match them to their dictionary definitions.

1 ________ try to find something
2 ________ wait with pleasure for something which is going to happen
3 ________ be responsible for or take care of somebody or something

b Complete the sentences with *after*, *for*, or *forward to*.

1 A nurse is a person who looks ____ people who are ill.
2 She's going to New York next month. She's really looking ____ it.
3 I can't find my keys. Can you help me to look ____ them?
4 I'm not looking ____ the exam – it's going to be very difficult.
5 Our house is a bit too small. We're looking ____ a new one.
6 Could you look ____ our dog this weekend? We want to go away.

c Tell your partner...

- something you are looking forward to
- something you often have to look for in the morning
- somebody or something that you (occasionally) look after

5 PRONUNCIATION sentence stress

a Underline the words which are important for communication in these questions (the stressed words).

1 Where are you going?
2 When are you leaving?
3 How are you getting there?
4 Where are you staying?
5 When are you coming back?

b 3.2 Listen and check. Listen again and repeat. Copy the rhythm.

6 SPEAKING

a Write down three plans or arrangements that you have for this week. Work in pairs. **A** tell **B** your plans. **B** listen and ask for more information. Then swap roles.

I'm going to the cinema on Friday night.

What are you going to see?

b **Communication** *Where are you going on holiday?* *p.116.* Find a travelling companion for an exotic holiday.

ON THEIR HONEYMOON

Maki, 25, and Koji, 27, from Nagasaki, Japan

Why are you here?

We're on our honeymoon. We got married last Saturday.

Congratulations!

7 ____________

We're staying at the Hyde Park Hotel. We're just here for a few days.

8 ____________

Everything is organized for us. Tomorrow we're doing a tour of London on a double-decker bus, and in the evening we're seeing a show. Then on Tuesday we're going to Oxford and Cambridge and on Wednesday we're flying to Edinburgh.

9 ____________

On Friday. We're going to Paris next, and then to Rome...

Well, have a good time!

3B The pessimist's phrase book

G *will / won't*
V opposite verbs
P contractions (*will / won't*), /ɒ/ and /əʊ/

I'm doing my driving test today.
You'll fail.

	YOU	THE PESSIMIST
1	We're having the party in the garden.	*It'll rain.*
2	I'm doing my driving test this afternoon.	*You won't pass.*
3	We're meeting Ana and Daniel at 7.00.	
4	I'm having my first skiing lesson today.	
5	My brother has a new girlfriend.	
6	I lent James some money yesterday.	
7	I'm going to see a film tonight in English.	
8	We're going to drive to the city centre.	
9	My team are playing in the cup tonight.	
10	I'm catching the 7.30 train.	

1 GRAMMAR *will / won't* for predictions

a Look at the picture. Who's the optimist? Who's the pessimist? Which are you?

b Read the YOU phrases. Find the THE PESSIMIST'S responses in the box below and write them in the phrase book.

He won't pay you back.	You'll miss it.	You won't understand a word.
~~You won't pass.~~	They'll be late.	It won't last.
They'll lose.	~~It'll rain.~~	You'll break your leg.
You won't find a parking space.		

c 3.3 Listen and check. Repeat the responses.

d Practise in pairs.
A (book open) read the **YOU** phrases.
B (book closed) say **THE PESSIMIST** phrase.
Then swap roles.

e Look at **THE PESSIMIST** phrases and answer the questions.
1 Do the sentences refer to the present or the future?
2 What are the full words in the contractions **'ll** and **won't**?

f **p.130 Grammar Bank 3B.** Read the rules and do the exercises.

2 VOCABULARY opposite verbs

a What's the opposite of the verbs in **A**? Use a verb from **B**.

b **p.149 Vocabulary Bank** *Verbs*. Do part 1.

A
pass
win
lose
lend

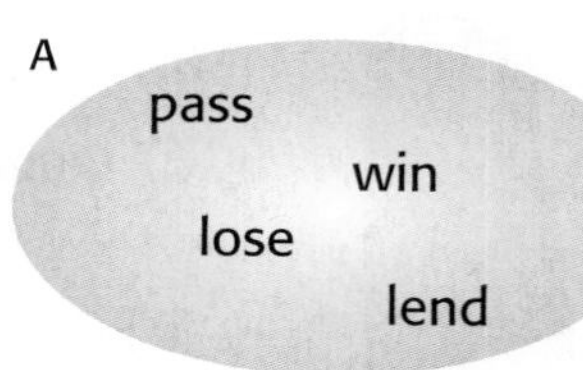

B
fail
borrow
find
lose

3 PRONUNCIATION contractions, /ɒ/ and /əʊ/

a 3.4 Listen and repeat the contractions. Copy the rhythm.

I'll	I'll be late	I'll be late for work.
You'll	You'll break	You'll break your leg.
She'll	She'll miss	She'll miss the train.
It'll	It'll rain	It'll rain tomorrow.
They'll	They'll lose	They'll lose the match.

b 3.5 Listen. Can you hear the difference?

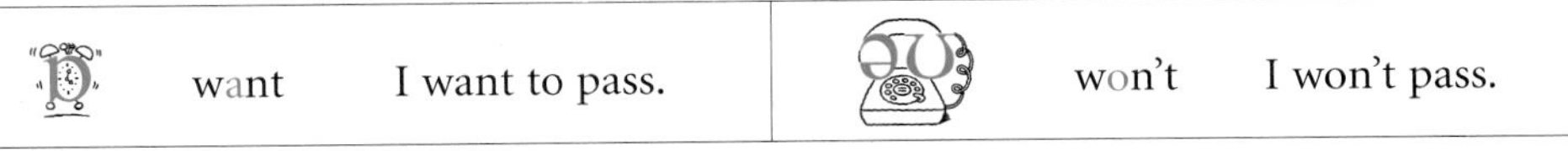

want	I want to pass.	
won't	I won't pass.	

c 3.6 Listen and write down the six sentences.

4 LISTENING

a 3.7 Listen to the introduction to a radio programme. Why is positive thinking good for you?

b Try to guess the missing words in these tips.

	Tip
Caller 1	Live in the ______, not in the ______.
Caller 2	Think ______ thoughts, not negative ones.
Caller 3	Don't spend a lot of time reading the ______ or watching the ______ on TV.
Caller 4	Every week make a list of all the ______ ______ that happened to you.
Caller 5	Try to use ______ ______ when you speak to other people.

c 3.8 Listen and check.

d Listen again. Write down any extra information you hear.

e Which tips do you think are useful?

5 SPEAKING

a In pairs match the positive phrases with the situations.
Make a positive prediction, *I'm sure you'll...*, *I'm sure it'll...*, etc.

Cheer up! Don't worry! Congratulations! That's great! Good luck!

Your friend says...	You say...	
1 I have an important exam tomorrow.	*Good luck!*	*I'm sure you'll pass.*
2 I'm getting married next month.		
3 I'm a bit depressed today.		
4 I'm going to New York next month.		
5 I can't go out tonight. I don't have any money.		

b Ask and answer with a partner. Use a phrase from the box and say why.

Are you a positive thinker?

Do you think...

- you'll go somewhere exciting for your next holiday?
- you'll pass your next exam?
- you'll get a good (or better) job?
- you'll do something nice this weekend?
- you'll get an interesting e-mail from someone tonight?
- you'll get to the end of this book?

I hope so. (I hope not.)
I think so.
I don't think so.
Maybe. / Perhaps.
Probably.
Definitely.

3C I'll always love you

G *will / won't* (promises, offers, decisions)
V verb + *back*
P word stress: two-syllable words

It's a secret.
OK, I won't tell anyone.

1 READING

a Look at the six promises below. What do you think they have in common?

I won't tell anyone.	**I'll write.**
I'll always love you.	**I'll pay you back tomorrow.**
I'll come back tomorrow.	**This won't hurt.**

b Read the article once and write the correct promise in the gaps 1–6.

c Read the text again. Find words to match to the definitions. Underline the stressed syllable.

1 ________ (n) a person who repairs water pipes, baths, etc.
2 ________ (n) studies to find more information about something
3 ________ (n) putting medicine under the skin with a needle
4 ________ (n) the act of travelling from one place to another
5 ________ (adv) one or the other
6 ________ (adj) something which lasts forever

2 PRONUNCIATION word stress: two-syllable words

⚠ Most two-syllable words are stressed on the first syllable, e.g *father*. When words are stressed on the second syllable, e.g *although*, underline the stress and learn them.

a Look at these two-syllable words from the text. Which **five** are stressed on the second syllable?

secret	forget	exist
always	complete	dentist
borrow	e-mail	money
promise	address	doctor
builder	journey	
worry	before	

b 3.9 Listen and check. Practise saying the words.

Promises, promises

We make them and we break them, because some promises are very hard to keep. Here are the top six most common broken promises ...

1 ________

You always hear this from builders, plumbers, and electricians. But the truth is very different. They won't come back until next week (or later). And you will probably need to phone them five times first.

2 ________

We love hearing secrets and we happily make this promise. And at the time we really mean it. 'Don't worry,' we say, 'your secret is safe with me.' But of course it isn't. Research shows that everybody will always tell one other person the secret. Very soon the whole street will know!

3 ________

A favourite phrase of doctors, dentists, and nurses. They usually say it just before they give you an injection. But the phrase is not complete. The full phrase is: 'This won't hurt me (but it will probably hurt you a lot).'

4 ________

You make a new friend on holiday or on a bus journey, you swap e-mail addresses, and you make this promise. Six months later you find a name and e-mail address on a card or an old piece of paper. 'Oh dear!' you think – but then you remember that they didn't write to you either!

5 ________

In *Hamlet*, Shakespeare told us never to borrow or lend money. He was right. When we lend people money they always make this promise, but then they forget. If we then ask for the money back, they think we are mean. If we don't ask, we never get the money back.

6 ________

Whitney Houston sang a song about this and every day, all over the world thousands of people make the same promise to each other. We know eternal love exists, but is this promise the most difficult one to keep of them all?

Adapted from a British newspaper

3 GRAMMAR *will / won't* for promises, offers, and decisions

a Look at the cartoons. What do you think the people are saying?

b Complete sentences 1–6 with a verb from the box and match them with the cartoons (A–F).

have	help	love	open	pay	take

1 I'll _____ the steak, please.
2 I'll _____ you back tomorrow.
3 I'll _____ you!
4 I'll always _____ you.
5 Shall I _____ the window?
6 Yes, it's very nice. I'll _____ it.

c Look at the sentences again. In which two are people…?

making a promise _2_ and ___
making a decision ___ and ___
offering to do something ___ and ___

d p.130 Grammar Bank 3C. Read the rules and do the exercises.

4 VOCABULARY verb + *back*

a Look at the sentences.What's the difference between *go* and *go back*?

I'm **going** to Italy. I'm **going back** to Italy.

b Complete the dialogues with a phrase from the box.

call back	come back	give it back	pay me back	take it back

1
A I love that shirt you gave me for my birthday. But it's a bit small.
B Don't worry. I'll _________ to the shop and change it.

2
A Can I speak to Bart, please?
B I'm sorry. He's not here at the moment.
A OK. I'll _________ later.

3
A Excuse me. Could I talk to you for a moment?
B I'm really busy at the moment. Could you _________ in five minutes?

4
A That's my pen you're using!
B No, it's not. It's mine.
A No, it's mine. _________!

5
A Can you lend me 50 euros, Nick?
B It depends. When can you _________?
A Tomorrow. I'll go to the bank first thing in the morning.

c 3.10 Listen and check. In pairs, practise the dialogues.

5 SPEAKING

Communication *I'll / Shall I? game* *p.117*. Play the game.

6 3.11 SONG ♫ *White Flag*

3D I was only dreaming

G review of tenses: present, past, and future
V verbs + prepositions
P sentence stress

I dreamt about a road. That means you're going to travel.

1 READING & LISTENING

a In pairs, say if you think these statements are true or false.

1 We can only remember a dream if we wake up in the middle of it.
2 We always appear in our dreams.
3 People often have the same dream many times.
4 Psychoanalysts use dreams to help their patients.
5 Dreams can predict the future.

b 3.12 You're going to listen to a psychoanalyst talking to a patient about his dreams. Cover the dialogue and listen and number the pictures 1–6 in the correct order.

Dr Muller	So, *tell* me, what did you dream about?
Patient	I was at a party. There were a lot of people.
Dr Muller	What _____ they _____?
Patient	They were _____ and _____.
Dr Muller	Were *you* drinking?
Patient	Yes, I _____ _____ champagne.
Dr Muller	And then what _____?
Patient	Then, suddenly I _____ in a garden. There _____ a lot of flowers...
Dr Muller	Flowers, yes... what kind of flowers?
Patient	I _____ really see – it was dark. And I _____ hear music – somebody _____ _____ the violin.
Dr Muller	The violin? Go on.
Patient	And then I _____ an owl, a big owl in a tree...
Dr Muller	How _____ you _____? Were you frightened?
Patient	No, not frightened really, no, but I _____ I felt very cold. Especially my feet – they were freezing. And then I _____ _____.
Dr Muller	Your feet? Mmm, very interesting, very interesting indeed...
Patient	So what _____ it _____, doctor?

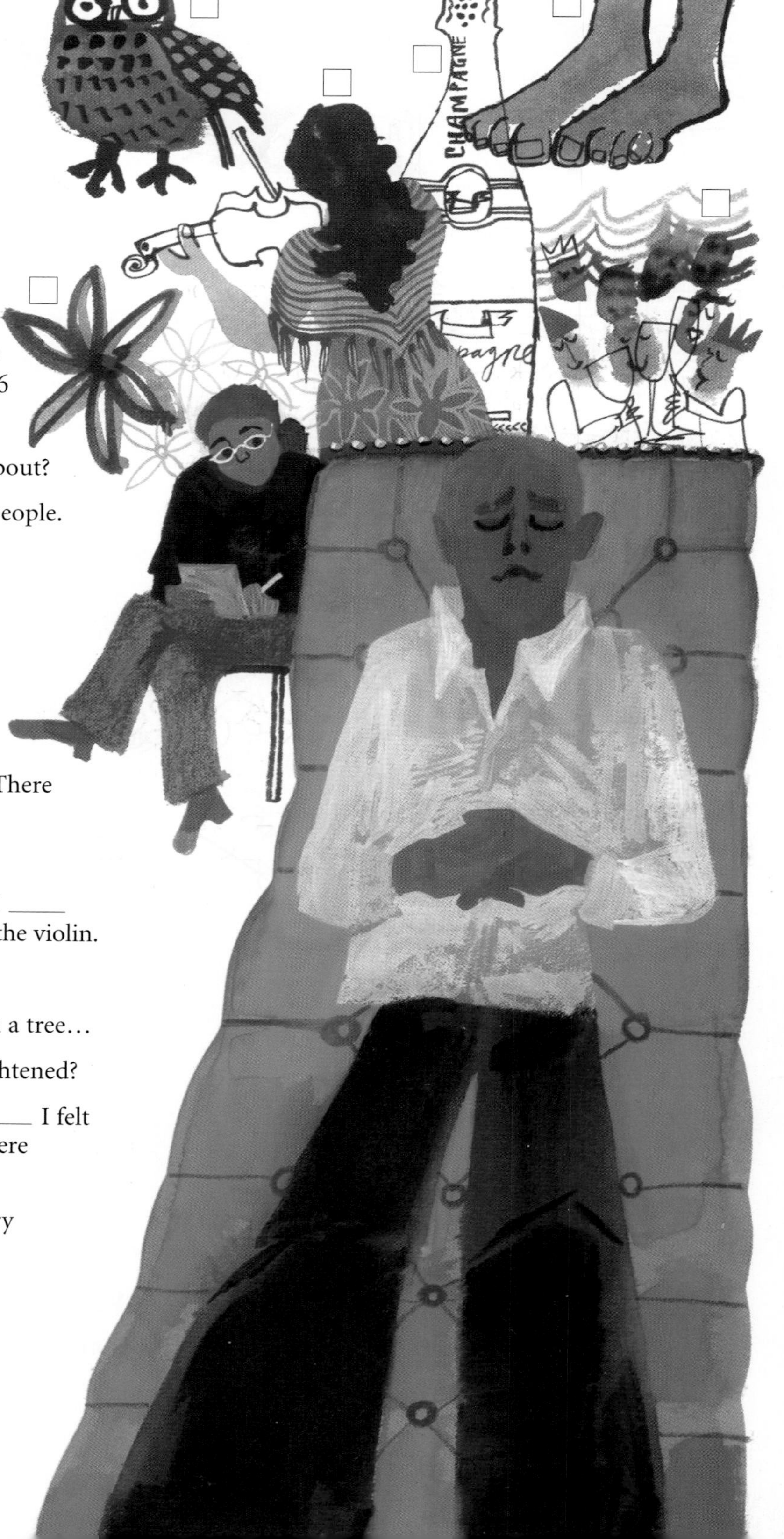

c Now uncover the dialogue. Listen again and fill the gaps with a word or phrase.

d What do you think the patient's dream means? Match the things in his dream with interpretations 1–6.

Understanding your dreams

You dream ...		This means ...
that you are at a party.	☐	1 the person you love doesn't love you.
that you are drinking champagne.	☐	2 you are going to be very busy.
about flowers.	☐	3 you'll be successful.
that somebody is playing the violin.	☐	4 you're feeling positive about the future.
about an owl.	☐	5 you want some romance in your life.
that you have cold feet.	☐	6 you need to ask an older person for help.

e 3.13 Now listen to Dr Muller interpreting the patient's dream and check your answers to **d**.

f Listen again. Look at the pictures again and remember what Dr Muller said about each thing. Compare with your partner.

The party means he's going to meet people.

2 GRAMMAR review of tenses

a Look at the chart. Write the sentences below the chart in the correct place in the **Example** column.

Tense	Example	Use
present simple	*You work in an office.*	D
present continuous	______	__
past simple	______	__
past continuous	______	__
going to **+ infinitive**	______	__
will / won't **+ infinitive**	______	__

I was drinking champagne.
You'll have a meeting with your boss.
I saw an owl.
You're going to meet a lot of people.
~~You work in an office.~~
I'm meeting her tonight.

b Now complete the **Use** column with uses A–F.

A Future plans and predictions.
B Finished actions in the past.
C Things happening now, or plans for a fixed time/place.
~~**D** Things that happen always or usually.~~
E Future predictions, decisions, offers, and promises.
F Actions that were in progress at a past time.

c **p.130 Grammar Bank 3D.** Read the rules and do the exercises.

3 PRONUNCIATION sentence stress

a 3.14 Listen to sentences 1–6 and underline the stressed (information) words.

1 You'll have a meeting with your boss.
2 Somebody was playing the violin.
3 You're going to meet a lot of people.
4 How did you feel?
5 I'm meeting her tonight.
6 She doesn't love me.

b Listen and repeat the sentences. Copy the rhythm.

4 SPEAKING

Communication *Dreams A p.110 B p.114.*
Roleplay interpreting your partner's dream.

5 VOCABULARY verbs + prepositions

Complete the questions with a preposition from the box.

about (x3)	for	of	to (x3)	with (x2)

1 What did you **dream** ______ last night?
2 What radio station do you usually **listen** ______?
3 What do you **talk** ______ with your friends?
4 Did you **wait** ______ a bus or a train today?
5 Who do you usually **agree** ______ in your family?
6 Are you going to **write** ______ anybody tonight?
7 What do you **think** ______ this book?
8 What are you **thinking** ______ now?
9 Do you often **argue** ______ people?
10 Who was the first person you **spoke** ______ this morning?

3 Restaurant problems

ORDERING A MEAL

3.15 Listen to Allie and Mark at the restaurant. Answer the questions.

1 What do they order for starters?
2 What does Allie order for her main course?
3 What kind of potatoes do they order?
4 How does Mark want his steak – rare, medium, or well done?
5 What are they going to drink?

Menu

Starters	Main courses
Tomato and mozzarella salad	Fried chicken
Mushroom soup	T-bone steak
Grilled prawns	Grilled salmon

All main courses served with a baked potato or fries.

PROBLEMS WITH A MEAL

a 3.16 Cover the dialogue and listen. What three problems do they have?

YOU HEAR	YOU SAY
Chicken for you ma'am, and the steak for you, sir.	I'm sorry, but I asked for a baked potato, not fries.
No problem. _____ _____ _____.	
	Excuse me.
Yes, sir?	I asked for my steak rare and this is well done.
I'm very sorry. _____ _____ _____ back to the kitchen.	
	Could we have the check, please?
Yes, sir.	
Your check.	Thanks. Excuse me. I think there's a mistake in the check. We only had two glasses of wine, not a bottle.
Yes, you're right. I'm very sorry. It's not my day today! _____ _____ _____ a new check.	Thank you.

US English	*fries*	*check*
UK English	*chips*	*bill*

b Listen again. Complete the YOU HEAR phrases.

c 3.17 Listen and repeat the YOU SAY phrases. Copy the rhythm.

d In pairs, roleplay the dialogue. **A** (book open) you're the waiter, **B** (book closed) you're Mark and Allie. Swap roles.

SOCIAL ENGLISH after dinner

a 3.18 Listen to Mark and Allie. Mark the sentences T (true) or F (false).

1 Jennifer is Mark's ex-wife.
2 Mark was married for three years.
3 His wife left him for another man.
4 Allie met her previous boyfriend at work.
5 After dinner they're going to go dancing.

b Complete the USEFUL PHRASES. Listen again and check.

c 3.19 Listen and repeat the phrases. How do you say them in your language?

USEFUL PHRASES

A That was a l_____ dinner.
M I'm g_____ you enjoyed it.
A Can I ask you s_____?
M Shall we go for a w_____?
A Where s_____ we go?
M We could have a _____ cup of coffee.

An informal letter

1 *28 Randalls Road*

2 ____________________

3 ____________________

4 ____________________,

Thank you for your letter. We're very happy that you're coming to stay with us in August, and we're sure you'll have a good time.

What time are you arriving at Gatwick airport? You can get a train to Brighton from there. Do you have a mobile phone? Then you can phone us when you're on the train, and we'll meet you at the station.

Could you also tell me a few more things about yourself? Is there anything you can't eat or drink? Do you smoke? Do you want a single room, or do you prefer to share a room with another student? Are you going to go back to Russia immediately after the end of the course? If not, how many more days are you going to stay with us?

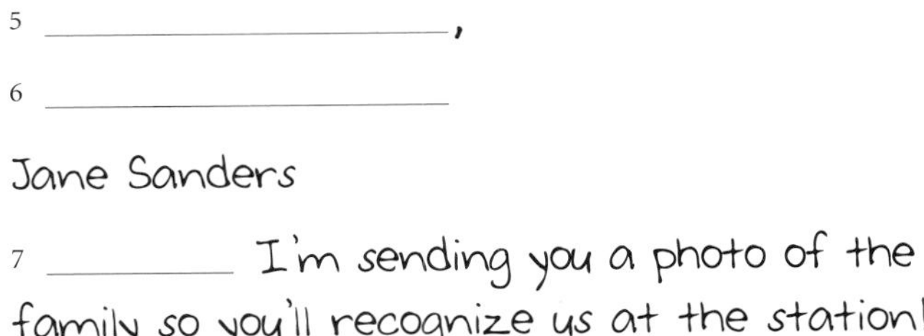

5 ____________________,

6 ____________________

Jane Sanders

7 __________ I'm sending you a photo of the family so you'll recognize us at the station!

a Ivan is a Russian student who's going to study English in Brighton. He's going to stay with a family. Read the letter from Mrs Sanders and complete it with expressions from the box.

Brighton BN3 1HJ	Best wishes	~~28 Randalls Road~~	14th April 2005
Dear Ivan	PS	Looking forward to hearing from you	

b Read the letter again and answer the questions.

1. When's Ivan coming to Britain?
2. How is he going to get there?
3. How many questions does Mrs Sanders ask him?
4. Does *Looking forward to hearing from you* mean…?
   a. I hope you will write soon.
   b. I'm going to write again soon.
5. Why does Mrs Sanders send Ivan a photo?

c What differences are there between an informal letter and an e-mail?

Imagine you are going to stay with Mrs Sanders. Answer her letter using your own information. Remember to include your address and the date.

WRITE three paragraphs:

Paragraph 1 Thank her for her letter.
Paragraph 2 Say when you are arriving, etc.
Paragraph 3 Answer her other questions.

End the letter with *Best wishes* and your name.

CHECK your letter for mistakes (grammar, punctuation, and spelling).

3 What do you remember?

GRAMMAR

Circle the correct answer, a, b, or c.

What's ______ name?

a yours (b) your c you

1 We ______ live with John's parents.
   a 're going
   b 're going to
   (c) go to
2 What time ______?
   (a) you are leaving
   b are you leaving
   c are you leave
3 I'm sure ______ lose the match.
   a they
   b they'll
   c they going to
4 It's very late. They probably ______ come now.
   a won't to
   b won't
   c don't
5 I ______ pass the exam.
   a don't think she'll
   b think she won't
   c don't think she won't
6 It's very hot in here. ______ I open the window?
   a Will
   b Shall
   c Won't
7 **A** I don't have a car.
   B Don't worry. ______ take you.
   a We
   b We are
   c We'll
8 I ______ about my grandmother.
   a dream often
   b often am dreaming
   c often dream
9 I ______ in the park when I saw an enormous dog.
   a walked
   b was walking
   c 'm walking
10 Where ______ go next summer?
   a are you going to
   b you will
   c are you

[ ] **10**

VOCABULARY

a prepositions

Complete the sentences with the correct preposition.

Where do you come *from*?

1 Last night I dreamed ______ being alone on a desert island.
2 I'm looking ______ my grandchildren next week while my daughter is on holiday.
3 I'm looking ______ to the weekend.
4 I waited ______ the bus for half an hour.
5 I often argue ______ my dad about politics.

b verbs + *back*

Match the phrases.

'I'm going tomorrow.'		'When are you coming back?'
1 'Could you lend me 50 euros?'	[ ]	A 'Yes, I'll give it back tomorrow.'
2 'I'm sorry, she's not at home.'	[ ]	B 'No. Go away and don't come back.'
3 'Do you have my book?'	[ ]	C 'OK, I'll call back later.'
4 'My new mobile doesn't work.'	[ ]	D 'If you can pay me back before Friday.'
5 'Don't you want to see me again?'	[ ]	E 'Take it back to the shop.'

c opposite verbs

Write the opposite verb phrase.

push the door *pull the door*

1 lose a match ______
2 remember to pay ______
3 buy a car ______
4 learn Spanish ______
5 get a letter ______

[ ] **15**

PRONUNCIATION

a Underline the word with a different sound

1	love	come	home	one
2	lose	too	good	do
3	offer	won't	want	sorry
4	go	know	don't	down
5	borrow	awful	open	remember

b Underline the stressed syllable.

information

pessimist prediction remember important interesting

[ ] **10**

CAN YOU UNDERSTAND THIS TEXT?

2020 woman the hunter, man the househusband

A new report on life in 2020 was published yesterday. This report predicts big changes, not just in technology but also changes in the way we live. These are some of the predictions for work and family life.

Family life

☐ One in five fathers will be househusbands, while the mothers go out to work.

☐ People will live near other people who have the same interests as them, for example in golf villages.

☐ There will often be three generations living in the same house, e.g. grandparents, parents, and children.

☐ People will live until their mid-eighties, but women will still live slightly longer than men.

Work and study

☐ One in five school classes will be on-line via the Internet. Pupils will also often have video classes with a 'superteacher' from another city or country.

☐ Most workers will only have short-term contracts. They will have to learn to do lots of different jobs because they will change jobs frequently.

☐ Most people will work a twenty-five hour week. This will usually mean working five hours a day, although some people may work three eight-hour days and have four days off.

Adapted from a British newspaper

a Read the article about 2020. Tick (✓) the predictions that you think would be a good thing.

b Read the article again. Mark the sentences T (true), F (false), or DS (doesn't say).

According to this report, in 2020…

1 20% of fathers will stay at home and look after the children.
2 People will live near other people who like the same things they do.
3 Grandparents will look after their grandchildren.
4 Men and women will live until they're 80.
5 'Superteachers' will sometimes travel to give classes.
6 Many people will work in the same job all their life.
7 Everybody will work five hours a day.

c Underline and learn six new words or expressions from the article. Use your dictionary to check the meaning and pronunciation.

CAN YOU UNDERSTAND THESE PEOPLE?

a 3.20 Listen to five short conversations. Circle a, b, or c.

1 On Saturday the woman is going to ________.
 a stay at home b go swimming
 c play volleyball
2 Who do they think will win the League?
 a Arsenal b Manchester United c Liverpool
3 Next weekend the weather is going to be ________.
 a wet and cold b sunny but cold
 c warm and sunny
4 The woman is going to buy ________.
 a the red sweater b the blue sweater
 c the black sweater
5 Last night the student ________.
 a had a bad dream b had a good dream
 c didn't dream

b 3.21 Listen and complete the flight details.

Supertravel

Flight from London to [1] ________

Departure	Tuesday May 6th
Return	[2] ________
Flight times	Outward: leaves 08.30, arrives [3] ________
	Return: leaves [4] ________, arrives 12.30
Passenger's name	Robert [5] ________

CAN YOU SAY THIS IN ENGLISH?

a In English, can you...? Yes (✓)

☐ talk about your plans for tonight
☐ talk about your plans for next year
☐ make three future predictions about your town
☐ make three promises about your English

b Re-order the words to make questions.

1 doing weekend this what you are ?
2 English year you next going study to are ?
3 think do who will elections next you win the ?
4 rain think tomorrow will you do it ?
5 you dreams how your remember do often ?

c Ask your partner the questions in **b**. Ask for more information.

G present perfect (experience) + *ever, never*; present perfect or past simple?
V clothes
P vowel sounds

Have you ever been to that shop? What did you buy?

From rags to riches

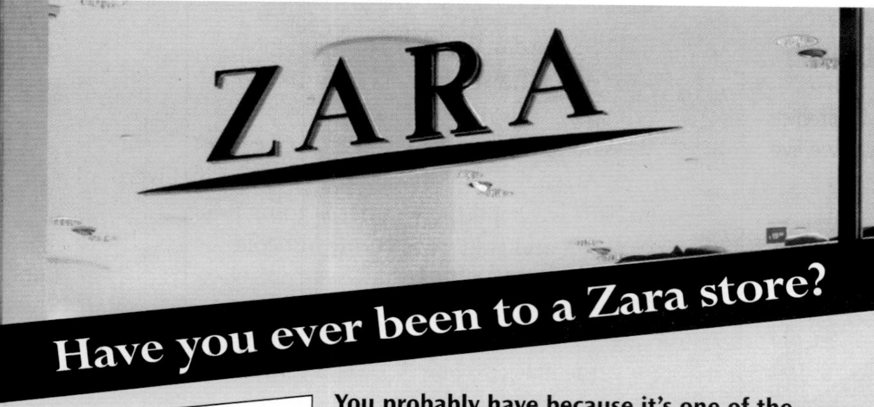

Have you ever been to a Zara store?

You probably have because it's one of the fastest-growing chains in the world. The person behind Zara is Amancio Ortega. He is the richest man in Spain, but very few people know his face. There are only two official photographs of him, and he rarely gives interviews. Although he is a multimillionaire businessman, he doesn't look like one – he doesn't like wearing suits or ties, and prefers to wear jeans and a shirt.

When he was young he worked as a shop assistant in a clothes store, but he always dreamed of having his own business. In 1963 he started a small company which made women's pyjamas. In 1975, at the age of 40, he opened his first clothes shop in La Coruña, a small city in north-west Spain, and named it *Zara*. Now you can find *Zara* shops all over the world, from New York to Moscow to Singapore. So why is *Zara* so successful?

The main reason is that *Zara* reacts incredibly quickly to the latest designer fashions, and produces clothes which are fashionable but inexpensive. *Zara* can make a new line of clothes in three weeks. Other companies normally take about nine months. The clothes also change from week to week – so customers keep coming back to see what's new. It produces 20,000 new designs a year – and none of them stay in the shops for more than a month.

So if you've seen a new jacket or skirt you like in a *Zara* store, hurry up and buy it, because it won't be there for long.

1 READING & VOCABULARY

a What's the most popular place to buy clothes in your town? Do you buy your clothes there? If not, where?

b Read the text about *Zara*. Then cover it and answer the questions below from memory.

1. Who is Amancio Ortega?
2. What is unusual about him?
3. What was his first job?
4. When did he open the first *Zara* shop?
5. Where are there *Zara* shops now?
6. What are the secrets of *Zara's* success?

c Read the text again and underline any words that are connected with clothes.

d ➲ **p.150 Vocabulary Bank** ***Clothes.***

2 PRONUNCIATION vowel sounds

a 4.1 Put two clothes words in each column. Listen and check. Practise saying the words.

belt blouse clothes coat pyjamas scarf
shirt shoes skirt suit sweater trousers

ɜː	əʊ	uː

aʊ	ɑː	e

b Ask and answer with a partner.

What did you wear yesterday?
What are you going to wear tonight?
What were the last clothes you bought?
What's the first thing you take off when you get home?
Do you always try on clothes before you buy them?
How often do you wear a suit?

3 LISTENING

4.2 Listen to three people being interviewed about *Zara*. Complete the chart with their information.

	Woman 1	Woman 2	Man	Your partner
1 Have you ever been to a *Zara* store?				
2 When did you last go there?				
3 Where?				
4 What did you buy?				
5 Are you happy with it?				

4 GRAMMAR present perfect or past simple?

a Interview your partner about *Zara* (or another shop in your town) and write his / her answers in the chart.

b Look at questions 1 and 2 above.

What tense are they?
Which question refers to a specific time in the past?
Which question is about some time in your life?

c **p.132 Grammar Bank 4A.** Read the rules and do the exercises.

5 SPEAKING

a Complete the questions with the past participle of the verb.

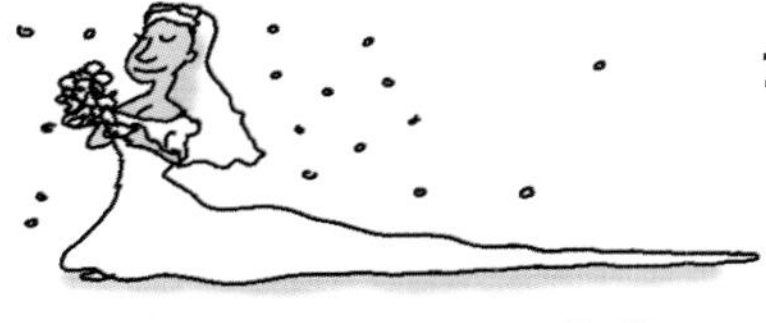

1 Have you ever _worn_ (wear) something only once? What? When / wear it?

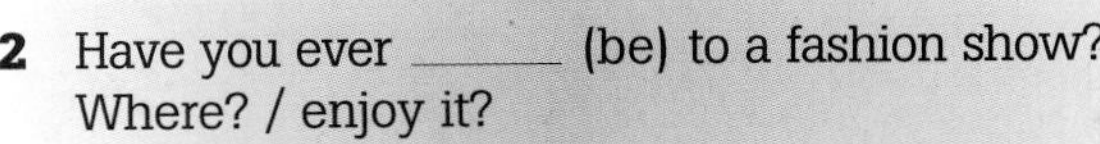

2 Have you ever ______ (be) to a fashion show? Where? / enjoy it?

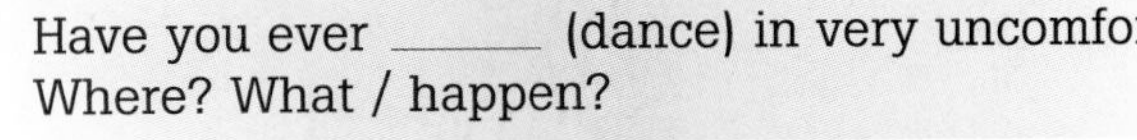

3 Have you ever ______ (dance) in very uncomfortable shoes? Where? What / happen?

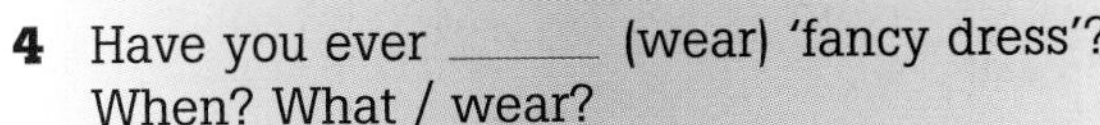

4 Have you ever ______ (wear) 'fancy dress'? When? What / wear?

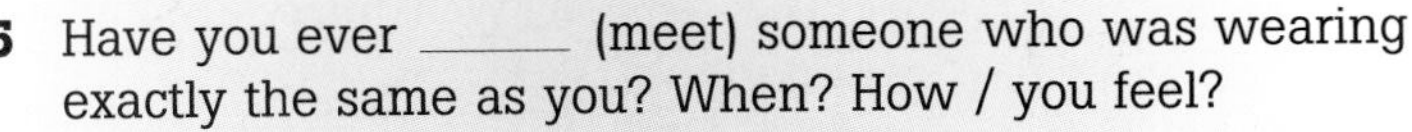

5 Have you ever ______ (meet) someone who was wearing exactly the same as you? When? How / you feel?

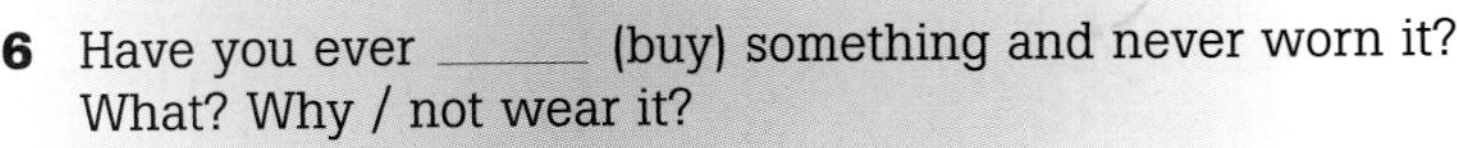

6 Have you ever ______ (buy) something and never worn it? What? Why / not wear it?

7 Have you ever ______ (ruin) clothes in the washing machine? What? What / happen?

8 Have you ever ______ (have) an argument with your family about clothes? What about?

b Interview a partner with the questions. If he / she answers 'Yes, I have', make follow-up questions in the past simple.

Have you ever worn something only once?
Yes I have. A suit.
When did you wear it?
For an interview for a job.

6 4.3 SONG ♫ *True Blue*

4 B

G present perfect simple + *yet, just, already*
V verb phrases
P /h/, /j/, /dʒ/

Have you tidied your room yet?
Yes, I've just done it.

Family conflicts

1 VOCABULARY verb phrases

a Read the magazine article and complete it with these verbs.

changes cleaned does (x2) leaves
~~makes~~ take tidies

Parents of teenagers wrote in to tell us what drives them mad.

Here are some of the top 'hates'.

1 He never *makes* his bed. If I make it, I find strange things in it like dirty socks, CDs without their boxes...

2 He never ______ his room – it's always a mess. The floor is covered with empty Coke cans, dirty socks...

3 She______ wet towels on the bathroom floor and doesn't pick them up.

4 She walks around the house eating food without a plate, usually just after I've ______ the floor. She then says 'Sorry' with an angelic smile.

5 He has breakfast, lunch, and dinner at home, but he never ______ the washing up.

6 When she comes into the living room she always ______ the channel on the TV – usually when I'm watching my favourite programme.

7 We bought a dog for him, because he promised to ______ it for a walk every day. Guess who always does it?

8 She always ______ her homework at the last minute – usually late on Sunday night. This means she needs the Internet, just when her sister is 'chatting' with her friends.

Adapted from a British magazine

b Cover the text. Can you remember the eight bad habits?

c In pairs, say which of these things are a problem in your house and why. What else is a problem?

housework	food
the TV / computer	the bathroom
pets (e.g. a dog)	homework

2 GRAMMAR present perfect + *just, yet, already*

a 4.4 Listen and number the pictures 1–4.

b Listen again and complete the dialogues with a past participle.

1 **A** Have you ______ yet?
B No, not yet.
A Well, hurry up! I'm going to be late for work.

2 **A** You've ______ a towel on the floor.
B Well, I haven't finished yet.
A Well, don't forget to pick it up.

3 **A** When are you going to do your homework?
B I've already ______ it.
A Really? When?
A I did it on the bus this evening.

4 **A** Can you get a plate for that sandwich? I've just ______ the floor.
B OK. Oops – sorry. Too late.

c Look at the conversations and underline *just*, *yet*, and *already*. What tense is the verb with them? What do you think they mean?

d **p.132 Grammar Bank 4B.** Read the rules and do the exercises.

3 PRONUNCIATION & SPEAKING

a **4.5** Listen and repeat. Practise saying the sentences.

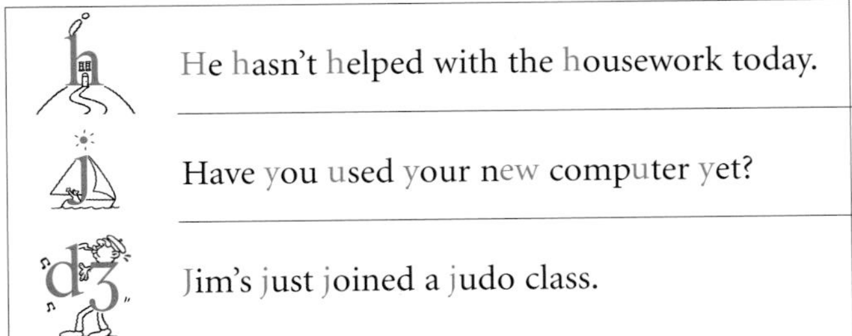

He hasn't helped with the housework today.

Have you used your new computer yet?

Jim's just joined a judo class.

b **Communication** *Has he done it yet? p.116.*

c **4.6** Listen. What's just happened?

4 READING

a Answer the questions in pairs.

1 At what age do young people usually leave home in your country?

2 What do you think is the right age for a young person to leave home? Why?

b Read the paragraphs and put them in order. Number them 1–5.

c Now read the whole article in order. Choose the best summary, A, B, or C.

A Mr and Mrs Serrano argued with their children. The children decided to leave home.

B Mr and Mrs Serrano argued a lot. Their children were unhappy so they left home.

C Mr and Mrs Serrano argued with their children a lot. They told their children to leave home.

d In pairs, underline any words or phrases you don't know. Try to guess their meaning. Then check with the teacher or with your dictionary. Choose five to learn.

e Do you think Mr and Mrs Serrano were right or wrong? Why? Do you think the story has a happy ending?

f **4.7** Listen and check.

Problems with your teenage children?

Why not throw them out?

A ☐ What did the Serranos' boys do? In fact they didn't go very far from home. The oldest boy David went to live with his girlfriend and has just started work in her father's construction company. The youngest son has rented a flat near the family home (his mother paid the first month's rent only).

B ☐ So Maria and Mariano asked their sons to leave the family home in Zaragoza in Spain. But the two boys didn't want to go. Then, Mr and Mrs Serrano took an unusual decision – they went to court.

C ☐ Do you have rude and moody teenage children living in your house? Have you ever secretly wanted to throw them out? A Spanish couple, Mr and Mrs Serrano, from Zaragoza in Spain, have done exactly that.

D ☐ Maria and her husband Mariano lived with their two sons, David, 20 and Mariano, 18. 'The situation was impossible,' said Maria. 'We were always arguing, our children were treating our house like a hotel, and they weren't contributing anything. Also they weren't studying or looking for work. They were complaining all the time and insulting us. They didn't respect us. I love my children, but in the end it was ruining our lives.'

E ☐ Normally, under Spanish law parents do not have the right to make their children leave home. But in this case the judge decided that the situation in the Serrano family was 'intolerable'. He gave Mr and Mrs Serrano the right to tell their children to go.

Elizabeth Nash, *The Independent* 18/10/99

G comparatives, *as…as, less… than…*
V time expressions: *spend time*, *waste time*, etc.
P sentence stress

We work harder and we have less free time.

Faster, faster!

1 GRAMMAR comparatives, *as… as, less… than…*

a Read the introduction to the article *We're living faster…* Is it optimistic or pessimistic? Why?

b Read it again and cross out the wrong word.

According to James Gleick, today we…

1 work **longer / shorter** hours.
2 have **more / less** free time.
3 talk **faster / more slowly**.
4 are **more relaxed / less relaxed**.
5 will probably have **longer / shorter** lives than our parents.

c Complete the sentences with *as* or *than*. Then check with the text.

1 We sleep less ____ previous generations.
2 If we don't slow down, we won't live ____ long ____ our parents.

d **p.132 Grammar Bank 4C.** Read the rules and do the exercises.

2 PRONUNCIATION sentence stress

⚠ Remember! *-er*, and unstressed words like *a, and, as,* and *than* have the sound /ə/

4.8 Listen and repeat the sentences. Copy the rhythm.

1 I'm busier than a year ago.
2 Life is more stressful than in the past.
3 We work harder than before.
4 We walk and talk faster.
5 I'm not as relaxed as I was.
6 We won't live as long as our parents.

3 READING & VOCABULARY

a You're going to read about some ways in which our lives are faster. Work in pairs. A read 1–3, B read 4–6.

b A tell B about paragraphs 1–3, B tell A about paragraphs 4–6. Use the pictures to help you. Are any of these things true in your country?

c Now read paragraphs 1–6. In pairs, look at the highlighted expressions with the word *time* and guess their meaning.

WE'RE LIVING FASTER,

NOT LONG AGO people believed that in the future we would work less, have more free time, and be more relaxed. But sadly this has not happened. Today we work harder, work longer hours, and are more stressed than ten years ago. We walk faster, talk faster, and sleep less than previous generations. And although we are obsessed with machines which save us time, we have less free time than our parents and grandparents had. But what is this doing to our health? An American journalist James Gleick in a new book, *Faster: the acceleration of just about everything*, says that people who live in cities are suffering from 'hurry sickness'– we are always trying to do more things in less time. As a result, our lives are more stressful. He says that if we don't slow down, we won't live as long as our parents. For most people, faster doesn't mean better.

Adapted from a British newspaper

4 LISTENING & SPEAKING

a 4.9 Look at the questionnaire. Listen to four people answering question 1. Which activity (working, studying, etc.) are they talking about?

1 ____________
2 ____________
3 ____________
4 ____________

b Listen again. Why do they spend more (or less) time on these things?

c In pairs, interview each other using the questionnaire.

ARE YOU LIVING FASTER...?

1 Compared to two years ago, do you spend more or less time on these things? Say why.

working or studying	sitting in traffic	cooking
talking on the phone	seeing friends	eating
working on a computer	shopping	sleeping

2 Do you have more or less free time than a year ago? Why? What don't you have enough time for?

3 How do you get to work / school? How long does it take you? Is this longer than a year ago?

4 Do you usually arrive on time...? Why (not)?
at work/school   for your English class   to meet your friends

5 What machines do you have which save you time? Do they make your life simpler or more complicated?

6 Do you waste a lot of time every day? Doing what?

BUT ARE WE LIVING BETTER?

1 No time for the news

Newspaper articles today are shorter and the headlines are bigger. Most people don't have enough time to read the articles, they only read the headlines! On TV and the radio, newsreaders speak more quickly than ten years ago.

2 No time for stories

In the USA there is a book called *One-Minute Bedtime Stories* for children. These are shorter versions of traditional stories, specially written for 'busy parents' who want to save time!

3 No time to listen

Some answerphones now have 'quick playback' buttons so that we can re-play people's messages faster – we can't waste time listening to people speaking at normal speed!

4 No time to relax

Even when we relax we do everything more quickly. Ten years ago when people went to art galleries they spent ten seconds looking at each picture. Today they spend just three seconds!

5 No time for slow sports

In the USA the national sport, baseball, is not as popular as before because it is a slow game and matches take a long time. Nowadays many people prefer faster and more dynamic sports like basketball.

6 ...but more time in our cars

The only thing that is slower than before is the way we drive. Our cars are faster but the traffic is worse so we drive more slowly. We spend more time sitting in our cars, feeling stressed because we are worried that we won't arrive on time. Experts predict that in ten years' time the average speed on the road in cities will be 17 km/h.

G superlatives (+ *ever* + present perfect)
V opposite adjectives
P word stress

It's the most beautiful city I've ever been to.

The world's friendliest city

1 READING & LISTENING

a Read the introduction to the article. In pairs, answer the questions.

1 What are the three tests?
2 Do you think they are good ones?
3 Which city do you think will be the friendliest / most unfriendly?

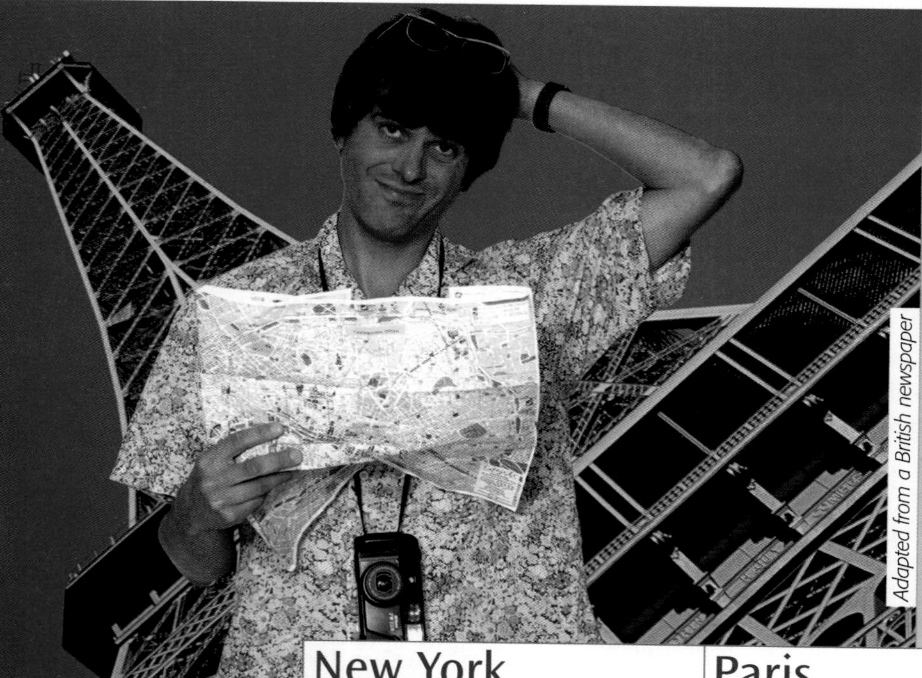

Adapted from a British newspaper

Big cities often have a reputation for being rude, unfriendly places for tourists. Journalist Tim Moore went to four cities, London, Rome, Paris, and New York, to find out if this is true. He went dressed as a foreign tourist and did three tests to see which city had the friendliest and most polite inhabitants. The three tests were:

1 The photo test

Tim asked people in the street to take his photo (not just one photo, but several – with his hat, without his hat, etc.). Did he find someone to do it?

2 The shopping test

Tim bought something in a shop and gave the shop assistant too much money. Did the shop assistant give back the extra money?

3 The accident test

Tim pretended to fall over in the street. Did anybody come and help him?

	New York	Paris	Rome
The photo test	I asked an office worker who was eating his sandwiches to take a photo of me. 'Of course I'll take your picture. Again? Sure! Again? No problem. Have a nice day!'	I asked some gardeners to take some photos of me in front of the Eiffel Tower. They couldn't stop laughing when they saw my hat.	I asked a very chic woman in sunglasses. She took a photo of me with my hat on, then without my hat. Then with my sunglasses. Then she asked me to take a photo of her!
The shopping test	I bought an *I love New York* T-shirt and drinks from two different people. I gave them too much money but they both gave me the extra money back.	I bought some fruit in a greengrocer's and gave the man a lot of coins. He carefully took the exact amount.	I bought a copy of *The Times* from a newspaper seller near the railway station. It was three euros. I gave the man four and he didn't give me any change.
The accident test	I fell over in Central Park. I didn't have to wait more than thirty seconds. 'Oh dear,' a man said. 'Is this your camera? I think it's broken.'	I fell over in the Champs Elysées. A minute passed before someone said, 'Are you OK?' And he was Scottish!	When I fell over about eight people immediately hurried to help me.

b Read about what happened in New York, Paris, and Rome. Answer the questions with **NY**, **P**, or **R**.

1 Which city do you think was the friendliest in the photo test? ____
2 In which city did he take a photo too? ____
3 In the shopping test, where didn't he get the right change? ____
4 Where did he buy a souvenir? ____
5 In the accident test, where did he wait longest for help? ____
6 In which city were people most helpful? ____

c 4.10 Now listen to Tim Moore talking about what happened in London. Answer the questions.

	London
The photo test	1 Who did he ask first?
	2 What did the man say?
	3 Who did he ask next? What happened?
The shopping test	4 What did he buy? Where?
	5 How much was it?
	6 Did he get the right change?
The accident test	7 Where did he do the accident test?
	8 Did anyone help him?
	9 What did the man say?

2 GRAMMAR superlatives (+ *ever* + present perfect)

a Cross out the wrong form in these questions.

1 Which city was **the friendlier / the friendliest** of the four?
2 Which city was **the more unfriendly / the most unfriendly**?
3 What's the friendliest place you've ever **been to / gone to**?

b Ask and answer the questions with a partner.

c **p.132 Grammar Bank 4D.** Read the rules and do the exercises.

3 VOCABULARY opposite adjectives

a What are the opposites of these adjectives?

friendly rude noisy boring

b **p.145 Vocabulary Bank** *Adjectives.* Do part 2.

c In pairs, choose five questions and ask a partner.

What's ...
the ________ (unfriendly)
the ________ (beautiful)
the ________ (ugly)
the ________ (expensive)
the ________ (polluted)
the ________ (exciting)
the ________ (dangerous)
the ________ (noisy)

place you've ever been to?

4 PRONUNCIATION word stress

a Underline the stressed syllable in the adjectives below.

1 It's the most **polluted** city I've ever been to.
2 He's the most **impatient** person I've ever met.
3 This is the most **comfortable** hotel I've ever stayed at.
4 It's the most **interesting** book I've ever read.
5 They're the most **expensive** shoes I've ever bought.
6 It's the most **beautiful** place I've ever seen.

b 4.11 Listen and check. What other words are stressed?

c Listen and repeat the sentences. Copy the rhythm.

5 SPEAKING

a **Communication** *The best and the worst A p.110 B p.114.* Read your instructions and write the names of people, places, etc. in the ovals.

b Ask and answer about what your partner has written in the ovals. Ask for more information.

Because it's the hottest place I've ever been to.

When did you go there?

4 Lost in San Francisco

DIRECTIONS

4.12 Listen to Allie talking to the hotel receptionist. Order the directions 1–5.

It's the third street on the left. ☐
Go straight ahead, down Sutter Street. ☐
Go out of the hotel and turn left. ☐
Union Square will be right in front of you. ☐
Turn left at Stockton. ☐

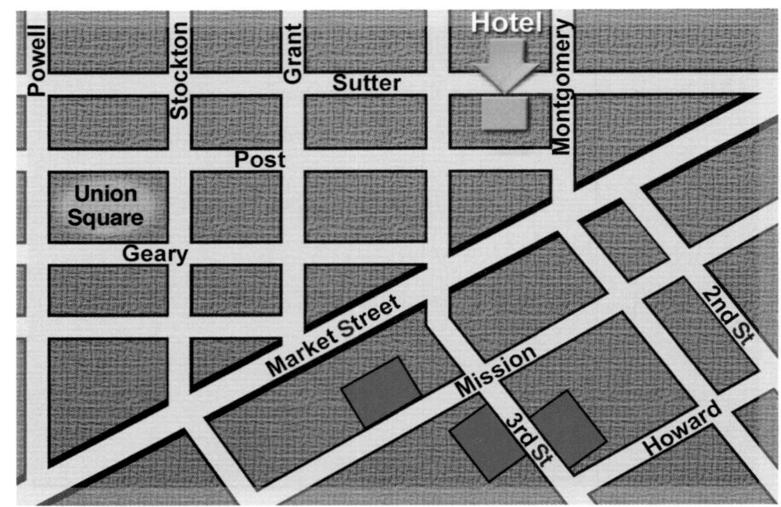

ASKING FOR INFORMATION

a 4.13 Cover the dialogue and listen. Where does Allie want to go? How is she going to get there? Mark the route from Union Square on the map.

YOU SAY	YOU HEAR
Can you recommend a good museum?	Well, SFMOMA is fantastic.
Sorry? Where did you say?	SFMOMA. The San Francisco ________ of Modern Art.
Where is it?	On ________ Street.
How far is it from Union Square?	Not far. It's just a ________ of blocks.
Can I walk from there?	Sure. It'll ________ you ten minutes.
Can you show me on the map?	Yes, Union Square is here, and the museum is here. From Union Square you go down Geary to the ________ and turn right. That's Third Street. Go down Third and you'll see SFMOMA on the ________.
What time does it open?	It opens at ________.
Thanks very much.	Have a good day. I'm sure you'll ________ the museum!

b Complete the YOU HEAR phrases. Listen and check.

c 4.14 Listen and repeat the YOU SAY phrases. Copy the rhythm.

d In pairs, roleplay the dialogue. A (book open) you're the receptionist, B (book closed) you're Allie. Swap roles.

SOCIAL ENGLISH looking for Union Square

a 4.15 Listen and circle a or b.

1 Allie and the man... **a** have met before. **b** haven't met before.
2 Mark is... **a** meeting Allie later. **b** in a meeting.
3 Del Monico's is... **a** a coffee bar. **b** a restaurant.
4 Brad wants to... **a** go shopping with Allie. **b** take Allie to Union Square.
5 Brad loves... **a** Allie's conversation. **b** Allie's pronunciation.

b Complete the USEFUL PHRASES, Listen again and check.

c 4.16 Listen and repeat the phrases. How do you say them in your language?

USEFUL PHRASES

B Don't I k______ you?
A I don't t______ so.
B What are you d______ here?
A I'm l______ for (Union Square).
A That's really k______ of you.
A Are you s______?

Study Link MultiROM

Describing where you live

a Read the text and match the questions with paragraphs 1–5.

What's it famous for? ☐
What's the weather like? ☐
What's the best thing about it? Do you like living there? ☐
Describe your home town. ☐
Where do you live? Where is it? How big is it? ☐

b Complete the text with these words.

atmosphere beach ~~city~~ festival museums
population river streets tourist weather

c Find one grammar mistake in each highlighted phrase. Correct it.

The place where I live

1 I live in Porto, which is a [1] *city* on the coast in the north of Portugal. It has a [2]______ of 300,000 people and it's the second ~~bigger~~ city in Portugal. *biggest*

2 It's a beautiful city, and it's great for walking around. There are lots of narrow [3]______, and it's full of churches, [4]______, and markets. There's an area called Foz where there is a lot of outdoor bars and restaurants – people go there at the weekend to sit in the sun, drink coffee, and watch the Atlantic.

3 The [5]______ here is very different from the south of Portugal. The winter can be very wet, and it sometimes rain for days. The summer is wonderful – it's sunny but not usually too hot, and it's great for going to the mountains or the [6]______.

4 Porto is famous for port wine, who is only produced here (but I don't like it much!). The biggest [7]______ attraction in Porto is probably the [8]______ – there are some beautiful bridges, including one designed by Eiffel, and lots of tourists goes on boat trips. There's a [9]______ in June called São Joao, with a lot of fireworks and people in the streets, and everybody spends most of the evening hitting each other with plastic hammers!

5 But I think the best things about Porto are the people and the [10]______. It's quite small and it's very safe and friendly. It's a working city and it has a real sense of history, and that's the main reason why I like live here so much.

WRITE a description of the place where you live.
Write five paragraphs. Answer the questions in **a** in the right order.

CHECK your description for mistakes (grammar, punctuation, and spelling) and attach a photo if you can.

4 What do you remember?

GRAMMAR

Circle the correct answer, a, b, or c.

What's ______ name?

a yours (b) your c you

1 ______ ever been to a *Zara* shop?
  a Do you
  b Have you
  c Did you
2 I've never ______ him in a suit and tie.
  a seen
  b see
  c saw
3 You haven't done the washing up ______.
  a already
  b just
  c yet
4 **A** Would you like a coffee?
  B No, thanks. ______ four cups today.
  a I've had already
  b I've already had
  c I already have had
5 I've ______ cleaned the floor. It's wet.
  a already
  b just
  c yet
6 The traffic is ______ than it was.
  a badder
  b worse
  c more bad
7 Radio newsreaders speak more ______ than before.
  a quickly
  b quick
  c quicker
8 Baseball isn't as ______ it was in the past.
  a popular than
  b popular that
  c popular as
9 What's the ______ city you've ever seen?
  a most beautiful
  b more beautiful
  c beautifulest
10 This is the ______ city in the world.
  a most noisy
  b noisiest
  c noisier

10

VOCABULARY

a verb phrases

Complete the phrases.

make your bed

do pick up take tidy waste

1 ______ your room
2 ______ things on the floor
3 ______ the dog for a walk
4 ______ the washing up
5 ______ time

b clothes

Complete the sentences.

That's a very nice j*acket*.

1 Levi's are famous for their j______.
2 Business people usually have to wear a s______ to work.
3 I always t______ on clothes before I buy them.
4 Take o______ your coat. It's very hot in here.
5 I wear my t______ when I do sport.

c adjectives

Write the opposite adjective.

big *small*

1 rude ______
2 noisy ______
3 possible ______
4 dangerous ______
5 patient ______

15

PRONUNCIATION

a Underline the word with a different sound.

1 (ɜː)	shirt	work	coat	skirt
2 (aʊ)	bought	blouse	trousers	mouth
3 (e)	friendly	pretty	men	many
4 (eɪ)	make	trainers	great	earn
5 (j)	yet	yellow	already	your

b Underline the stressed syllable.

information

pyjamas already nearly busier friendliest

10

CAN YOU UNDERSTAND THIS TEXT?

IN 1952, Audrey Hepburn was in Rome, making the film *Roman Holiday* with Gregory Peck. She was engaged to James Hanson, a London 'playboy', and she asked a famous Italian designer, Zoe Fontana, to make her a dress for the wedding.

Signora Fontana said, 'Audrey was 23. She was so young and so beautiful then. She tried the dress on many times. It was in white lace, with a lot of tiny buttons down the back, and she wanted to wear flowers on her head.'

But two weeks before the wedding, Audrey Hepburn decided not to get married. She phoned Zoe Fontana and said, 'I've cancelled the wedding. But I want another girl to wear my wedding dress, perhaps a poor girl who could never pay for a dress like this one. Find a beautiful girl and give the dress to her.'

Signora Fontana found a poor 20-year-old girl in Latina, a town near Rome. She was exactly the same size as Hepburn and the dress fitted her perfectly. Her name was Amabile Altobello.

Signora Altobello said, 'I wanted to get married, but my fiancé and I didn't have enough money for a wedding. When Audrey Hepburn gave me the dress it was like a dream come true. Everybody in the town was very excited, and they also gave us furniture, and even organized a honeymoon for us in Paris.'

Today Signora Altobello is over 70 years old but she still has the dress. 'We are still poor and we have had a hard life, but we have three daughters and five grandchildren. We have had a happy marriage, so the dress brought me luck.'

Adapted from a British newspaper

a Read the article and mark the sentences T (true), F (false), or DS (doesn't say).

1. Audrey Hepburn was going to marry a playboy.
2. She wanted to get married in Rome.
3. Her wedding dress was white with flowers on it.
4. Before the wedding she fell in love with another man.
5. She asked Zoe Fontana to give the dress to a friend.
6. Amabile Altobello was the same age as Audrey Hepburn.
7. The people of Latina also gave her things for her house.
8. She and her husband are still married.

b Guess the meaning of the highlighted words.

CAN YOU UNDERSTAND THESE PEOPLE?

a 4.17 Listen and circle the correct answer, a, b, or c.

1. He thought the fashion show was ________.
   a exciting b interesting c boring
2. The woman bought ________.
   a a shirt b a skirt c some shoes
3. The floor is ________.
   a wet b dry c dirty
4. What time does he finish work?
   a 7.00 b 8.00 c 9.00
5. The most beautiful city he's been to is ________.
   a Venice b Prague c Amsterdam

b 4.18 Listen to an interview with a model. Mark the sentences T (true) or F (false).

1. She often wears clothes she doesn't like.
2. She broke her leg during a fashion show.
3. She hasn't been to Africa.
4. She went to Argentina two years ago.
5. She would like to go to India again.

CAN YOU SAY THIS IN ENGLISH?

a Can you...? Yes (✓)

- ☐ say what clothes you wore yesterday
- ☐ say what housework you / other people in your family do
- ☐ say if you have more or less free time than last year, and why

b Make five questions with the present perfect and a superlative.

What / good book / ever / read?
What's the best book you've ever read?

1. What / hot place / ever / be to?
2. What / bad film / ever / see?
3. Who / generous person / ever / meet?
4. What / good restaurant / ever / be to?
5. What / long journey / make?

c Ask your partner the questions in **b**.

5 A

G uses of the infinitive (with *to*)
V verbs + infinitive
P word stress

I want to go to the party.

Are you a party animal?

How to survive at a party...
(when you don't know anybody!)

Has this ever happened to you? You arrive at a party or wedding reception where you don't know anybody. Everybody there seems to know each other. What can you do? Here are five simple tips.

- Don't stand in the corner. You need [1] *to be* positive. Find somebody you think you would like [2] ______ and go and introduce yourself.
- Try [3] ______ impersonal questions like 'I love your bag. Where did you get it?' That will help [4] ______ a conversation.
- Try [5] ______ the conversation. When you are nervous, it's very easy [6] ______ about yourself all the time. Nobody wants [7] ______ to your life story when they've only just met you.
- Smile, smile, smile. Use your body-language [8] ______ a positive, friendly impression. That way people will want [9] ______ to you.
- If you want [10] ______ from a really boring person, say that you are going to the bar [11] ______ another drink or that you need [12] ______ to the bathroom. Don't come back!

Adapted from a British magazine

1 SPEAKING

Interview a partner with the questionnaire. Ask for more information. Is your partner a 'party animal'?

Do you like going to parties? Why (not)?
Do you like giving parties? Why (not)?

When was the last time you went to a party or celebration? (for example, a wedding, a birthday party, etc.)

Whose party was it?

Did you have a good time?

What did you wear?

What kind of music did they play?

Did you dance?

Did you meet anybody new?

What did you have to eat and drink?

Did you stay until the end?

2 GRAMMAR uses of the infinitive (with *to*)

a Read the article about parties. Complete the five rules with an infinitive.

to ask ~~to be~~ not to dominate to escape to get
to give to go to listen to meet to start to talk (x2)

b Read the article again and then cover it. Can you remember the tips?

c Match the examples A–C from the text with rules 1–3.

A It's very easy **to talk** about yourself all the time.
B Say that you're going to the bar **to get** another drink.
C Try **to ask** impersonal questions.

Use the infinitive (with *to*)...
1 after some verbs (e.g. *want*, *try*, etc.) ☐
2 after adjectives ☐
3 to say why you do something. ☐

d ➲ **p.134 Grammar Bank 5A.** Read the rules and do the exercises.

3 READING & LISTENING

a Read this article about the right things to say to different people at parties. In pairs, guess how to complete the **Don't say** phrases.

What to say
(and what not to say)
to people at parties

If you're talking to a doctor…
Don't say: I have a ____________. Could you ____________?
Say: You look tired. Would you like a drink?

If you're talking to a teacher…
Don't say: You're so lucky! You have ____________.
Say: I'm sure it's very difficult to motivate teenagers.

If you're talking to a travel agent…
Don't say: Can you recommend ____________?
Say: What's the most interesting place you've ever been to?

If you're talking to a hairdresser…
Don't say: What do you think of ____________? Is it too ____________?
Say: What do you think will be the new style this year?

If you're talking to a psychiatrist…
Don't say: Are you ____________?
Say: Do you work with children or adults?

b 5.1 Now listen to some people at a party who say the wrong things. Complete the **Don't say** phrases. Did you guess any of them?

c Listen to the people at the party again. Complete the conversations with an infinitive.

Conversation 1	I want ______ ______ him a 'Happy Birthday'.
Conversation 2	Perhaps you would like ______ ______ my class one day.
Conversation 3	I'd like ______ ______ somewhere ______.
Conversation 4	You're just the person I want ______ ______ to.
Conversation 5	I need ______ ______ to the ______.

4 VOCABULARY verbs + infinitive

a ➲ **p.154 Vocabulary Bank** *Verb forms* (Verb + infinitive). Look at some other verbs followed by the infinitive. Highlight any that you didn't know.

b ➲ **Communication** *Guess the infinitive A p.110 B p.114.*

5 PRONUNCIATION & SPEAKING

> ⚠ Two- and three-syllable words usually have the stress on the first syllable. Always underline the stress in new words.

a In pairs underline the stressed syllable in these words.

dangerous	decide	difficult	forget	important
interesting	possible	pretend	promise	remember

b 5.2 Listen and check. Practise saying the words.

c Choose five questions and ask a partner.

Do you find it **difficult to remember** people's names?

Do you think it's **important to learn** to cook?

What's the most **interesting place to visit** in your town?

Have you ever **forgotten to turn off** your mobile in a cinema or a concert?

Do you think it's **possible to learn** a foreign language without going to the country?

Is there any part of your town where it's **dangerous to go** at night?

Do you always **remember to phone** your friends on their birthdays?

When was the last time you **promised not to come** home late?

Have you ever **pretended to be** ill (when you weren't)?

Have you **decided to go** anywhere next summer?

5 B

G verb + *-ing*
V verbs followed by *-ing*
P *-ing*

I love waking up on a sunny morning.

What makes you feel good?

We asked readers from all over the world to tell us what makes them feel good

- Eating outside. I love sitting at street cafés or having meals in the garden, even when the weather's not perfect – which it often isn't.
- Being with people I like (and not being with people I don't like).
- Sitting on a plane when it takes off – you can't control what's going to happen for the next 2–3 hours so you can really relax.
- Waking up on a sunny morning during my holidays when I know I have a whole day ahead to do the things I really like doing.
- Getting out of the city. It doesn't matter where to, to the beach, or to the country, or to the forest. Being in the middle of nature makes me feel alive.

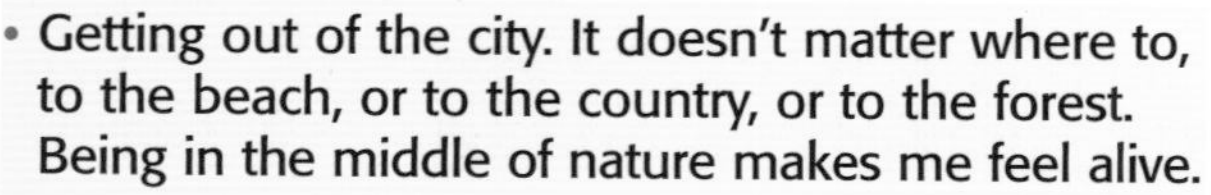

- Watching heavy rain storms through the window from a comfortable, warm room with a fire, and knowing I don't need to go out.
- Talking to intelligent people: good conversation is one of life's great pleasures.
- Having time for myself. Unfortunately, it doesn't happen very often.
- Reading books or magazines in English – I'm Hungarian, and I still find it hard to believe that I can enjoy reading without using a dictionary in a language that once was a complete mystery.
- Tidying a cupboard. It stops me from thinking about my problems.

1 READING

a Read the article once. How many people mention...?

1 the weather
2 holidays and travelling
3 housework
4 nature
5 other people

b Read the article again and tick (✓) the *three* things you agree with most. Then put a cross (✗) next to any you don't agree with. Compare with a partner. Say why.

c Underline five new words or phrases you want to learn from the text.

2 GRAMMAR verb + *-ing*

A **Being** with people I like (makes me feel good).
B I love **sitting** at cafés...
C I can enjoy reading without **using** a dictionary.

a Match sentences A–C with rules 1–3.

Use the *-ing* form...

1 after some verbs (e.g. *like, love*, etc.) ☐
2 when we use a verb as a noun (e.g. as the subject of a sentence) ☐
3 when we use a verb after a preposition ☐

b Look at the **highlighted** verbs. Can you remember the spelling rules for making the *-ing* form?

c ➲ **p.134 Grammar Bank 5B.** Read the rules and do the exercises.

d Now write two things that make *you* feel good (that are not in the article). Compare with a partner.

3 PRONUNCIATION *-ing*

a 5.3 Listen and repeat the sound picture and the words.

thing bring wrong language
sitting watching thanks think

b **p.159 Sound Bank.** Look at the typical spellings for this sound.

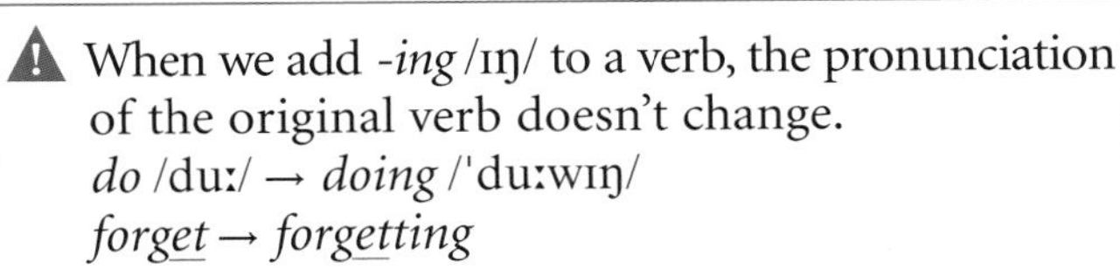

When we add *-ing* /ɪŋ/ to a verb, the pronunciation of the original verb doesn't change.
do /duː/ → *doing* /ˈduːwɪŋ/
forget → *forgetting*

c 5.4 Listen and say the *-ing* form of the verbs you hear.

4 VOCABULARY & SPEAKING

a **p.154 Vocabulary Bank** *Verb forms* **(Verb + *-ing*).** Look at other verbs which are followed by the *-ing* form.

b Work in pairs. Choose five things to talk about from the list below.

a job you **don't mind** doing in the house
a sport you **enjoy** watching
something you **like** doing with your family
something you **love** doing in the summer
something you **hate** doing at work / school
something you **spend** a lot of time doing
somebody you **dream of** meeting
something you **don't like** doing alone
a country you are **interested in** visiting
something you are **thinking of** doing this weekend
something you have **stopped** doing
something you are not very **good at** doing

c A tell B about the five things. Say why. B ask for more information. Then swap roles.

I don't mind cooking. It's quite relaxing.

Do you cook every day?

5 LISTENING

a Ask and answer these questions in pairs.

Do you ever sing…?
in the shower
in the car
at karaoke bars
while you're listening to a CD
in a choir /kwaɪə/ or a band

b In pairs, say if you think sentences 1–7 are T (true) or F (false).

1 Singing is good for your health.
2 To sing well you need to learn to breathe correctly.
3 People who sing are fatter than people who don't.
4 Not everybody can learn to sing.
5 You need to know how to read music to be able to sing well.
6 If you make a surprised face, you can sing high notes better.
7 It takes a long time to learn to sing better.

c 5.5 Now listen to an interview with the director of a singing school and a student who did a course there. Were you right?

d Listen again. Choose the right answer.

1 When you are learning to sing you need to ______ correctly.
a stand **b** dress **c** eat

2 Singing well is 95% ______.
a repeating **b** listening **c** breathing

3 Gemma's course lasted ______.
a one day **b** one week **c** one month

4 Gemma has always ______.
a been good at singing **b** been in a choir **c** liked singing

5 In the morning the students learnt to ______.
a breathe and sing **b** listen and breathe **c** listen and sing

6 At the end of the afternoon they could sing ______.
a perfectly **b** much better **c** a bit better

5 C

G *have to, don't have to, must, mustn't*
V modifiers: *a bit, really*, etc.
P sentence stress

You have to come to all the classes. You don't have to do an exam.

How much can you learn in a month?

1 GRAMMAR *have to, don't have to, must, mustn't*

a Look at these notices. Have you seen any like these in your school?

A **SILENCE** Exam in progress

B Tonight's film: ***Pirates of the Caribbean*** Entrance free

C **Course fees** to be paid in advance

D 

E No food here please

F Extra pronunciation class **5pm**

b Match the notices with the rules.

1 You have to pay before you start. ☐
2 You don't have to come if you don't want to. ☐
3 You mustn't eat in here. ☐
4 You must turn off your mobiles before you come in. ☐
5 You mustn't talk near here. ☐
6 You don't have to pay to see this. ☐

c Look at the highlighted expressions and answer the questions.

1 Which two phrases mean...?
It is a rule. There's an obligation to do this. *You have to*
____

2 Which phrase means…?
It isn't obligatory. It isn't necessary. ______________

3 Which phrase means…?
It isn't permitted. It is against the rules. ______________

d **p.134 Grammar Bank 5C.** Read the rules and do the exercises.

2 PRONUNCIATION sentence stress

a 5.6 Listen and write the six sentences.

b Listen again and repeat the sentences. Copy the rhythm. Which letter is 'silent' in *mustn't*?

c Make true sentences about the rules in the school where you are studying English. Use *We have to, We don't have to,* or *We mustn't.*

1 ______________ come to lessons on time.
2 ______________ turn off our mobile phones.
3 ______________ eat or drink in the classroom.
4 ______________ come to class on Saturday.
5 ______________ bring a dictionary to class.
6 ______________ do an exam at the end of the year.
7 ______________ smoke in the building.
8 ______________ do homework after each lesson.
9 ______________ do a test every week.

3 READING & LISTENING

a Do you think people from your country are good at learning languages? Why (not)?

b Read about Anna, a British journalist who did an intensive Polish course. Then cover the article and answer the questions.

1 What languages did Anna already know?
2 Why did she choose to learn Polish?
3 Where did she do the course?
4 What did she think was the most difficult thing about Polish?
5 Where is she going to do the 'tests'?
6 What five things does she have to do?
7 What are the rules?

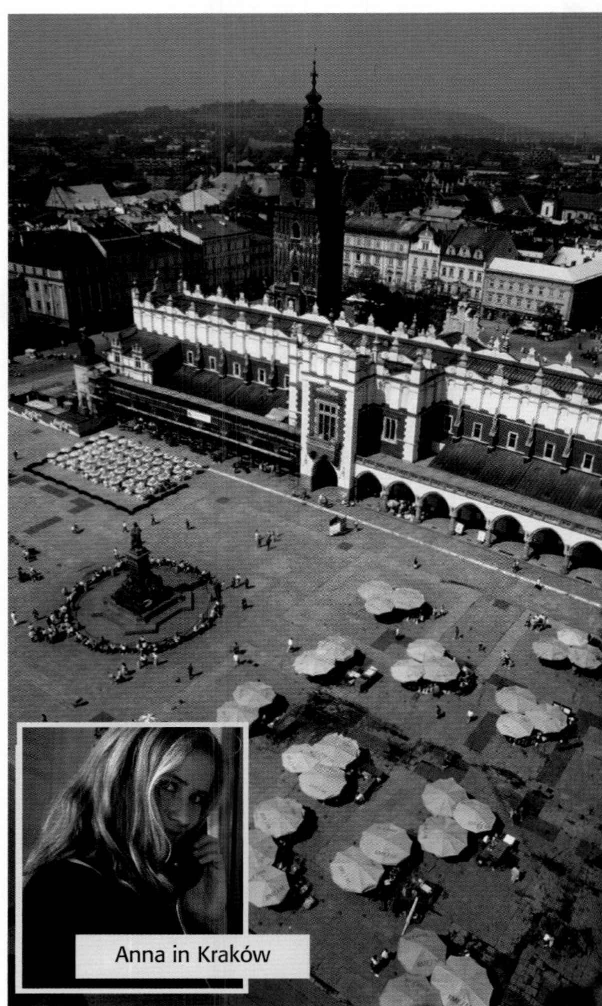

Anna in Kraków

How much can you learn in a month?

I work for a magazine, which was doing an article about British language learners. As an experiment, they asked me to learn a completely new language for one month. Then I had to go to the country and do some 'tests' to see if I could 'survive' in different situations. I decided to learn Polish because my great-grandmother was Polish and I have some relatives there. I can already speak French and Spanish quite well but Polish isn't a Latin-based language so I knew it would be completely different.

I did a one-month intensive course at a language school in Birmingham. I thought I was good at languages before I started learning Polish, but now I'm not so sure. I found it incredibly difficult. The grammar was really complicated and the words were not like any other language I know so it was very hard to remember them. For example, I thought 'football' was more or less an international word, but in Polish it's *piłka nożna*. And the pronunciation is unbelievable! Every word is full of z's where you don't expect them, like *jeździsz* which means 'you go'.

My course finished yesterday and I'm going to Kraków for the weekend to do my tests. A local guide called Kasia is coming with me and is going to give me a mark out of 10.

These are the tests and the rules:

Tests

You have to...

1 get a taxi.
2 order a drink in a bar.
3 ask for directions (and follow them).
4 phone and ask to speak to someone.
5 ask somebody the time.

Rules

– you mustn't use a dictionary or phrasebook.
– you mustn't speak English at any time.
– you mustn't use your hands or mime.

c 5.7 Which test do you think will be the easiest for Anna? Which will be the most difficult? Listen to Anna doing the tests in Kraków and check your answers.

d Listen again. Mark the sentences T (true) or F (false). Correct the false ones.

1 The taxi driver couldn't speak English.
2 Anna understood the waitress's question.
3 She ordered a small Coke.
4 Anna asked for directions to a bank.
5 She couldn't understand what the woman said.
6 Anna couldn't understand everything the woman on the phone said.
7 Anna thought telling the time in Polish was very easy.
8 She didn't find out what the time was.
9 Kasia gave her eight out of ten for her Polish.

4 SPEAKING

a How well could you do Anna's five tests in English? How much do you think you can learn in a month?

b Talk to a partner.

Have you ever...

spoken in English on the phone? Who to? What about?
seen a film in English? Which? How much did you understand?
spoken to a tourist in English? When? Why?
read an English book or magazine? Which ones?
asked for directions in a foreign city? Where? What happened?
learnt another foreign language? How well can you speak it?

5 VOCABULARY modifiers

I found Polish **incredibly** difficult.
I felt **a bit** stupid when the taxi driver spoke perfect English.

a Complete the chart with the words in the box.

a bit   incredibly   ~~not very~~   quite   really   ~~very~~

Polish is
______
______
very   difficult
______
______
not very

b Complete the sentences with one of the words so they are true for you. Compare with a partner.

1 I'm ______ good at learning languages.
2 I'm ______ motivated to improve my English.
3 English pronunciation is ______ difficult.
4 English grammar is ______ complicated.
5 I'm ______ worried about the next English exam.
6 English is ______ useful for my work / studies.

G expressing movement
V prepositions of movement, sport
P prepositions

5D The name of the game

The ball went over the net.

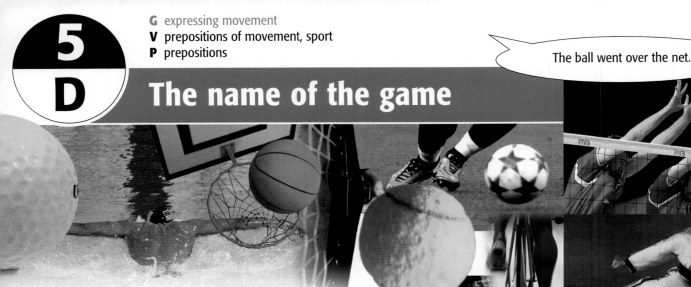

1 VOCABULARY & SPEAKING sport, prepositions of movement

a Look at the photos. Can you name the sports? Write them in the correct column.

play	go	do

b 5.8 Listen and check.

c In pairs, say…

Which of the sports in **a** are usually team sports?
How many **players** are there?
In which sports do you…?
a **hit** the ball b **throw** the ball c **kick** the ball d **shoot**

d Ask and answer with a partner.

Do you do any sports? Which one(s)?
Which sports do you enjoy watching?
Which sports do you hate watching?
Are you (or anyone in your family) a fan of a sports team? Which one?
Do you (or they) watch their matches? Where?

e Where did the ball go? Complete with a preposition.

across along down into ~~over~~

The ball went *over* the wall, _______ the street, _______ the steps, _______ the road, and _______ the river.

f p.148 **Vocabulary Bank** *Prepositions*. Do part 2.

2 GRAMMAR expressing movement

The rules of the game

1 You play this sport outside with one, two, or more players. You have to hit the ball into a small hole. You mustn't hit the ball into the water.

2 You can play this sport outside or inside with two or four players. You have to hit the ball over a net and the ball mustn't go 'out'.

3 You usually do this sport outside (but it can be inside). You have to go round a track many times and be the first one to go past the finish line. Sometimes you have to go round a country, for example, France.

4 You play this sport outside with two teams. You have to pass the ball to other players with your foot and try to kick the ball into the goal. You mustn't touch the ball with your hands.

5 You play this sport outside with two teams. You have to throw the ball to other players and take the ball over the other team's line. You can also get points by kicking the ball through two very high posts.

a Match the rules to the sports in 1. What are the sports?

b 5.9 Listen and check.

c Look at the sports rules again and the highlighted words. How do you express movement in English?

d **p.134 Grammar Bank 5D.** Read the rules and do the exercises.

3 PRONUNCIATION prepositions

a Match the prepositions with the phonetics. How do you pronounce the words?

across along into over
round through towards

1 /ˈɪntuː/ ________
2 /əˈlɒŋ/ ________
3 /raʊnd/ ________
4 /təˈwɔːdz/ ________
5 /əˈkrɒs/ ________
6 /θruː/ ________
7 /ˈəʊvə/ ________

b 5.10 Listen and check. Underline the stressed syllable, and practise saying the prepositions.

c **Communication** *Cross country p.117.* Tell your partner where the runner went.

4 READING & SPEAKING

a How long does a normal football match last? How many minutes are added after each half?

b Read the article and complete it with a word from below.

champions fans goal ~~match~~ pitch
players referee scored stadium team

c Read the text again. Number the sentences 1–6.

A Manchester United scored their first goal. ☐
B The Bayern Munich fans started celebrating. ☐
C The 90 minutes finished and the referee added three minutes. ☐
D Bayern Munich scored a goal. *1*
E Manchester United scored their second goal. ☐
F The UEFA president left his seat to go to present the cup. ☐

d What is the most exciting sporting event you've ever seen? Prepare your answers to these questions.

1 What sport was it?
2 When and where was it?
3 Who was taking part?
4 Were you there or did you see it on TV?
5 What happened?

e Ask and answer with a partner.

5 5.11 SONG ♫ *We are the champions*

Your most exciting sporting moments...

This week, Duc from Vietnam writes:

The most exciting football [1] *match* I have ever seen was the 1999 Champions' League Final between Manchester United and Bayern Munich in the Nou Camp [2] ________ in Barcelona.

After 90 minutes Manchester United were losing 1–0. The Bayern Munich [3] ________ in the stadium were already celebrating their [4] ________'s victory. The Manchester United fans in the stadium and millions around the world were watching in despair.

There were now just three minutes of added time. 20 seconds passed and United got a corner. The atmosphere in the stadium was incredibly intense. All the Manchester United [5] ________ (including their goalkeeper) were in the Bayern Munich penalty area. David Beckham took the corner and Teddy Sheringham [6] ________. It was 1–1!

The Manchester United fans were ecstatic. There was only about one minute left now but United attacked again and scored another [7] ________. Now it was 2–1! 30 seconds later we heard the [8] ________ blow his whistle. The match was over. United were the [9] ________! Many of the Bayern fans and players were crying. They had lost the match in less than three minutes.

The next day I read that the UEFA president missed both Manchester United's goals. He was going down to the [10] ________ to give the cup to the German team when United scored their first goal and he was going back up to his seat when they scored their second! He missed the most exciting and unforgettable three minutes of football I have ever seen.

BUYING CLOTHES

5.12 Listen to Allie shopping. Answer the questions.

1 What does Allie want to buy?
2 What size is she?
3 Does she try it on?
4 How much does Allie think it costs?
5 How does she pay?

TAKING SOMETHING BACK

a 5.13 Cover the dialogue and listen. What's the problem with Allie's sweater? Does she change it or ask for her money back?

YOU HEAR	YOU SAY
Can I help you?	Yes, I bought this sweater about half an hour ago.
Yes, I remember. Is there a ______?	Yes, I've decided it's too big for me.
What ______ is it?	Medium.
So you need a ______. I don't see one here.	Do you have any more?
I'll go and check. Just a ______.	
I'm sorry but we don't have ______ one in black.	Oh dear.
We can order one for you. It'll only take a few ______.	No, I'm leaving on Saturday.
Would you like to exchange it for ______ else?	Not really. Could I have a refund?
No problem. Do you ______ the receipt?	Yes, here you are.

b Listen again. Complete the YOU HEAR phrases.

c 5.14 Listen and repeat the YOU SAY phrases. Copy the rhythm.

d In pairs, roleplay the dialogue. A (book open) you're the shop assistant, B (book closed) you're Allie. Swap roles.

SOCIAL ENGLISH the conference cocktail party

a 5.15 Listen and complete with *Mark*, *Allie*, or *Brad*.

1 *Allie* tells ______ about the shopping and museum.
2 ______ comes to say hello to ______ and ______.
3 ______ is surprised that ______ and ______ met this morning.
4 ______ asks ______ if she wants a drink.
5 ______ is annoyed, but goes to get the drinks.

b Complete the USEFUL PHRASES, Listen again and check.

c 5.16 Listen and repeat the phrases. How do you say them in your language?

USEFUL PHRASES

M What did you t______ of it?
A Never m______.
A What a l______ evening!
A I got l______.
M What would you like to d______?
B What a good i______.

A formal e-mail

a Read the e-mail to a language school. Tick (✓) the questions that Adriano wants the school to answer.

- ☐ How much do the courses cost?
- ☐ When do the courses start and finish?
- ☐ How many students are there are in a class?
- ☐ Are there Business English classes?
- ☐ Where can I stay?
- ☐ Where are the teachers from?

b Look at the highlighted expressions. How would they be different in an informal e-mail (or letter)?

Formal e-mail	Informal e-mail
Dear Sir / Madam	________
I am writing	________
I would like	________
I look forward to hearing from you	________
Yours faithfully	________

From: Adriano Ruocco [adrianor@tiscali.net]
To: The Grange Language School [enquiries@grangeedinburgh]
Subject: Information about courses

Dear Sir / Madam,

I am writing to ask for information about your language courses. I am especially interested in an intensive course of two or three weeks. I am 31 and I work in the library at Milan University. I can read English quite well but I need to improve my listening and speaking. The book I am currently studying is 'pre-intermediate' (Common European Framework level A2).

I have looked at your website, but there is no information about intensive courses next summer. Could you please send me information about dates and prices? I would also like some information about accommodation. If possible I would like to stay with a family. My wife is going to visit me for a weekend when I am at the school. Could she stay with me in the same family?

I look forward to hearing from you.

Yours faithfully

Adriano Ruocco

c Read the advertisements and choose a course. Think of two or three questions you would like to ask.

Thai Cookery courses in Chiang Mai

Learn to cook Thai food in northern Thailand. One week courses, from April to October. Your accommodation in Chiang Mai is included. Beginners welcome. E-mail us for more information at thaicook@blueelephant.com

Tennis courses in France

One- or two-week courses in different parts of the country. Professional tennis coaches. All levels, beginners to advanced. Small groups or private lessons. For more information e-mail us at info@tennisinfrance.com

WRITE a formal e-mail asking for information. Write two paragraphs.

Paragraph 1 Explain why you are writing and give some personal information.

Paragraph 2 Ask your questions, and ask them to send you information.

CHECK your e-mail for mistakes (grammar, punctuation, and spelling).

5 What do you remember?

GRAMMAR

Circle the correct answer, a, b, or c.

What's ______ name?

a yours (b) your c you

1 We want ______ a party next month.
a have
b to have
c having

2 It's often difficult ______ new friends.
a to make
b make
c for make

3 She bought a new dress ______ at the party.
a for to wear
b for wear
c to wear

4 ______ early on a sunny morning makes me feel good.
a Waking up
b Wake up
c To wake up

5 My brother doesn't enjoy ______ by plane.
a travel
b to travel
c travelling

6 I'm tired of ______ TV. Let's do something different.
a to watch
b watching
c watch

7 I like Saturdays because I ______ work.
a mustn't
b don't have to
c haven't to

8 She can't come to the cinema because she ______ to study.
a must
b have
c has

9 You ______ be late for class tomorrow. You have an exam.
a mustn't
b mustn't to
c don't must

10 The golf ball ______ the hill and into the river.
a down
b downed
c went down

10

VOCABULARY

a verb phrases

Complete the sentences.

I don't *enjoy* going to parties.

decide dream of forget hate hope learn mind need start try

1 **A** Which film do you want to see? **B** I don't ________. You choose.
2 Don't ________ to buy some milk at the supermarket.
3 I ________ finding the perfect job.
4 Your hair's very long. You ________ to go to the hairdresser's.
5 What did you ________? Are you coming or not?
6 I'd like to ________ to play chess. Can you teach me?
7 I always travel by train or car because I ________ flying.
8 I ________ to see you soon.
9 ________ to read in English as much as you can.
10 Don't ________ running until you hear 'Go'.

b prepositions of movement

Complete the sentences with a preposition.

In the 100 metres race the athletes have to run *along* a track.

1 In golf you have to hit the ball ______ the hole.
2 In tennis you have to hit the ball ______ the net.
3 In football you have to pass the ball ______ the other players on your team.
4 In Formula 1 you have to drive ______ a track.
5 In rugby you have to kick the ball ______ the posts.

c sport verbs

Complete the sentences with *play*, *do*, and *go* in the correct form.

1 We ______ football every Saturday.
2 I ______ skiing last year.
3 He ______ judo twice a week.
4 She often ______ cycling after work.
5 They love ______ aerobics.

20

PRONUNCIATION

a Underline the word with a different sound

1	ɪ	hit	mind	kick	finish
2	aɪ	promise	like	decide	tired
3	eɪ	hate	have	game	race
4	aʊ	out	round	down	throw
5	uː	through	mustn't	doing	music

b Underline the stressed syllable.

infor<u>ma</u>tion

promise decide forget enjoy practise

10

CAN YOU UNDERSTAND THIS TEXT?

a Read the article. Is Alexandra Kosteniuk…?

1 beautiful but not very good at chess.
2 not very beautiful but good at chess.
3 beautiful and good at chess.

b Read the article again and mark the sentences T (true), F (false), or DS (doesn't say).

1 The International Chess Federation wants chess to have a more modern image.
2 Alexandra never wears glasses.
3 Alexandra's father taught her to play chess.
4 She became a grandmaster after playing chess for five years.
5 She thinks that chess should be more popular.
6 If you have Internet access, you can play chess with Alexandra.
7 Nigel Short has an attractive personality.

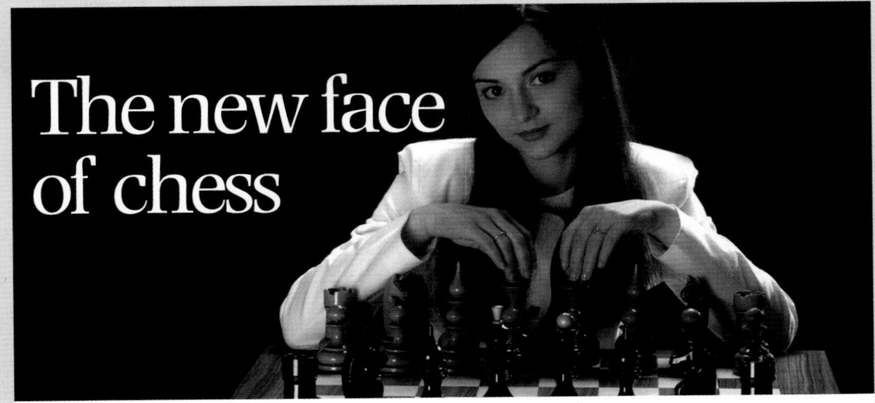

The new face of chess

17-year-old Alexandra Kosteniuk is sometimes called the Anna Kournikova of the chess world. The International Chess Federation have asked her to be the new face of the game, which traditionally has had an image of middle-aged men wearing glasses.

Alexandra started playing chess when she was five. She learnt to play from her father, and became a grandmaster when she was only 14. Experts say that her game is one of the most exciting they have seen for a long time.

'Chess is not as popular as it should be, and I think I could help it,' Kosteniuk said last week. 'It is an honour for me to be described as the face of the game.' She has her own website with pictures, poems, and the opportunity to play chess against her.

Making the game faster is another part of the campaign to make chess more popular. There are now strict time limits for making moves. Games that before lasted for hours can now take place in five minutes. The longest international tournament games, which sometimes took days, now last only four to seven hours.

Nigel Short, the British grandmaster, says, 'There are a lot of attractive women in chess, but Alexandra Kosteniuk has made a very big impression. She is obviously very talented. Any sport needs attractive personalities, and I have no problem with marketing the game through her.'

Adapted from a British newspaper

CAN YOU UNDERSTAND THESE PEOPLE?

a 5.17 Listen to five short conversations. Circle a, b, or c.

1 Anna ______ to go to the party.
a wants b doesn't want c isn't sure if she wants
2 The concert was ______.
a awful b quite good c very good
3 Maria is ______ late for class.
a never b hardly ever c often
4 The woman speaks ______ very well.
a French b German c Italian
5 Henry kicked the ball ______.
a into the goal b over the top of the goal c to the left of the goal

b 5.18 Listen and complete the form for the Milford Sports Centre.

Sport:	1 ______	Day:	2 ______
Time:	from 3 ______	to	4 ______
Name:	5 ______	Cost:	6 ______

CAN YOU SAY THIS IN ENGLISH?

a Can you…? Yes (✓)

☐ talk about the last party you went to
☐ talk about what makes you feel good and why
☐ say what you have to do to learn a language
☐ describe the rules for a sport you know

b Complete the questions with a verb in the *-ing* form or infinitive.

1 Where do you want ______ for your next holiday?
2 Have you ever tried to learn ______? What happened?
3 Do you enjoy ______? Why (not)?
4 Do you have to ______ at work / school?
5 What sport would you like ______?

c Ask your partner the questions in **b**. Ask for more information.

G *if* + present, *will* + infinitive (first conditional)
V confusing verbs
P long and short vowels

If you change queues, the other one will move faster.

If something bad can happen, it will

1 GRAMMAR *if* + present, *will* + infinitive

a Read the beginning of the story. Why do you think the Italian doesn't want to lend his newspaper to the American?

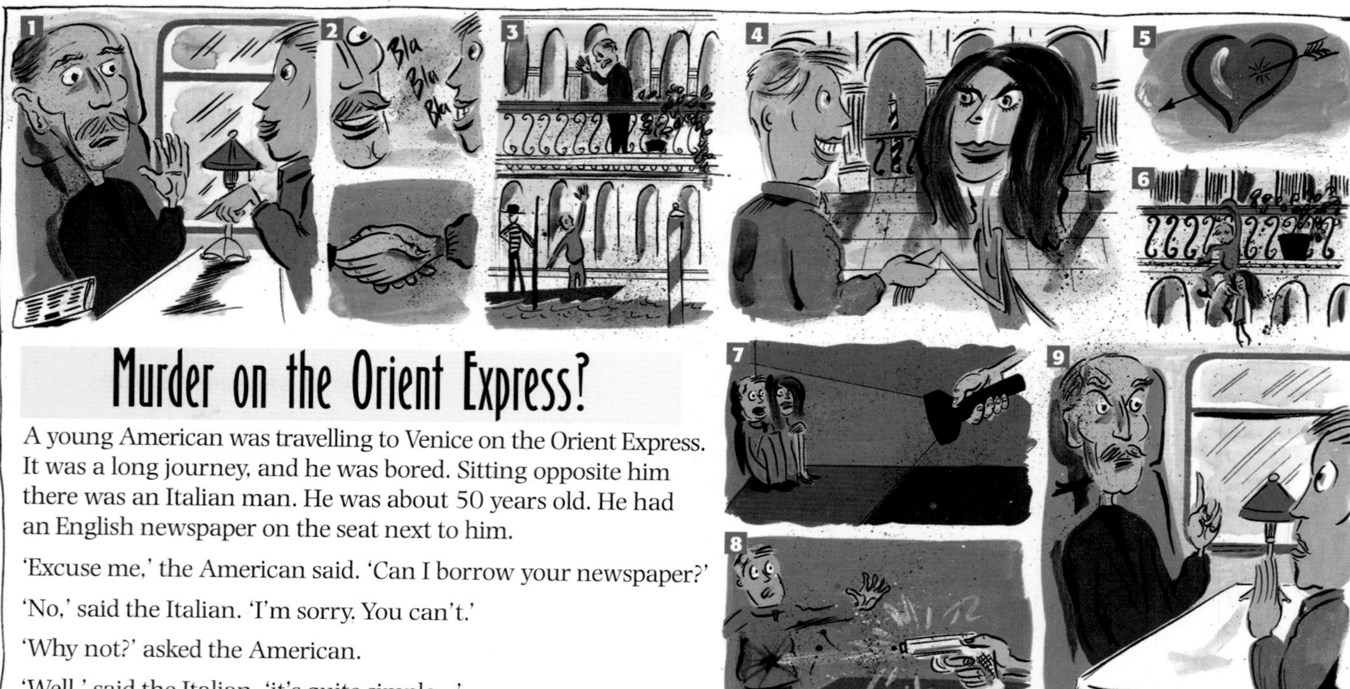

Murder on the Orient Express?

A young American was travelling to Venice on the Orient Express. It was a long journey, and he was bored. Sitting opposite him there was an Italian man. He was about 50 years old. He had an English newspaper on the seat next to him.

'Excuse me,' the American said. 'Can I borrow your newspaper?'

'No,' said the Italian. 'I'm sorry. You can't.'

'Why not?' asked the American.

'Well,' said the Italian, 'it's quite simple...'

b Look at the pictures. Number the rest of the story 1–9.

- ☐ 'If you meet Nicoletta, you'll fall in love with her.'
- ☐ 'If we start talking, we'll become friends.'
- ☐ 'If I invite you to my house, you'll meet my beautiful daughter, Nicoletta.'
- ☐ 'So that's why I won't lend you my newspaper.'
- ☐ 'If I find you, I'll kill you.'
- ☐ 'If you fall in love with her, you'll run away together.'
- ☐ 'If we become friends, I'll invite you to my house in Venice.'
- *1* 'If I lend you my newspaper, we'll start talking.'
- ☐ 'If you run away, I'll find you.'

c **6.1** Listen and check. Then cover sentences 1–9 and look at the pictures. Try to remember the sentences.

d Look at the sentences again. What tense is the verb after *if*? What tense is the other verb?

e ➲ **p.136 Grammar Bank 6A.** Read the rules and do the exercises.

2 VOCABULARY confusing verbs

a What's the difference between *know* and *meet*, and *borrow* and *lend*? Underline the right verb.

1 You'll **know** / **meet** my beautiful daughter Nicoletta.
2 Do you **know** / **meet** my sister's boyfriend?
3 Can I **borrow** / **lend** your newspaper?
4 If I **borrow** / **lend** you my newspaper, we'll start talking.

b ➲ **p.149 Vocabulary Bank** *Verbs*. Do part 2.

3 READING

a If you are in a supermarket and you change queues, what will happen?

b Read the first paragraph of the article *Murphy's Law*. Who was Murphy? What exactly is his law?

c Read the rest of the article. Can you guess how the examples 1–8 of Murphy's Law finish?

Murphy's Law

If you change queues in a supermarket, what will happen? The queue you were in before will move more quickly. You know what will happen, because there's a law of life that says, 'if something bad can happen, it will happen'. It's called Murphy's Law, and it took its name from Captain Edward Murphy, an American aeroplane engineer from the 1940s. He was investigating why planes crashed, and not surprisingly, he got a reputation for always thinking of the worst thing that can happen in every situation…

At home

1 If you wash your car,… ☐
2 If you look for something you've lost,… ☐

Social life

3 If you wear something white,… ☐
4 If someone near you is smoking,… ☐

Shopping

5 If you find something in a shop that you really like,… ☐
6 If you take something that doesn't work back to a shop,… ☐

Transport

7 If you stop waiting for a bus and start walking,… ☐
8 If you get to the station and a train is just leaving,… ☐

d Now match them with A–H from the box below.

A you'll spill wine or coffee on it.
B it'll rain.
C they won't have it in your size.
D it'll be your train.
E the bus will come.
F it'll start working.
G you'll find it in the last place you look.
H the smoke will always go directly towards you.

e In pairs, look only at the first half of the sentences in the text. How many of the 'laws' can you remember? Can you think of any others?

4 PRONUNCIATION long and short vowels

a 6.2 Listen and repeat the pairs of long and short vowels. Practise making the difference.

b Put these words into the chart.

beautiful borrow if law leave look
meet move push queue stop story
talk took wash we'll will win

c 6.3 Listen and check. Practise saying the words.

d ➲ **p.157 Sound Bank.** Look at the typical spellings for these sounds.

5 SPEAKING

In pairs or small groups, invent some new 'Murphy's Laws' beginning with the sentence halves below.

If you're single and you meet somebody you really like,…
If you throw something away,…
If you park a long way from where you're going,…
If your baby goes to sleep late,…
If you're driving somewhere and you're in a hurry,…
If you arrive very early to catch a plane,…
If you get to work late,…
If you leave your mobile phone at home,…
If you push a door,…

G *if* + past, *would* + infinitive (second conditional)
V animals
P stress and rhythm

If I saw a bear, I'd run away.

Never smile at a crocodile

Would *you* survive?

We all enjoy seeing wild animals on the television. But what would happen if we met one in real life? Do our animal quiz and see if you would survive.

1 What would you do …
… if you were in the middle of a river and suddenly you saw a crocodile swimming quickly towards you?

a I would try to swim to the bank as quickly as possible. ☐
b I wouldn't move. I'd stay still and wait for the crocodile to go away. ☐
c I would try to hit the crocodile in the face. ☐

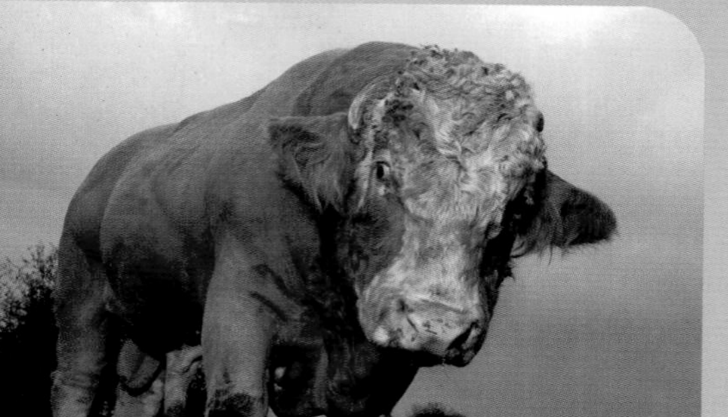

2 What would you do …
… if you were in a forest and a very large bear came towards you?

a I would climb up the nearest tree. ☐
b I would lie on the ground and pretend to be dead. ☐
c I would run away as fast as I could. ☐

3 What would you do …
… if you were in the middle of a field and a bull started running towards you?

a I would run. ☐
b I would throw something (e.g. my hat) in another direction. ☐
c I would shout and wave my arms. ☐

1 SPEAKING & LISTENING

a Read the quiz and tick (✓) your answers, **a**, **b**, or **c**. Compare with a partner.

b 6.4 Now listen to a survival expert. Did you choose the right answer?

c Listen again. Why are the other two answers wrong? Compare what you heard with a partner.

2 GRAMMAR *if* + past, *would* + infinitive

a Look at question 1 in *Would you survive?* and answer these questions.

1 Is the crocodile situation...?
   a one which could easily happen to you
   OR
   b one which is not very probable.
2 What tense of the verb goes after *if*?
3 What's the form of the other verbs in the question and in the answers?

b **p.136 Grammar Bank 6B.** Read the rules and do the exercises.

3 PRONUNCIATION stress and rhythm

a 6.5 Listen and repeat the sentence halves and then the whole sentence. Copy the rhythm.

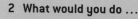

1 If I saw a crocodile,	I'd climb a tree.
2 What would you do	if you saw a snake?
3 We could have a dog	if we had a garden.
4 If a bear attacked me,	I wouldn't move.
5 If I were you,	I'd go on a safari.

b Cover the right-hand column. Try to remember the sentences.

4 VOCABULARY animals

a Answer the questions with a partner.

1 Do (or did you) have a pet? What?
2 What's the most dangerous animal in your country?
3 What's your favourite film about an animal?
4 What's your favourite cartoon animal?
5 If you went on a safari, what animal would you most like to see?
6 Are there any animals or insects you are really afraid of?
7 If you were an animal, what would you like to be?

b ➲ **p.151 Vocabulary Bank** *Animals*.

c 6.6 Listen. Which animal can you hear?

5 SPEAKING

Choose five questions and ask your partner.

What would you do...

... if there was a mouse in your bedroom?
... if you were driving and a bee or a wasp came into the car?
... if you saw a spider in the bath?
... if you were on a beach that was famous for shark attacks?
... if someone offered to buy you a fur coat?
... if you went to your friends' house for dinner and they gave you horse meat?
... if your neighbour's dog barked all night?
... if a friend asked you to look after their cat or dog?

6 READING

a Can you remember the best way to survive a crocodile attack?

b Read the article about crocodiles and mark the sentences T (true), F (false), or DS (doesn't say).

1 The Australian crocodile is bigger than all other kinds.
2 Crocodiles can run faster than horses.
3 Crocodiles only attack you if you are in the water.
4 The German tourist didn't know that there might be crocodiles in the lake.
5 The crocodile also attacked the girl's friends.
6 The Australian boy was killed when he and his friends went swimming in a river.
7 His friends escaped by climbing a tree.
8 Norman Pascoe's aunt was attacked by a crocodile.
9 She hit it on the nose, and it opened its mouth.

NATURE'S
PERFECT
KILLING
MACHINE

THE AUSTRALIAN CROCODILE is the largest crocodile in the world. It can grow up to seven metres long and the biggest can weigh up to 1000 kilos. It has only two muscles to open its mouth but 40 to close it!

What makes crocodiles so dangerous is that they attack incredibly quickly and they take their victims under the water to drown them. They usually attack in the water, but they can suddenly come out of a river and attack animals or people, and they can run on land at 17 km/h.

Every year in Australia there are crocodile attacks on humans. Two years ago a 24-year-old German tourist died when she went for a swim in a lake. Although there were signs warning people that there might be crocodiles, the girl and her friends decided to have a midnight swim. The girl suddenly disappeared and next morning her body was found. Near it was a four-metre crocodile. And only last month two Australian boys watched in horror as their friend was killed by a crocodile when they were washing their mountain bikes in a river. They climbed a tree and stayed there for 22 hours while the crocodile waited below.

But you CAN survive a crocodile attack. Last year Norman Pascoe, a 19-year-old, was saved from a crocodile when his aunt hit it on the nose. Norman's aunt said: 'I hit it and I shouted, "Help!" The crocodile suddenly opened its mouth and my nephew escaped.'

Adapted from a British newspaper

c Cover the text. In pairs, can you remember what these numbers refer to?

7	1000	40	17	24	22	19

d Read the text again and check your answers.

7 6.7 SONG ♫ *Wouldn't it be nice*

6C Decisions, decisions

G *may / might* (possibility)
V word building: noun formation
P sentence stress, *-ion endings*

I might go, but I might not.

1 SPEAKING

a Complete the definitions with words from the box. Underline the stressed syllable.

decision   decisive   indecisive   decide

1 ________ /dɪˈsaɪd/ *verb* think about two or more possibilities and choose one
2 ________ /dɪˈsɪʒn/ *noun* from 1
3 ________ /dɪˈsaɪsɪv/ *adj* good at making decisions
4 ________ /ɪndɪˈsaɪsɪv/ *adj* not good at making decisions

b Interview your partner with the questionnaire. Ask for more information. Which of you is more indecisive?

Are you indecisive?

	Yes	No	Sometimes
Do you find it difficult to make decisions?			
Do you have problems deciding…			
– what to wear when you go out?			
– what to eat in a restaurant?			
– what to do in your free time?			
– where to go on holiday?			
– what to buy when you go shopping?			
Do you often change your mind about something?			

Do you think you are indecisive?
Yes **No** **I'm not sure**

2 GRAMMAR *may / might*

a 6.8 Cover the dialogue and listen. Who's indecisive, Roz or Mel? What about?

R Hi Mel. It's me... Roz.
M Hi Roz.
R Listen Mel. It's about the party tonight.
M You're going, aren't you?
R I don't know. I'm not sure. I might _____ but I might not. I can't decide.
M Oh come on. You'll love it. And you might _____ somebody new.
R OK. I'll go then.
M Good. So what are you going to wear?
R That's the other problem. I'm not sure what to wear. I might _____ my new black trousers. Or perhaps the red dress – what do you think?
M If I were you, I'd wear the red dress.
R But the red dress may _____ too small for me now…
M Well, wear the black trousers then.
R OK. I'll wear the black trousers.
M How are you getting there?
R I might _____ with John… or Ruth… or I may _____ there… I'm not sure yet.
M OK, I'll see you there. Bye.
R Bye.

M Hello?
R Mel? It's me again. Roz. Listen. I've changed my mind. Sorry. I'm not going to go to the party.

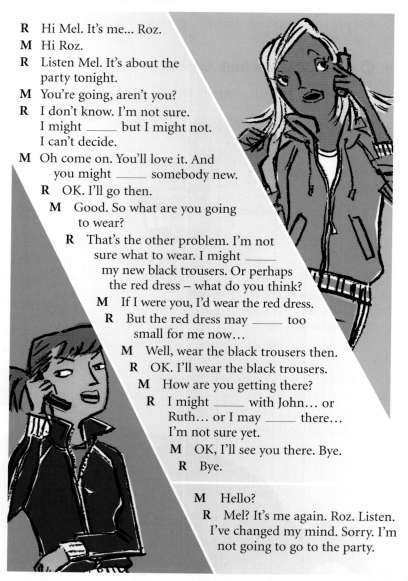

b Listen again and complete the conversation.

c Underline the verb phrases in the dialogue with *may / might*. Do we use them for…?

1 an obligation   OR   2 a possibility

d **p.136 Grammar Bank 6C.** Read the rules and do the exercises.

3 PRONUNCIATION & SPEAKING

a 6.9 Listen and repeat the *may / might* phrases from the dialogue. Copy the rhythm. Are *may* and *might* stressed?

b **Communication** *Decisions, decisions A p.110 B p.115.* In pairs, roleplay being indecisive.

4 READING

a You're going to read some tips to help people to make decisions. Before you read, cover the text. In pairs, try to predict what one of the tips will be.

b Quickly look through the article. Is your tip there? Then complete the text with these verbs from the box.

ask	compare	confuse	feel	have
make (x2)	~~take~~	use	wait	

c Read the article again. In pairs, try to decide which tip is the best. Can you think of one other tip?

How to make decisions

When you have to choose between two possibilities:

- [1] *Take* your time. The most important thing is not to make a decision in a hurry.
- [2] ________ a list of the positive and negative points for both options. Then decide which points are most important and [3] ________ the two lists.
- If you [4] ________ other people for their advice, don't ask more than one or two. If you ask a lot of people, this will probably [5] ________ you.
- [6] ________ your imagination to help you. Imagine yourself in both situations. How do you [7] ________? Relaxed or stressed?
- When you've made a decision, [8] ________ a bit before you tell other people, to see how you feel. If you feel comfortable with your decision after an hour, you have probably made the right decision.
- Finally, remember that you can't [9] ________ everything. Choosing one of two possibilities always means that you can't have the one you didn't choose. And it's impossible to *always* [10] ________ the right decision!

Adapted from a British newspaper

5 VOCABULARY noun formation

⚠ With some verbs you can make a noun by adding *-ion*, *-sion*, or *-ation*, for example, *decide > decision*; *imagine > imagination*

a Complete the chart.

Verb	Noun
confuse	confusion
decide	decision
imagine	imagination
inform	________
elect	________
invite	________
organize	________
educate	________
translate	________
communicate	________

b 6.10 Listen and check. Underline the stressed syllable in the verbs and nouns.

1 How do you pronounce *-sion* and *-tion*?
2 Where is the stress in nouns which finish in *-ion*?

c Complete the questions with a noun from **a**.

1 When was the last time you had to make a big ________?
2 What kind of ________ do you often get from the Internet?
3 When was the last time you had an ________ to a wedding?
4 Which party won the last general ________ in your country?
5 Do you belong to any ________ (for example, *Greenpeace*, etc.)?
6 What do you think is the best form of ________, e-mail, phone, or text-message?

d In pairs, ask and answer the questions. Ask for more information.

6D What should I do?

G *should / shouldn't*
V *get*
P /ʊ/, sentence stress

You should talk to her.

1 LISTENING & READING

a Read this extract from a TV and radio guide.

1 What kind of programme is it?
2 Why do people call the programme?
3 Would you call a programme like this?

RADIO GUIDE

WHAT'S THE PROBLEM?
Weekdays 8.00–8.45p.m.

Daily advice programme with Julian Greenwood. Whatever your problem, call the programme and ask for help. Listeners can e-mail their suggestions to the *What's the problem?* website. Today's subject is 'friends'.

b 6.11 Listen to three people phoning *What's the Problem?* and complete the sentences with one word.

clothes jealousy money

Barbara's problem is about ________.
Kevin's problem is about ________.
Catherine's problem is about ________.

c Now listen again. What exactly are their problems? Compare what you understood with your partner.

d Read the e-mails which listeners sent to the *What's the problem?* website. Match two e-mails to each problem. Write Barbara, Kevin, or Catherine.

RADIO FM **MESSAGE BOARDS**

AUTHOR	MESSAGE
1 Malcolm	Hi ________, I think you should talk to your girlfriend, not your friend. She might like the way your friend treats her. Perhaps that's why he does it. Why don't you tell her to ask him to stop? Malcolm
2 Maria	*Dear ________, If I were you, I wouldn't say anything to your friend. I think you should lock your clothes in a cupboard. She'll soon get the message, and that way you'll stay friends. Maria*
3 Darren	Hi ________, You shouldn't be so sensitive. It's not really a problem, it just shows your friend thinks you have good taste. And don't argue with your friend. Women aren't worth it. Darren
4 Silvia	*Hi ________, I think it depends if your friend is good company or not. If he is then I think you should pay for him. If not, don't tell him where you're going when you go out. Silvia*
5 Sandy	Dear ________, When your friend gets home tonight I think you should talk to her. Say 'I'm really sorry but I'm a bit obsessive about my things. I don't like other people touching them.' That way she'll stop but she won't get angry or offended. Sandy
6 Martyn	Hi ________, You definitely shouldn't pay for him. When the waiter brings the bill, pretend that nobody has money to pay for him. Then he'll have to make an excuse to the waiter and maybe he'll learn that he has to pay for himself. Martyn

e Now read the e-mails again. In pairs, say which advice you think is best for each person and why.

2 GRAMMAR *should / shouldn't*

a Highlight examples of *should* and *shouldn't* in the e-mails on p.70.

b Does *You should talk to your girlfriend* mean…?

1 You have to talk to your girlfriend.
2 I think it's a good idea if you talk to your girlfriend.

c **p.136 Grammar Bank 6D.** Read the rules and do the exercises.

3 PRONUNCIATION & SPEAKING /ʊ/

a 6.12 Listen and repeat. Write the words.

1 /ʃʊd/ = *should*	4 /'wʊdnt/ =
2 /'ʃʊdnt/ =	5 /kʊd/ =
3 /wʊd/ =	6 /'kʊdnt/ =

b 6.13 Listen and repeat these sentences. Copy the rhythm.

1 You should talk to your friend.
2 You shouldn't be so sensitive.
3 You should lock your clothes in a cupboard.
4 You definitely shouldn't pay for your friend.
5 What should I do?
6 Should I write to him?

4 WRITING & SPEAKING

a Choose one of the problems and write a short note giving advice.

1 It's my girlfriend's birthday next week and I want to give her a surprise with a special present or a special evening somewhere. What should I do?

2 My friend has gone away on holiday for two weeks and I'm looking after her cat. Yesterday I couldn't find the cat anywhere. My friend is coming home in three days. I'm desperate. Should I phone her now and tell her? What should I do?

3 My best friend wants to borrow some money to help her buy a car. I have the money, and she says she'll pay me back next year. But I'm worried that it's not a good idea to lend money to friends. What should I do?

4 I really want to get fit and do more exercise. The problem is I hate going to gyms, and they're very expensive. And there are no parks near me to go running. What should I do?

b In pairs, read other student's notes. Decide which problem they refer to. Do you agree with the advice? Why (not)?

5 VOCABULARY *get*

a Look at these sentences from 1. Match the examples of *get* with meanings A–D.

1 I'm sure you'll soon **get** some e-mails with good advice. ☐
2 When your friend **gets** home tonight you should talk to her. ☐
3 She won't **get** angry with you. ☐
4 I **get on** very **well** with her. ☐

A receive	B be friendly with
C become	D arrive

b **p.152 Vocabulary Bank** *get*

c In pairs, do the **get** questionnaire.

1 Do you ever **get to** school / work late? When was the last time?

2 When was the last time you **got lost**? Where were you trying to go? What happened?

3 What makes you **get angry**? When was the last time you got really angry? Why?

4 When was the last time you **got a present**? What was it? Who was it from?

5 Who do you **get on with** best in your family? Is there anybody you don't get on with?

6 What do you think is the best age to **get married**? Why?

7 Which problems in your country are **getting better**? Which are **getting worse**?

6 At the pharmacy

ASKING FOR HELP

6.14 Listen and underline the right phrase.

1 Allie asks the receptionist for some **aspirin / painkillers**.
2 Allie has a **headache / backache**.
3 The receptionist **gives / doesn't give** her medicine.
4 Allie **wants / doesn't want** a doctor.
5 The pharmacy **is / isn't** near the hotel.

US English	*pharmacy*
UK English	*chemist's*

ASKING FOR MEDICINE

a 6.15 Cover the dialogue and listen. What does the pharmacist give her? How often does she have to take them? How much are they?

YOU HEAR	YOU SAY
Good morning. Can I help you?	I have a bad cold. Do you have something I can take?
What ______ do you have?	I have a headache and a cough.
Do you have a ______?	No, I don't think so.
Does your back ______?	No.
Are you allergic to any drugs?	I'm allergic to penicillin.
No problem. These are ______. These will make you feel ______.	How many do I have to take?
Two every four hours.	Sorry? How often?
Every four hours. If you don't feel better in ______ hours, you should see a doctor.	OK, thanks. How much are they?
$4.75, please.	Thank you.
You're welcome.	

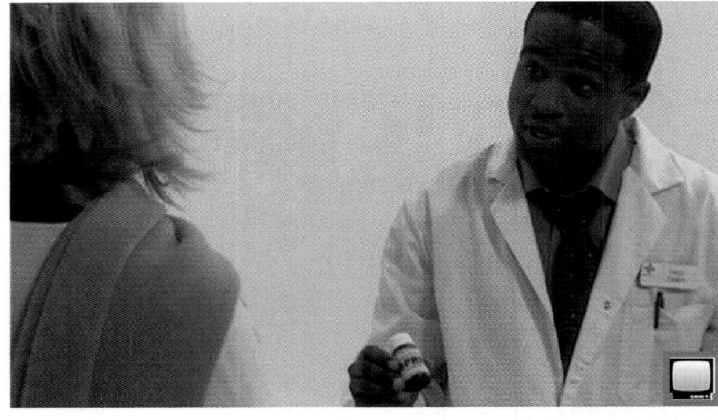

b Listen again. Complete the YOU HEAR phrases.

aspirin better hurt symptoms temperature twenty-four

c 6.16 Listen and repeat the YOU SAY phrases. Copy the rhythm.

d In pairs, roleplay the dialogue. **A** (book open) you're the pharmacist, **B** (book closed) you're Allie. Swap roles.

SOCIAL ENGLISH talking about the party

a 6.17 Listen and mark the sentences T (true) or F (false).

1 Mark apologizes for getting angry last night.
2 Allie thinks Brad is annoying.
3 Brad isn't Allie's type of man.
4 Today is Allie's last day.
5 They're going to have dinner on a boat.

b Complete the USEFUL PHRASES. Listen again and check.

c 6.18 Listen and repeat the phrases. How do you say them in your language?

USEFUL PHRASES

M B______ you!
M I'm really sorry a______ (last night).
A I don't m______. You choose.
M H______ about (a boat trip around the bay)?
A That s______ fantastic.
A It's a p______.

Writing to a friend

From: Daniel
To: Alessandra
Subject: Exams

Hi Alessandra!

Thanks for your last e-mail. I hope your exams went well. I have some exciting news and I'm writing to [1] *ask* for your advice.

I [2] ______ to go on holiday to Argentina next year. What do you [3] ______ is the best month for me to come? I can only come for three weeks, so which places do you think I should [4] ______? Do you think I should [5] ______ a car or travel around by bus or train?

I'm planning to [6] ______ a few days in and around Mendoza, and it would be great if we could [7] ______. Can you [8] ______ a good hotel (not too expensive)?

Hope to hear from you soon!
Best wishes,
Daniel

a Read the e-mail and complete it with these verbs.

~~ask~~ hire meet recommend spend think visit want

b Imagine that Daniel has written to *you* about visiting *your* country. Plan how you're going to answer his questions. Compare with a partner.

c Look at the **USEFUL PHRASES**. What are the missing words?

USEFUL PHRASES

1 Thanks ______ your e-mail.
2 It was great to hear ______ you again.
3 I'm really happy that you want ______ visit my country.
4 I think you should come ______ July.
5 If I were you, I'd travel ______ bus.
6 I'm looking forward ______ seeing you soon.

WRITE an e-mail to Daniel. Use the phrases in **c** to help you.

Paragraph 1 Thank him for his e-mail, etc.
Paragraph 2 Answer his questions about your country. Give reasons.
Paragraph 3 Answer his question about your town. Give reasons.

CHECK your e-mail for mistakes (grammar , punctuation , and spelling).

6 What do you remember?

GRAMMAR

Circle the correct answer, a, b, or c.

What's ______ name?

a yours (b) your c you

1 If we start walking, the bus ______.
a come
b came
c will come

2 James ______ come to the party if his ex-girlfriend is there.
a won't
b don't
c doesn't

3 If we ______ queues, the other will move more quickly.
a change
b will change
c changed

4 What would you do if you ______ a bear?
a saw
b will see
c see

5 If we had a garden, we ______ a dog.
a 'll have
b 'd have
c had

6 I ______ go to the party. I'm not sure.
a might
b will
c may to

7 The petrol station ______ open today. It's a holiday.
a may not be
b may not to be
c may to

8 I think you ______ go to the doctor.
a would
b should to
c should

9 She ______ come home so late.
a not should
b shouldn't
c shouldn't to

10 If I ______ you, I'd talk to your girlfriend.
a were
b be
c am

10

VOCABULARY

a confusing verbs

~~Cross out~~ the wrong verb.

I don't **watch** / ~~**look at**~~ TV very often.

1 Where did you **know** / **meet** your husband?
2 Shh! They're **making** / **doing** an exam.
3 How much money does he **earn** / **win**?
4 He was **carrying** / **wearing** a black umbrella.
5 You **look** / **look like** your sister. You have the same eyes.

b animals

Write the names of the animals.

It's a popular pet and it barks. *dog*

1 It's a big cat and it lives in Africa. ______
2 It has eight legs and it eats flies. ______
3 People ride this animal in races. ______
4 It's the largest animal in the sea. ______
5 It's a male cow and it can be dangerous. ______

c noun formation

Make nouns from these verbs.

imagine *imagination*

1 communicate ______
2 organize ______
3 discuss ______
4 translate ______
5 decide ______

15

PRONUNCIATION

a Underline the word with a different sound

1	rob	lose	borrow	problem
2	we'll	meet	lion	sheep
3	carry	camel	wasp	happen
4	ask	start	fall	shark
5	zoo	food	you'll	mouse

b Underline the stressed syllable.

information

advice crocodile decision happen translation

10

CAN YOU UNDERSTAND THIS TEXT?

a Read the article and match the questions and answers.

A question of principles

The first of a new series in which celebrities answer questions on moral dilemmas. This week, radio presenter Stephen Bruce.

A ☐ If your girlfriend was allergic to the dog you've had for ten years, would you give your dog away?

B ☐ If your boss gave you tickets to the theatre and you forgot to go, would you tell him the truth when he asked?

C ☐ If your young daughter's hamster died, would you buy an identical one or tell her the truth?

D ☐ If a colleague at work told everyone that he was 45 but you knew he was five years older, would you keep his secret?

E ☐ If a celebrity was having a secret affair with your neighbour, would you sell the story to a newspaper?

1 I'd tell everybody the truth, probably in front of him. I think telling lies about your age is ridiculous.

2 No, I'd say that it was the best show I've ever seen! I wouldn't want to offend him. But he would probably guess I was lying.

3 I'm afraid the dog would win! I'd tell my girlfriend that my dog and I had been together for a long time but that she might not be here next week.

4 It would be an interesting story – my neighbour is a 92-year-old, bald Swedish man! No, I wouldn't. I'd just tell my partner.

5 I'd buy another one. It happened to me once when the children's goldfish died. I bought another one but they saw that it was different. I told them it had put on weight.

b Read the article again. Guess the meaning of the highlighted words or phrases. Check with the teacher or your dictionary.

CAN YOU UNDERSTAND THESE PEOPLE?

a 6.19 Listen and circle the correct answer, a, b, or c.

1 The man and woman decide to ________.
a walk b wait c get a taxi
2 The woman ________ Deborah.
a knows b hasn't met c wouldn't like to meet
3 Is the woman afraid of mice?
a Yes b No c We don't know
4 Where does the man decide to go?
a home b to the pub c to the cinema
5 What pet does the woman think he should buy?
a a fish b a cat c a hamster

b 6.20 Listen and mark the sentences T (true) or F (false).

1 Dave got married five years ago.
2 His wife has just had a baby.
3 Dave's wife doesn't give him much attention.
4 Dave is more tired than his wife.
5 The advice he gets is to help his wife more.

CAN YOU SAY THIS IN ENGLISH?

a Can you...? Yes (✓)

☐ say three things you'll do if it rains tomorrow
☐ say what you would do if you were attacked by a crocodile
☐ say what you might do this weekend
☐ say what you should or shouldn't do if you have problems sleeping

b Write second conditional questions.

1 What / you do if / lose / wallet?
2 What / you do if / win the lottery?
3 What / you do if / find some money in the street?
4 What / you do if / have more free time?
5 What / you do if / can speak perfect English?

c Ask your partner the questions in **b**. Ask for more information.

G present perfect + *for* and *since*
V words related to fear
P /ɪ/ and /aɪ/, sentence stress

I've been afraid of spiders since I was a child.

Famous fears and phobias

1 READING & VOCABULARY

a Match the words with the pictures.

flying ☐
heights ☐
closed spaces ☐
open spaces ☐
snakes ☐
spiders ☐
wasps ☐
water ☐

1 2 3 4 5 6 7 8

b Are you afraid of any of these things? Why? Do you know any people who are?

I'm afraid of flying.

I have a friend who is afraid of water. He can't swim.

c Read the article and complete each paragraph with a word from **a**.

d Underline the four words in the text related to being afraid.

2 GRAMMAR present perfect + *for* and *since*

a Read about Winona Ryder again and answer the questions.

When did she begin to be afraid of water?
In ______.

Is she afraid of water now? YES/NO

b Complete the answers with a year or a number of years.

How long has she been afraid of water?
She has been afraid of water **since** ______.
She has been afraid of water **for** ______ years.

c Complete the rule with *for* and *since*.

Use ______ with a period of time.
Use ______ with a point in time.

d ➲ **p.138 Grammar Bank 7A.** Read the rules and do the exercises.

We're all afraid...

Famous people have phobias like the rest of us, and sometimes they seriously affect their lives.

Winona Ryder, American actress

Winona Ryder has been afraid of ______ since 1983. When she was 12 years old she fell into a lake and nearly died. Luckily someone pulled her out, and after a few minutes she came back to life again. It can be a real problem when she's making a film. For example, in some of the scenes in *Alien III*, she had to go in a boat and she was terrified.

Rupert Grint, British actor

Rupert Grint has been afraid of ______ since he was a child. In this respect he is like the character he played in the *Harry Potter* films, Ron Weasley, who is also frightened of them. Rupert had a very hard time in the second *Harry Potter* film where he and Harry had to fight a giant one (the size of an elephant) with very hairy legs!

Dennis Bergkamp, ex-international footballer

Dennis Bergkamp has been afraid of ______ since 1994. He was on a plane in the USA with the Dutch national team during the World Cup. A journalist said that there was a bomb on the plane (there wasn't), and everybody started to panic, including Dennis. He decided never to travel by plane again. Because of his fear Bergkamp could not play in many important matches for Holland, Inter Milan, and Arsenal.

3 LISTENING

a **7.1** Listen to Scott, a doctor talking about his cat phobia. What happens if he sees a cat?

b Listen again and answer the questions.

1 What's the medical name of his phobia?
2 How long has he had his phobia?
3 How did it start?
4 Does his phobia affect his work?
5 What treatment is he having?
6 Does he think his phobia will disappear?

4 PRONUNCIATION /ɪ/ and /aɪ/, sentence stress

a Put these words in the right column.

child children in I've like life line
live (v) mine minute since win

b **7.2** Listen and check. Practise saying the words.

c Practise saying the sentences.

I've lived here since I was a child.
I've liked wine since I lived in Italy.

d **7.3** Listen and repeat the questions. Copy the rhythm.

1 lived here	have you lived here	How long have you lived here?
2 known him	have you known him	How long have you known him?
3 been married	have they been married	How long have they been married?
4 had his dog	has he had his dog	How long has he had his dog?

5 SPEAKING

Ask and answer in pairs.

A ask **B** six *How long ...?* questions with a verb phrase.
B answer with *for* or *since*.
Give more information if you can.
Then swap roles.

How long have you known your oldest friend?

Since we were at primary school together.

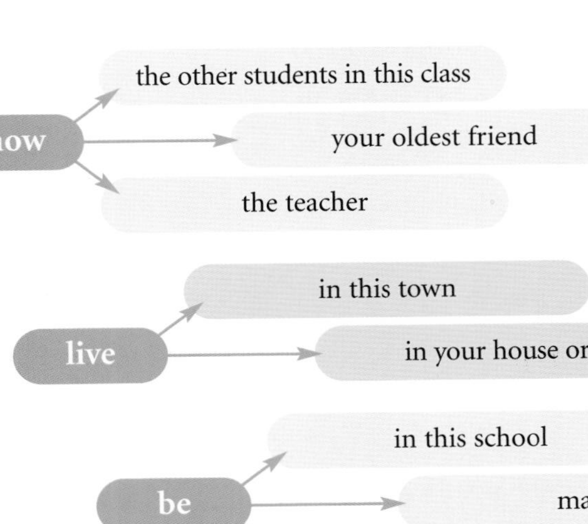

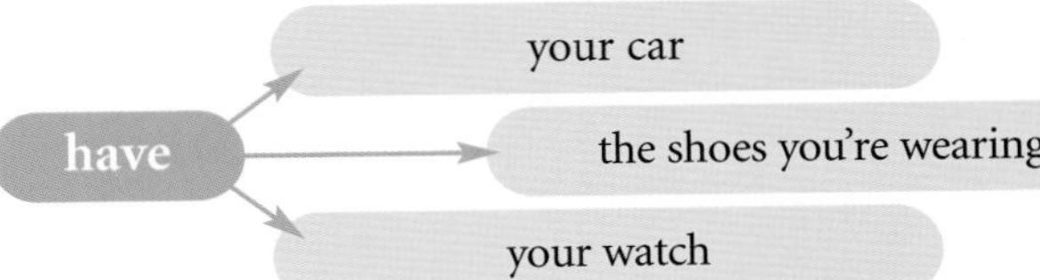

G present perfect or past simple?
V biographies
P word stress

He was born in Knoxville, Tennessee.

Born to direct

1 VOCABULARY & PRONUNCIATION

a Underline the stressed syllable in the highlighted words below.

Events in your life

go to university	☐	fall in love	☐
be born	☐	get divorced	☐
go to primary school	☐	have children	☐
start work	☐	get married	☐
leave school	☐	go to secondary school	☐
die	☐	separate	☐
retire	☐		

b 7.4 Listen and check. Practise saying the phrases.

c Number the expressions in what you think is a logical order. Compare with a partner. Do you agree?

2 READING & SPEAKING

a Look at the film photos. In pairs, answer the questions.

1 Who directed the films?
2 Have you seen either of the films? What kind of films are they?

b Read fifteen facts about the lives of the two directors. In pairs, decide which eight are about Hitchcock, and which seven are about Tarantino. Write **H** or **T**.

c **A** re-read the facts about Hitchcock, and **B** about Tarantino.

d Work in pairs.

A (Book closed) in your own words say everything you can remember about Hitchcock.

B (Book open) listen and help. Then swap roles. **B** Say everything you can remember about Tarantino.

3 GRAMMAR present perfect or past simple?

a Answer the questions.

1 Look at the eight facts about Hitchcock's life. What tense are all the verbs? Why?
2 Look at the seven facts about Tarantino's life. What three tenses are there? Why?

b ➲ **p.138 Grammar Bank 7B.** Read the rules and do the exercises.

Hitchcock or Tarantino?

1 He appeared in small roles in almost all of his films. *H*

2 He was a very intelligent child, but he had difficulties with reading and writing. He left school when he was 15 and went to work in a cinema, where he checked tickets at the entrance. ☐

3 He was born in London in 1899. ☐

4 His muse is Uma Thurman, who he has directed in several of his most successful films. ☐

The Birds

5 He was married and his daughter Patricia appeared in several of his films. ☐

6 He went to school at St. Ignatius College, in London, and later studied art at the University of London. ☐

7 He was famous for not liking actors. He once said 'all actors are children and should be treated like cattle.' ☐

8 He was born in Knoxville, Tenesee in 1963. ☐

Kill Bill

Alfred Hitchcock

9 He spent a short time in prison because he could not pay a parking ticket. ☐

10 His muse was Grace Kelly (later Princess Grace of Monaco), who he directed in several of his most successful films. ☐

11 He died in 1980. ☐

12 He began his career as an actor. His biggest role was in an episode of the TV series *The Golden Girls*. He played the part of a man who impersonated Elvis Presley. ☐

Quentin Tarantino

13 He never won an Oscar for Best Director, although he was nominated five times. When the Academy finally gave him an honorary Oscar he received a standing ovation. He just said, 'Thank you' and left the stage. ☐

14 He has been nominated for an Oscar for Best Director but he hasn't won one yet. ☐

15 He says he hates drugs and violence but they appear a lot in his films. ☐

4 SPEAKING

a Think about a member of your family (who is alive), for example a parent, uncle, aunt, or grandparent. Prepare to answer the questions below about their life.

The past	**The present**
Where / born?	Where / live now? How long / live there?
Where / go to school?	Is he / she married? How long / be married?
What / do after (he/she) left school?	Is he / she retired? How long has he / she be retired?
When / start work?	How many children / have?
When / get married?	

b A interview B about their person. Ask for more information. Then swap roles.

5 LISTENING

a Look at the photo of Sofia Coppola and her father. What do they both do?

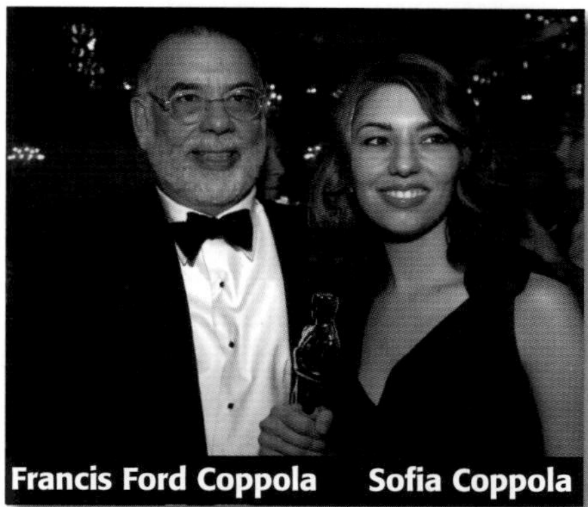
Francis Ford Coppola   Sofia Coppola

b You're going to listen to part of a TV programme about Sofia Coppola. Look at the information below. Before you listen guess what the connection is with her.

I think she directed *The Godfather*.

No, she was too young.

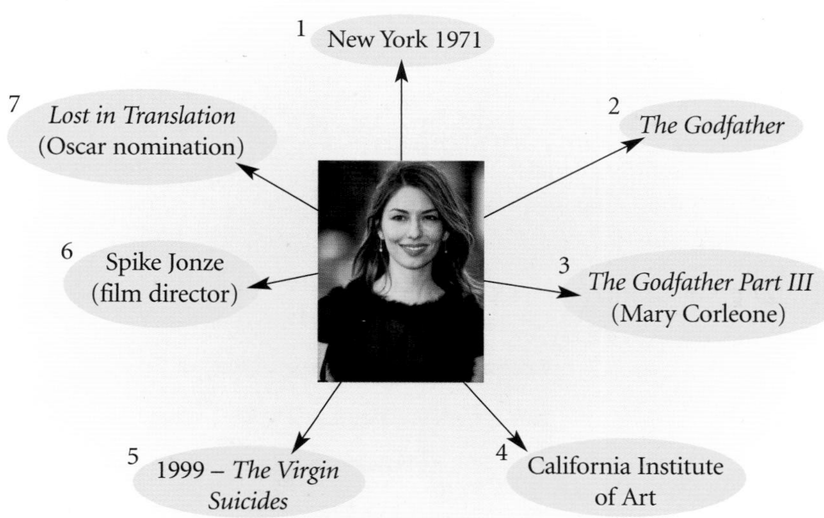

c 7.5 Now listen and make notes. Compare with a partner.

d In pairs, ask and answer the questions.

Have you seen any of the films in **b**? Which one(s)? Did you like them?
Have you seen a good film recently? Which one? Who was in it?
What's the best film you've seen this year? Who directed it?
What's the worst film you've seen this year? Who directed it?

7C I used to be a rebel

G *used to*
V school subjects: *history*, *geography*, etc.
P sentence stress: *used to* / *didn't use to*

Did you use to like primary school?
Yes, I did.

1 READING

a Look at the picture. Does it make you think of your school? Why (not)?

b Look at the photos and read the article about Mick Jagger. Do you think he was *really* a rebel when he was at school? Why (not)?

c Read the text again. In pairs, guess the meaning of the highlighted words.

2 GRAMMAR *used to*

a Underline six phrases with *used to* / *didn't use to* in the text. Does *used to* refer to…

1 the present or the past?
2 things that happened once or for a long time?

b **p.138 Grammar Bank 7C.** Read the rules and do the exercises.

A famous rebel – but was he really?

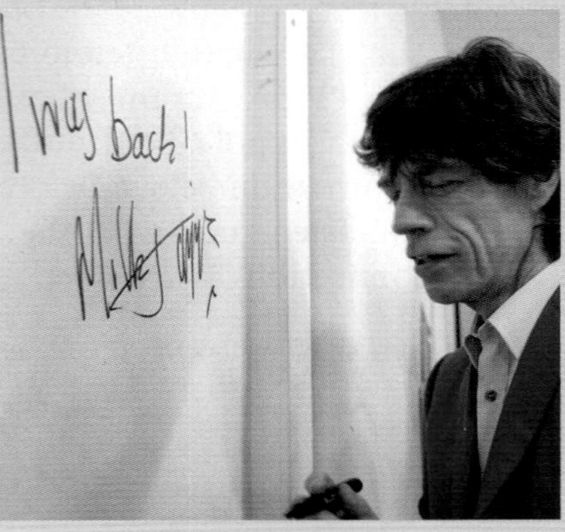

MICK JAGGER went back to his old school recently – for the first time since he left in 1961. He was invited to the school to open the 'Mick Jagger Performing Arts centre', a new music and drama department at Dartford Grammar School.

Jagger said that he was 'honoured' that the centre was named after him. But in a newspaper interview two days before he told a journalist that in fact he hated school and that he used to be a rebel.

He didn't use to do the homework – 'there was far too much'– and he was continually at war with the teachers. He used to break the rules all the time, especially rules he thought were stupid, about how to wear the school uniform and things like that. Once he even organized a mass protest against 'appalling' school dinners. 'It was probably the greatest contribution to school I ever made,' he said. Although he made a good start at school, Jagger said his school work deteriorated because of 'music and girls'.

Mick Jagger in his school basketball team

However, according to one of his old school friends, musician Dick Taylor, this is not true. He says that Mick didn't use to be a rebel at all – he was quite bright and used to work hard. He also used to do a lot of sport.

When Mick Jagger left school, he had seven O-levels and two A-levels, which at that time were good qualifications – so perhaps Dick's memory is better than Mick's…

Adapted from a British newspaper

3 LISTENING

a Look at the photos of Melissa when she was at school and today. How has she changed?

b 7.6 Listen to her talking about her school days. Was she a rebel or a 'good girl' at school? What does she do now?

c Listen again. Mark the sentences T (true) or F (false).

1 Melissa is a teenager in the photo.
2 She used to write things on the walls.
3 She didn't like any of the subjects at school.
4 Her least favourite subject was PE.
5 The PE teacher made them try to do difficult things.
6 She used to break the rules about the school uniform.
7 She wanted to be a doctor.
8 Her parents wanted her to be a teacher.

4 PRONUNCIATION sentence stress

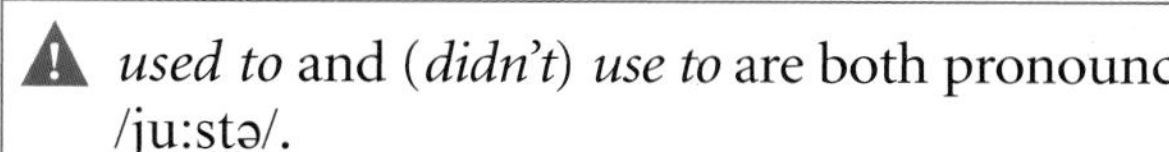

⚠ *used to* and (*didn't*) *use to* are both pronounced /ju:stə/.

a 7.7 Listen and underline the stressed words. Then listen and repeat.

1 I used to go out a lot.
2 He used to hate school.
3 They didn't use to be friends.
4 She didn't use to like him.
5 Did you use to wear glasses?

b 7.8 Now listen and write six more sentences.

5 VOCABULARY school subjects

a Match the words with the pictures.

PE (=physical education) ☐
geography ☐
technology ☐
maths ☐
history ☐
foreign languages (English, etc.) ☐
literature ☐
science (physics, chemistry, and biology) ☐

b 7.9 Listen and practise saying the words.

c Think about when you were 11 or 12 years old. Talk about each subject with one of the expressions below. Say why.

I used / didn't use to like _____.

I didn't use to like maths. I was really bad at it.

6 SPEAKING

a Think about when you were 11 or 12. Were these things true or false about you? Why?

I used to be a rebel.	I used to do a lot of sport.
I used to work hard.	I used to wear glasses.
I used to like all the teachers.	I used to wear a uniform.
I used to hate school.	I used to have longer hair.

b Work in groups of three.

A tell **B** and **C** about how you used to be. **B** and **C** listen and ask for more information. Then swap roles. Did you have anything in common?

I didn't use to be a rebel. I was a good boy.

7 7.10 SONG ♫ *It's all over now*

7 D

G passive
V verbs: *invent*, *discover*, etc.
P *-ed*, sentence stress

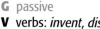

It was invented by a woman.

The mothers of invention

the dishwasher

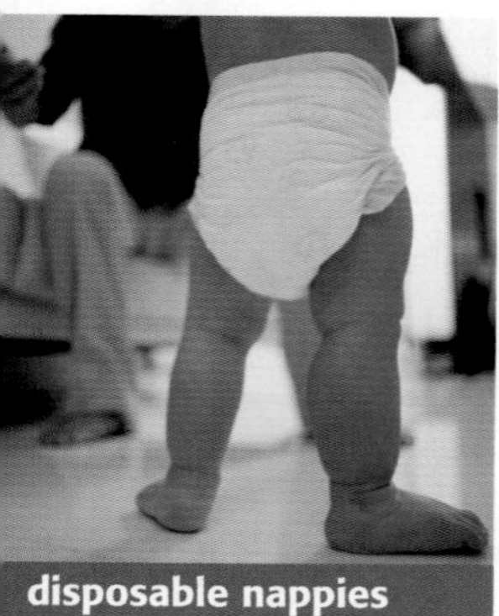
disposable nappies

nylon stockings

1 LISTENING

a Look at the photos. Five of these things were invented by women. In pairs, decide which five you think they are.

b 7.11 Now listen to a radio programme about inventions. Were you right? Complete the sentences with the invention.

1 ______________ was invented by Josephine Cochrane in 1886.
2 ______________ were invented by Mary Anderson in 1903.
3 ______________ were invented by Marion Donovan in 1950.
4 ______________ was invented by Bette Nesmith Graham in 1956.
5 ______________ was invented by Stephanie Kwolek in 1966.

c Listen again and answer the questions.

1 What happened after Josephine Cochrane's dinner parties?
2 What was the problem with cars in 1903 when it rained or snowed?
3 How many disposable nappies are used every day?
4 What was Bette Nesmith Graham's job?
5 What was special about the material Stephanie Kwolek invented?

d Which of the five inventions do you think was the best?

2 GRAMMAR passive

a Make five true sentences using the words in the chart.

The dishwasher	is called	Tipp-Ex today.
Disposable nappies	was invented	by Marion Donovan.
More than 55 million nappies	are protected	every day.
Mrs Graham's invention	were invented	by the bullet-proof vest.
Policemen all over the world	are used	by an American woman.

The dishwasher was invented by an American woman.

b Look at these two sentences and answer the questions.

a An American woman invented the dishwasher.
b The dishwasher was invented by an American woman.

1 Do the sentences have the same meaning?
2 Do the sentences have the same emphasis?
3 Which sentence is in the passive?

c ➲ **p.138 Grammar Bank 7D.** Read the rules and do the exercises.

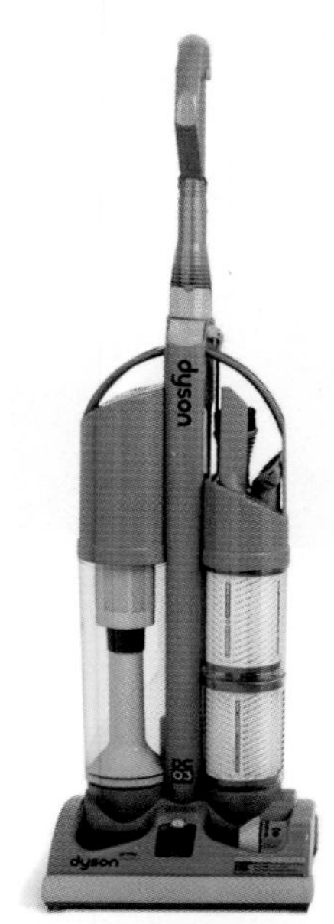

the vacuum cleaner

the bullet-proof vest

Tipp-Ex

windscreen wipers

the Biro

the washing machine

3 READING & VOCABULARY

a Complete the text below with the correct verb in the right form.

base create design (x2) discover ~~invent~~ name use write

Did you know...?

Text-messaging was [1] *invented* by the Finnish company Nokia. They wanted to help Finnish teenagers, who were very shy. They found it easier to text their friends than to phone them.

The first bikini was [2] __________ by two Frenchmen. It was [3] __________ after Bikini Atoll, the island where the atomic bomb was first tested. The Frenchmen thought that the bikini would have a similar effect on men as a bomb exploding.

Light bulbs are [4] __________ specially to last only a certain number of hours. It would be possible to make light bulbs that lasted forever, but then the manufacturers wouldn't make so much money.

The first Harry Potter book was [5] __________ in a café in Edinburgh. JK Rowling was unemployed, and she didn't have enough money to pay for heating, so she wrote it in the café where it was warmer.

Although penicillin was [6] __________ by Alexander Fleming, he didn't know how to make it into a medicine. It was first made into a medicine ten years later, by an Australian scientist Howard Florey.

Spiders were [7] __________ as a cure for toothache in the 17th century. They were first made into a paste, and then put on the bad tooth.

Sherlock Holmes, the great detective was [8] __________ by writer Arthur Conan Doyle. Holmes was [9] __________ on a real person – Doyle's teacher at medical school, who was famous for saying to his students, 'What can you tell me by just observing the patient?'

b Read the facts again. In pairs, say which one is the most surprising.

4 PRONUNCIATION *-ed*, sentence stress

a How is the *–ed* pronounced in these past participles? Put them in the right column.

based designed directed discovered invented
named painted produced used

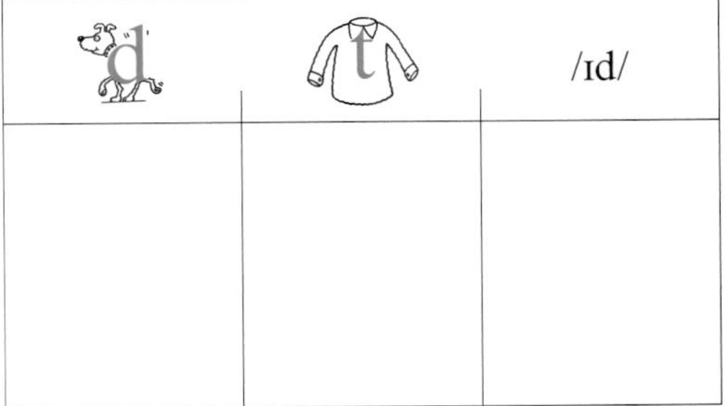

d	t	/ɪd/

b 7.12 Listen and check. Underline the stressed syllable in each multi-syllable verb.

c 7.13 Listen and repeat the sentences. Copy the rhythm. Which words are stressed?

1 The film was based on a true story.
2 These clothes were designed by Armani.
3 This wine is produced near here.
4 My sister was named after our grandmother.
5 These pictures were painted by my aunt.
6 Garlic is used a lot in French cooking.

5 SPEAKING

Communication *Passives quiz A p.111 B p.115.* Make sentences for your partner to decide if they are true or false.

HOW TO GET THERE

7.14 Listen to Mark and Allie and mark the sentences T (true) or F (false).

1 Allie's feeling worse.
2 Mark thinks Allie might get cold.
3 They're going to get a taxi to the bay.
4 Allie wants to be at the hotel again at 1.00 p.m.
5 She's expecting an important visitor.

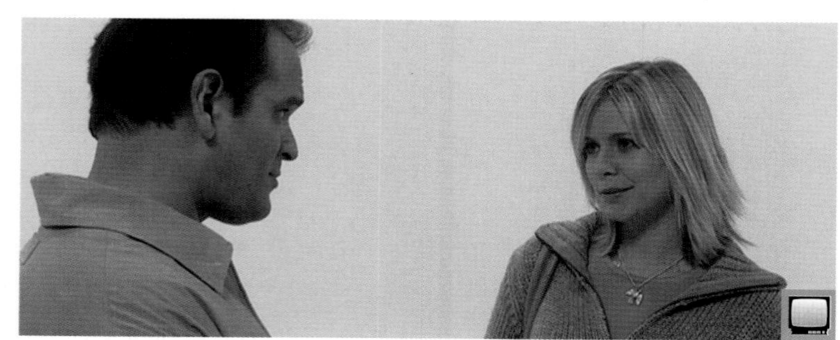

BUYING TICKETS

a 7.15 Cover the dialogue and listen. Complete the sentences.

The next boat leaves at ___ a.m. The trip takes ___ hour(s) and costs ___.

YOU SAY	YOU HEAR
Good morning.	Good morning, sir.
What time does the next boat leave?	At 10.00.
How long does it take?	______ an hour.
Where exactly does the boat go?	It goes ______ the bridge, ______ Angel Island and ______ Alcatraz, and then ______ here.
Can we get anything to eat or drink on the boat?	Yes, ma'am, there's a ______ bar.
Can I have two tickets, please?	Sure. Two ______.
How much is that?	That's $40.
Here you are.	Thank you, sir.
Thank you.	

b Listen again and complete the YOU HEAR phrases.

c 7.16 Listen and repeat the YOU SAY phrases. Copy the rhythm.

d In pairs, roleplay the dialogue. A (book open) you're the ticket seller, B (book closed) you're Mark and Allie. Swap roles.

SOCIAL ENGLISH on the boat

a 7.17 Listen and answer the questions.

1 Does Allie prefer San Francisco to London?
2 Does she think she could live there? Why (not)?
3 What did the building on Alcatraz use to be?
4 What's the weather like?
5 What does Mark ask the boatman to do?

USEFUL PHRASES

M What do you t______ of (San Francisco)?
A Why do you a______?
M Oh, no reason. I j______ wondered.
A I'm really l______ forward to it.
M C______ you take a photo of us, please?
B Are you r______?

b Complete the USEFUL PHRASES. Listen again and check.

c 7.18 Listen and repeat the phrases. How do you say them in your language?

Describing a building

a Read the description and complete it with words from the box.

~~cathedral~~ completed designed roof steps statue view windows

b Match the questions with paragraphs 1–6.

Is there a view from the building? ☐
Describe the building outside. ☐
Describe the building inside. ☐
How much does it cost to go in? ☐
What's the most beautiful building in your town? Where is it? ☐
Who was it designed by? When was it built? ☐

c Find one spelling mistake in each paragraph and correct it.

WRITE a description of a building in your town. Answer the questions in **b** in the right order.

CHECK your description for mistakes (grammar , punctuation , and spelling).

1 The most bea/tiful building in my town is the [1] *cathedral* (the Duomo). It is in the centre of Milan, in the Piazza del Duomo.

2 Nobody knows who it was [2] ________ by, but peopel think it was an architect from northern Europe. Construction began in 1386, but the building wasn't [3] ________ for another 500 years.

3 It is one of the largest cathedrals in the world and it has 135 spires and 3,400 statues. On top of the Duomo there is a gold [4] ________ of the Madonna which watches over the city. The statue is called the 'Madonnina', or the little Madonna, althought it is four metres tall.

4 Inside the Duomo it is quite dark. There are beautiful big [5] ________, and a lot of intresting statues and monuments. In the chapel of St Fina there are some wonderful frescoes by Ghirlandaio.

5 One of the best things you can do in Milan is to go up to the [6] ________ of the Duomo. The [7] ________ is fantastic – on a cleer day you can see the Italian Alps. You can get the lift, or if you are feeling energetic you can walk up the 250 [8] ________.

6 It is free to go in, but you must dress apropriately.

7 What do you remember?

GRAMMAR

Circle the correct answer, a, b, or c.

What's ______ name?

a yours (b) your c you

1 I ______ in this house since I was a child.
 a live
 b 'm living
 c 've lived

2 My father's had his car ______.
 a for two years
 b since two years
 c two years ago

3 How long ______ afraid of flying?
 a are you
 b have you been
 c you have been

4 Tom Cruise and Nicole Kidman ______ married for ten years, but divorced in 2001.
 a are
 b have been
 c were

5 When ______?
 a did Alfred Hitchcock die
 b is Alfred Hitchcock dead
 c has Alfred Hitchcock died

6 My brother ______ glasses.
 a used to wear
 b use to wear
 c used to wearing

7 I ______ like vegetables when I was a child.
 a don't use to
 b didn't use to
 c didn't used to

8 Radium ______ discovered by Pierre and Marie Curie.
 a is
 b were
 c was

9 *The Lord of the Rings* ______ by J.R.R. Tolkien.
 a wrote
 b was wrote
 c was written

10 Paper ______ the Chinese.
 a was invented by
 b invented for
 c was invented for

[ ] 10

VOCABULARY

a time expressions

Complete the sentences with *for* or *since*.

I've lived here *since* 1998.

1 I've had this pen ______ I was a child.
2 He's been married ______ last June.
3 They've known each other ______ a long time.
4 She's studied French literature ______ three years.
5 You've worn that sweater every day ______ Christmas!

b verb phrases

Complete the phrases with a verb.

be get fall ~~have~~ leave retire

have children

1 ______ in love
2 ______ school / university
3 ______ married / divorced
4 ______ when you're 65
5 ______ born

c school subjects

Complete the sentences with a school subject.

If you study *technology* you learn to use computers.

1 If you study ______ you learn about what happened in the past.
2 If you study ______ you learn about countries, mountains, rivers, etc.
3 If you study ______ you learn to add, multiply, etc.
4 If you study ______ you learn physics and chemistry.
5 If you study ______ you learn about plants and animals.

[ ] 15

PRONUNCIATION

a Underline the word with a different sound.

1	aɪ	since	time	child	life
2	uː	school	food	cartoon	book
3	juː	use	ugly	university	uniform
4	s	scene	science	scarf	since
5	tʃ	change	teacher	school	children

b Underline the stressed syllable.

infor<u>ma</u>tion

afraid favourite directed discovered invented

[ ] 10

CAN YOU UNDERSTAND THIS TEXT?

a Read the article quickly. What is surprising about Lady Morton?

The world's most experienced driver?

One of Scotland's most active [1] centenarians, Lady Morton, has been a driver for nearly 80 years, although she has never taken a driving test. But last week she had her first ever accident – she hit a traffic island when she took her new car for a drive in Edinburgh.

Lady Morton, who celebrated her 100th birthday in July, [2] was given the Nissan Micra as a surprise present. Yesterday she talked about the accident. 'I wasn't going fast, but I hit a traffic island. I couldn't see it, because it had no lights, which I think is [3] ridiculous. But I am all right and luckily my car wasn't badly [4] damaged.'

[5] In spite of the accident, she is not planning to stop driving. 'Some people are just born to drive, and I think I am one of them. I've never taken a test, but I've been a good driver since the first time I got in a car. I'm musical, so I listen to the sound of the car to know when to change gear. Some people are very rude – they ask me if I'm still driving at my age. [6] It really annoys me.'

Lady Morton bought her first car in 1927. The [7] main change she has noticed since then is the traffic. 'It's [8] appalling. I don't mind it, because I am experienced, but I feel very sorry for beginners.'

Adapted from a British newspaper

b Tick (✓) the things the article says.

1 Lady Morton has had a lot of accidents.
2 She bought a Nissan Micra recently.
3 She couldn't see the traffic island because she didn't have her lights on.
4 She wasn't badly hurt.
5 After her latest accident she needs a new car.
6 She thinks she's a safe driver.
7 The amount of traffic isn't a problem for her.

c Read the article again. Guess the meaning of the highlighted words or phrases. Check with the teacher or your dictionary.

CAN YOU UNDERSTAND THESE PEOPLE?

a 7.19 Listen. Circle a, b, or c.

1 How long has Matt lived in Glasgow?
a Since he was at university. b For six months. c For two years.
2 John's sister ______ married.
a is b is going to get c was
3 He started running ______.
a a few years ago b at school c a few days ago
4 What's her favourite subject?
a Geography b Literature c Maths
5 When was the White Tower completed?
a In the 17th century. b In 1068. c In 1285.

b 7.20 Listen and complete the table with a number or one word.

Ground floor:	1 a collection of ______ by Graham Richmond.
First floor:	2 children's ______
Entrance hall:	3 the museum ______
Price of guidebook:	4 ______
Museum closes at:	5 ______

CAN YOU SAY THIS IN ENGLISH?

a Can you...? Yes (✓)

☐ say how long you have lived in your town, worked in your job, etc.
☐ talk about the life of an old person in your family
☐ say three things you used to do when you were at (primary) school
☐ describe a famous building in your town

b Complete the questions with an auxiliary verb.

1 How long ______ you been in this class?
2 Where ______ your grandparents born?
3 What TV programmes ______ you use to watch when you were a child?
4 What's the oldest building in your town? When ______ it built?

c Ask your partner the questions in **b**. Ask for more information.

G *something, anything, nothing,* etc.
V adjectives ending *-ed* and *-ing*
P /e/, /əʊ/, /ʌ/

I didn't do anything at the weekend.

I hate weekends!

Most people say that Saturdays or Sundays are their favourite days of the week – but not everybody. For some people weekends are not much fun...

Marco from Brazil is a ________

'I hate the weekend. The weekend is when I'm busiest. I never go [1] **any***where* and I don't really do [2] **any**________ except work. On Friday and Saturday nights we're usually full, and I have to be on my feet for seven or eight hours both days. We're supposed to close at 1.00, but people often don't leave until 1.30 or even later – they never think that we might want to go home. Luckily we close after lunch on Sunday, but when I get home, usually at about 5.30, I'm so tired that I don't want to see [3] **any**________ or do [4] **any**________ except lie on the sofa and watch TV. The best day of the week for me is Wednesday – that's my day off.'

Kirsten from Germany is a ________

'I must admit that for me now the weekends are more tiring than the week. During the week I have [5] **some**________ to help me, but at the weekends we're on our own. My husband's always exhausted from his job and wants to relax, but [6] **no**________ can relax with two small kids around. Our flat isn't very big so there's [7] **no**________ you can go to have some peace and quiet. Before we had children I used to work too and weekends were perfect. We had [8] **no**________ to do except enjoy ourselves. Now I'm really happy when it's Monday morning.'

Steve from the UK is a ________

'My weekend is usually quite stressful, more stressful than during the week. If we're playing at home I can't go out on Friday night. All my friends know that, so [9] **no**________ invites me out on a Friday. I have [10] **some**________ light to eat, and watch TV, and go to bed early. Very boring! On Saturday morning I usually relax and prepare myself mentally, as our home matches are usually at 3.00 in the afternoon. What I do on Saturday night depends on whether we win or lose. If we win, I have to go out with the team to celebrate. If we lose, we're too depressed to go [11] **any**________. When we play away, the weekend doesn't exist. We travel [12] **some**________, play, and then travel back again. I look forward to having a weekend just for me.'

1 READING

a Is the weekend your favourite part of the week? Why (not)?

b Read the article. In pairs, guess what the three people do.

c **8.1** Listen and check.

d Complete the sentences with **Marco**, **Kirsten**, or **Steve**.

1 ____________ always gets home late on Saturdays.
2 ____________ goes to bed early on Friday night.
3 ____________ usually spends the weekend with the family.
4 ____________ sometimes goes out on Saturday night.
5 ____________ used to love the weekend.
6 ____________ prefers Wednesdays to Saturdays.

e Read the texts again. Complete the words 1–12 with **-thing**, **-body**, or **-where**.

2 GRAMMAR *something, anything, nothing,* etc.

a Look again at 1–12 in the text. Complete the rules with *things, places,* and *people.*

Use *something, anything,* and *nothing* for ________.

Use *somebody, anybody,* and *nobody* for ________.

Use *somewhere, anywhere,* and *nowhere* for ________.

b **p.140 Grammar Bank 8A.** Read the rules and do the exercises.

3 PRONUNCIATION /e/, /əʊ/, /ʌ/

a What are sounds 1–3?

1

2

3

b What sound do the pink letters make in each sentence? Write 1, 2, or 3.

1 Nobody knows where he goes. ☐
2 Somebody's coming to lunch. ☐
3 I never said anything. ☐
4 I've done nothing since Sunday. ☐
5 Don't tell anybody about the message. ☐
6 There's nowhere to go except home. ☐

c 8.2 Listen and check your answers. Practise saying the sentences.

4 VOCABULARY adjectives ending *-ed* and *-ing*

a Look at the two sentences from the article. What's the difference between *tired* and *tiring*?

I'm so **tired** that I don't want to see anybody.

Weekends are more **tiring** than week days.

b Look at the adjectives in **bold** in these sentences. How do you pronounce them?

1 Friday night is **bored** / **boring**. I never go out.
2 I'm **bored** / **boring** with my job. It's always the same.
3 If we lose we feel **depressed** / **depressing**.
4 My team never win. It's **depressed** / **depressing**.
5 Reading is very **relaxed** / **relaxing**.
6 I feel very **relaxed** / **relaxing** at the weekend.
7 His latest film is really **interesting** / **interested**.
8 I'm not very **interesting** / **interested** in sport.
9 I'm very **excited** / **exciting** about my holiday.
10 It was a really **excited** / **exciting** match.

c Cross out the wrong word.

5 SPEAKING

Ask and answer with a partner. Ask for more information too.

Every weekend

/ you normally have to work or study at weekends?
/ there anything you always watch on TV?
/ you normally have to buy anything on Saturdays?
/ have to do anything in the house (clean, etc.)?

Last weekend

/ you go anywhere exciting on Friday night?
/ do anything tiring on Saturday morning?
/ you meet anybody on Saturday night?
/ you do anything relaxing on Sunday?

Next weekend

/ you go away anywhere?
/ you do anything special on Saturday?
/ you go anywhere interesting on Sunday?

6 LISTENING

a 8.3 Listen and number the pictures 1–8.

b In pairs, use the pictures 1–8 to re-tell the story.

How old is your body?

I eat too much meat.
I don't drink enough water.

How old are you? How old is your body? The answer to these two questions isn't always the same. Our body age can be much younger or much older than our calendar age (even eighteen years different!). We can now calculate our body age by answering questions about the way we live. If our body age is older than our calendar age, we should change our lifestyle.

EXERCISE

I know I'm too fat because I don't do enough exercise. I spend too much time sitting in studios. All I do is play squash, but I don't play very often – about once a month. I would go to a gym if I had more time.

DIET

I eat quite a lot of fresh food and a lot of fruit, but I probably eat too much meat. My girlfriend says I don't drink enough water. I drink a little alcohol – just a glass of red wine with my dinner. But I don't drink any beer. I drink a lot of coffee. It goes with the job.

LIFESTYLE

Like everybody I'm too busy! There aren't enough hours in the day. I love my job but I work too much (sometimes I spend 14 hours a day in the studio – that's too many). I often feel a bit tense and irritable. I smoke a few cigarettes when I go out, but I'm not a regular smoker. I only wear sunscreen when I go to the beach. My skin is quite dark so I don't think it's a problem.

PERSONALITY

I'm quite pessimistic. I always think that things will go wrong – and they usually do, especially at work.

SOCIAL LIFE

I don't have much free time but I have a few close friends and I try to see them regularly. If I'm too busy then I phone them.

DOCTOR'S VERDICT:

Tariq should do more exercise, for example he could walk to work. This would help him to control his stress. His diet is quite healthy but he should drink more water and less coffee. He must give up smoking. Although his skin is quite dark he should wear sunscreen all year round, even in winter. And he should try to be more positive.

Tariq, a record producer
Calendar age 32

Body age ______

1 READING

a Read the introduction to the article and answer the questions.

1 Is our body age the same as our calendar age?
2 How can we calculate our body age?
3 What should we do if our body age is older than our calendar age?

b Look at the photo of Tariq and read about him. Underline the things he does that are good. Circle the things he does that are bad. Compare with a partner.

c Cover the *Doctor's verdict*. What do you think he should do?

d Now read the *Doctor's verdict*. Was the advice the same as yours? What do you think his body age is?

2 GRAMMAR quantifiers, *too*, *not enough*

a Can you remember how to use *much*, *many*, etc.? In pairs, choose the correct word or phrase for each sentence. Say why the other one is wrong.

1 How **much** / **many** coffee do you drink?
2 I don't eat **much** / **many** vegetables.
3 I eat **a lot of** / **many** bread.
4 I smoke **a lot** / **a lot of**.
5 **A** How much tea do you drink?
B **Any** / **None**. I don't like it.

b Match the phrases 1–6 with the meanings A–F.

1 ☐ I drink **too much** coffee.
2 ☐ I'm **too** fat.
3 ☐ I work **too many** hours.
4 ☐ I don't do **enough** exercise.
5 ☐ I drink **a little** alcohol.
6 ☐ I have **a few** close friends.

A I don't drink much.
B I need to do more.
C I have two or three.
D I work more than I want.
E I should be a bit thinner.
F I drink more than I should.

c ➲ **p.140 Grammar Bank 8B.** Read the rules and do the exercises.

3 PRONUNCIATION /ʌ/, /uː/, /aɪ/, /e/; linking

a Cross out the word with a different pronunciation.

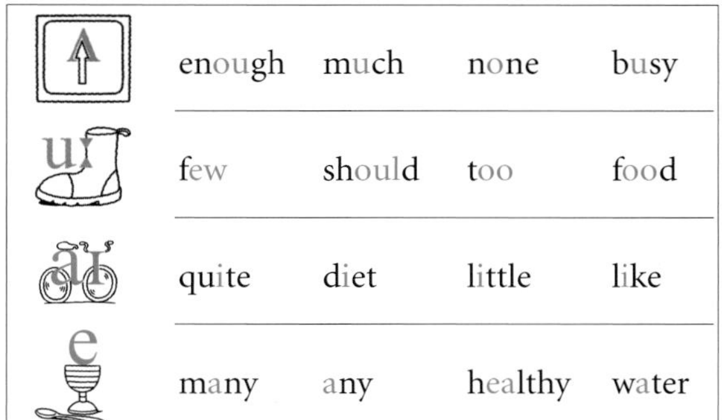

ʌ	enough	much	none	busy
uː	few	should	too	food
aɪ	quite	diet	little	like
e	many	any	healthy	water

b 8.4 Listen and check. Practise saying the words.

Remember! When people speak quickly they don't separate the words.

c 8.5 Listen and write the six sentences.

d Listen and repeat the sentences. Copy the rhythm.

4 SPEAKING

a Read the questionnaire and circle your answers.

b Interview your partner and underline his / her answers. Ask for more information.

How much sport or exercise do you do?
A lot.
What do you do?
I go to the gym three times a week.

c **Communication** *Body age p.111.* Work out your body age.

d Look at your partner's answers. Give him / her some good advice.

I think you should do more exercise. For example...

What's your body age?
Do our quiz and find out

EXERCISE

1 **How much do you walk a day?**
a a lot **b** quite a lot **c** not much **d** very little

2 **How much sport and exercise do you do a week?**
a a lot **b** quite a lot **c** a little **d** none

DIET

3 **How much fast food (processed and pre-prepared) do you eat?**
a I eat too much. **b** I eat quite a lot.
c I don't eat much. **d** I don't eat any.

4 **How many portions of fruit and vegetables do you eat per day?**
a only a few **b** quite a lot **c** a lot

5 **How much water do you drink?**
a a lot **b** quite a lot **c** a little

6 **What's your worst diet habit?**
a I eat too much fat. **b** I eat (or drink) too many sweet things.
c I eat (or drink) too much. **d** none of these

LIFESTYLE

7 **How many cigarettes do you smoke a day?**
a none **b** a few **c** a lot

8 **How would you describe yourself mentally?**
a I am a very positive person. **b** I am not positive enough.
c I'm quite pessimistic.

9 **How would you describe your stress level?**
a I am too stressed. **b** I am stressed, but it's under control.
c I am quite relaxed.

10 **How often do you wear sunscreen?**
a all year **b** only when I'm on holiday **c** when it's sunny

SOCIAL LIFE

11 **How many close friends do you see regularly?**
a a lot **b** quite a lot **c** a few **d** not many / none

12 **How much time do you have for yourself?**
a none **b** not enough **c** quite a lot

8C Waking up is hard to do

G word order of phrasal verbs
V phrasal verbs
P /g/ and /dʒ/

I wake up and I turn on the radio.

1 VOCABULARY phrasal verbs

a Match the questions 1–7 with the pictures A–G.

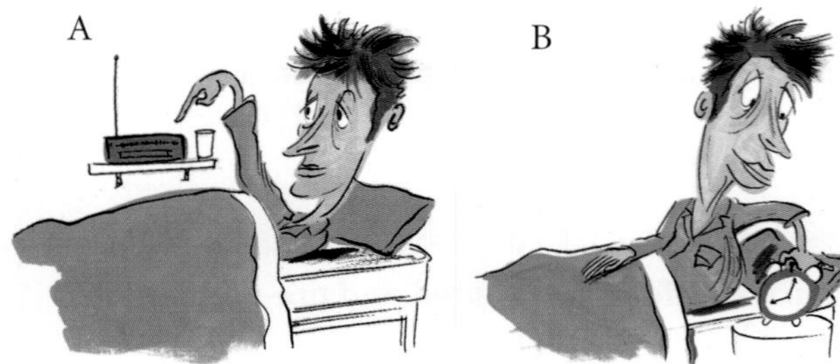

1 What time do you wake up in the morning? D
2 Do you use an alarm clock to wake up? ☐
3 Do you turn off the alarm clock immediately? ☐
4 What's the first thing you turn on after you wake up? ☐
5 Do you get up immediately after you wake up? ☐
6 How do you feel when you first get up? ☐
7 When you get dressed, what's the last thing you put on? ☐

b Cover the questions and look at the pictures. Try to remember the questions.

c In pairs, use the pictures to ask and answer the questions.

d **p.153 Vocabulary Bank** ***Phrasal verbs.***

2 GRAMMAR word order of phrasal verbs

a Look at the pictures 1–3 and underline the object of the phrasal verb in each sentence.

b Complete the rules about separable phrasal verbs with *noun* or *pronoun*.

1 If the object of a phrasal verb is a ______, you can put it **after** the verb +*up*, *on*, etc. OR **between** the verb and *up*, *on*, etc.
2 If the object of a phrasal verb is a ______, you **must** put it **between** the verb and *up*, *on*, etc.

c **p.140 Grammar Bank 8C.** Read the rules and do the exercises.

d Match the sentences. Then cover the sentences on the right. Try to remember them.

1 Your mobile's ringing.	E	A You need to give it up.
2 This is an important rule.	☐	B Put them away.
3 I can't hear the music.	☐	C Turn it up.
4 If you don't know what the words mean,	☐	D Throw it away.
5 This is an immigration form.	☐	E ~~Turn it off.~~
6 Coffee is bad for you.	☐	F Please fill it in.
7 Your clothes are on the floor.	☐	G Write it down.
8 That's rubbish.	☐	H look them up.

3 READING

a Do you know what these scientific words and expressions mean?

a gene DNA your 'body clock' research

b Read the article about morning and evening people. Choose **a**, **b**, or **c**.

1 Scientists say that if we are bad at getting up in the morning, this is because
 a we are born like that.
 b we go to bed too late.
 c we drink too much coffee.

2 Researchers asked people questions about
 a the way they lived.
 b science.
 c sport and exercise.

3 They discovered that people who have a short 'clock' gene
 a are better in the morning than in the evening.
 b get tired very early.
 c are better in the evening than in the morning.

4 They recommend that people who have a long 'clock' gene
 a should only work in the afternoon and evening.
 b should start work early and finish early.
 c should start work late and finish late.

Are you allergic to mornings?

Are you somebody who can't wake up in the morning? Do you need two cups of coffee before you can start a new day? Do you feel awful when you first wake up? Scientists say it's all because of our genes. How did they find this out? Researchers from the University of Surrey interviewed 500 people. They asked them questions about their lifestyle, for example what time of day they preferred to do exercise and how difficult they found it to wake up in the morning. Scientists then compared their answers to the people's DNA.

They discovered that we all have a 'clock' gene, also called a Period 3 gene. This gene can be long or short. People who have the long gene are usually people who are very good in the morning, but who get tired quite early at night. People who have the short gene are usually people who are more active at night but who have problems waking up early in the morning. How does it help us to know if we have the long or short gene? Scientists say that, if possible, we should try to change our working hours to fit our 'body clock'. If you are a 'morning person' then you could start work early and finish early. But if you are bad in the mornings, then it might be better to start work in the afternoon and work until late at night. So maybe, instead of nine to five it should be seven to three or twelve to eight.

Adapted from a British newspaper

4 LISTENING & SPEAKING

a 8.6 Listen to David being interviewed by a researcher. Is he a morning or evening person?

b Listen again and write down David's answers.

1 What do you do?
2 When do you work?
3 What time do you get up in the morning?
4 If you have an exam, do you study best in the morning, afternoon, or at night?
5 If you do exercise, when do you prefer to do it?
6 Do you like your working hours? (school/university timetable)?
7 Why (not)?
8 Would you like to change them (it)? How?

c Interview your partner using the questions in **b**. Is he / she a morning or evening person?

5 PRONUNCIATION /g/ and /dʒ/

a How is the letter *g* pronounced in these words? Put five words in each column.

gene get go change energetic
gym good give hungry age

b 8.7 Listen and check. Practise saying the words.

c Now practise saying the sentences.

1 She gets up early to go to the gym.
2 George and Greta are good at German.
3 I'm allergic to mornings. It's in my genes.
4 I generally feel hungry and energetic.

6 8.8 SONG ♫ *Say a little prayer*

8D

G *so, neither* + auxiliaries
V similarities
P vowel and consonant sounds, sentence stress

I like dogs.
So do I.

'I'm Jim.' 'So am I.'

1 LISTENING

a Look at the photos and describe the two men.

b Read about the two men and answer the questions.

1 Who are Jim Springer and Jim Lewis?
2 Why didn't they know each other?
3 When did they meet?

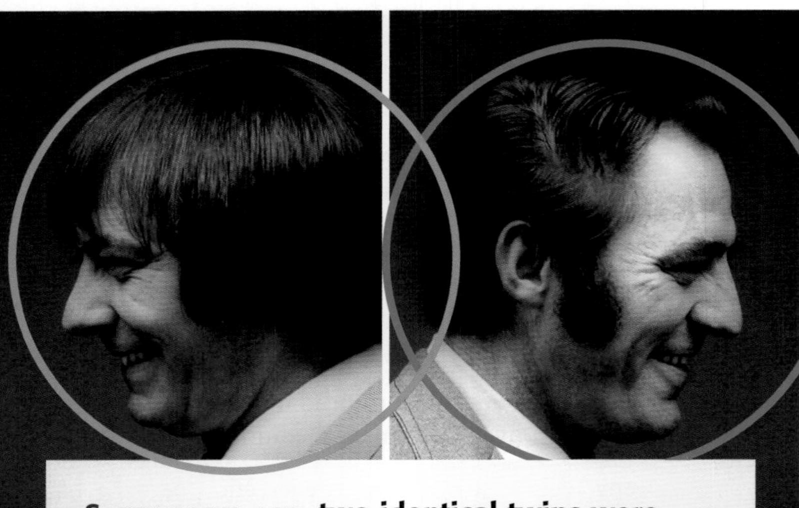

Some years ago, two identical twins were born in Minnesota USA. They were adopted by two different families. The two new families both called their babies Jim. Jim Springer never knew that Jim Lewis existed. But when they were 40 years old they met for the first time and they had a conversation something like this…

c 8.9 Cover the dialogue. Listen once. Try to remember **three** things they have in common.

d Uncover the dialogue. Listen again and fill the gaps.

A Hi! I'm Jim.
B So _____ I. Great to meet you. Are you married, Jim?
A Yes…well, I've been married twice.
B Yeah? So _____ I. Do you have any children?
A I have one son.
B So _____ I. What's his name?
A James.
B That's amazing! My son's name is James too.
A Did you go to university, Jim?
B No, I didn't.
A Neither _____ I. I was a terrible student.
B So _____ I. What do you like doing in your free time, Jim?
A I like making things, especially with wood.
B That's incredible! So _____ I.
A But I don't do any exercise at all. Look at me.
B Don't worry. Neither _____ I.
A Do you smoke?
B Yes. I smoke Salem cigarettes.
A So _____ I! What car do you have?
B A Chevrolet.
A Me too! Let's go and have a drink. What beer do you drink?
B Miller Lite.
A So _____ I!

2 GRAMMAR *so, neither* + auxiliaries

a Look at the dialogue again. Write one phrase that the twins use…

when they have something [+] in common. _________
when they have something [−] in common. _________

b **p.140 Grammar Bank 8D.** Read the rules and do the exercises.

3 READING & VOCABULARY

a Read the text and answer the questions.

1 Who reunited the two Jims?
2 What did Dr Bouchard want to find out?
3 What was he very surprised by?
4 What are their sons and their dogs called?
5 What do they both do for their wives?
6 What does Dr Bouchard believe, as a result of the case of the two Jims?

b Complete the phrases with these words.

as both like neither so similar

Similarities

1 Jim Springer looks exactly ________ Jim Lewis.
2 Jim Springer's son has the same name ________ Jim Lewis's son.
3 The two Jims ________ have dogs.
4 Jim Springer likes baseball and ________ does Jim Lewis.
5 Jim Lewis doesn't like basketball and ________ does Jim Springer.
6 Dr Bouchard didn't expect them to be so ________ to each other.

c Complete the sentences about you and your family. Tell your partner.

1 I have the same colour eyes as my ________.
2 I look like my ________.
3 My personality is quite similar to my ________'s.
4 My ________ and I both like ________.
5 I like ________ and so does my ________.
6 I don't like ________ and neither does my ________.

JIM SPRINGER AND JIM LEWIS were reunited after forty years by Dr Thomas Bouchard, Professor of psychology at the University of Minnesota. He was investigating how much of our personality depends on genes. Dr Bouchard was amazed by how many things the twins had in common. He had expected them to look identical and to have similar medical histories. But he and his team were very surprised to find the enormous similarities in the two Jims' personalities, their lifestyle, their hobbies, their religion, even their political beliefs.

Some of the similarities are incredible: Jim Springer's son is called James Allen, and Jim Lewis's is called James Alan. They both have dogs named Toy. They like and hate the same sports and they voted for the same President. And both Jims have the same romantic habit of leaving little love letters for their wives around the house.

Dr Bouchard is convinced that genes are probably much more important in determining our personality and preferences than people used to think.

4 PRONUNCIATION sounds, sentence stress

a The same or different? Circle the word with a different sound in each group.

1	so	no	do
2	they	neither	both
3	two	twice	twins
4	identical	incredible	immediately
5	food	good	wood
6	now	know	how
7	speak	great	each
8	beer	free	weekend

b 8.10 Listen and check. Practise saying the words.

c 8.11 Listen and repeat the dialogues. Underline the stressed words.

1 **A** I like tea. **B** So do I.
2 **A** I'm tired. **B** So am I.
3 **A** I don't smoke. **B** Neither do I.
4 **A** I'm not hungry. **B** Neither am I.

d 8.12 Listen and respond. Say you're the same. Use *So* ______ *I* / *Neither* ______ *I*.

5 SPEAKING

a Complete the sentences so they are true for you.

ME	WHO ELSE?
I love ________. (a kind of music)	________
I don't like ________. (a TV programme)	________
I'm ________. (star sign)	________
I'm not very good at ________. (a subject)	________
I'm going to ________ this weekend. (an activity)	________
I have to ________ every day. (an obligation)	________
I don't eat ________. (a kind of food)	________
I'm not very ________. (adjective of personality)	________

b Move around the class saying your sentences. For each sentence try to find someone like you, and write down their name. Respond to other people's sentences. Say *So do / am I* or *Neither do / am I* if you are like them.

I love classical music.
So do I.

CHECKING OUT

8.13 Listen to Allie talking to the receptionist. Answer the questions.

1 When is she leaving the hotel?
2 When does she want to pay?
3 What time is her flight?
4 What time does she have to be at the airport?
5 What is the message for her?

MAKING PHONE CALLS

a 8.14 Cover the dialogue and listen. Who does Allie want to speak to? What happens the first time she calls? Is the news good or bad? What is it?

YOU HEAR	YOU SAY
Hello.	Hello. Is that MTC?
Sorry, you've got the ______ number.	Oh sorry.
MTC New York. How can I help you?	Hello. Can I speak to Lisa Formosa, please?
Just a moment. I'll ______ you ______.	
Hello.	Hi, is that Lisa?
No, I'm sorry. She's not at her desk right now.	Can I leave a message, please?
Sure.	Tell her Allie Gray called. I'll call back in five minutes.
MTC New York. How can I help you?	Hello. Can I speak to Lisa Formosa, please?
Just a moment. I'm sorry, the line's ______. Do you want to ______?	OK, I'll hold.
Hello.	Hi Lisa. It's Allie Gray.
Allie, hi. How's California?	Great, great. Well? Is it good news or bad news?
It's good. You got the job in Paris!	Oh wonderful! That's fantastic!

b Listen again and complete the YOU HEAR phrases.

c 8.15 Listen and repeat the YOU SAY phrases. Copy the rhythm.

d In pairs, roleplay the dialogue. **A** (book closed) you're Allie, **B** (book open) you're all the other people. Swap roles.

SOCIAL ENGLISH saying goodbye?

a 8.16 Listen and mark the sentences T (true) or F (false).

1 Mark thinks that their relationship has a future.
2 She thinks it's a problem that Mark is very different from her.
3 Mark tells Allie he's going to move to another company.
4 Allie is very surprised.
5 Allie is going to be Mark's wife.

b Complete the USEFUL PHRASES. Listen again and check.

c 8.17 Listen and repeat the phrases. How do you say them in your language?

USEFUL PHRASES

A Thanks for e______.
M C______! To us.
A What do you m______?
M I______ that amazing?
M What's the m______?
M I don't b______ it.

Giving your opinion

a Read the article and complete it with these words.

above all although another ~~but~~ general however secondly which who

The weekend

The good side

For me the first good thing about the weekend is that I don't have to go to work. I like my job, [1] *but* I have to spend all day inside, in an office, and I'm a person [2] ______ loves being outside. [3] ______ good thing is that I don't have to get up early. During the week I have to get up at half past six every day. It's not too bad in the summer but I hate it in the winter when it's dark in the morning. But [4] ______, I like the weekend because I have time to do all the things I really enjoy doing, like listening to music, reading, or going out with friends.

The bad side

[5] ______, there are some things I don't like about the weekend. Firstly, I have to go shopping on Saturday morning, and the supermarket is always crowded. [6] ______, on Sundays we always have lunch with my husband's family. [7] ______ my mother-in-law is a good cook and her food is delicious, I don't usually have a good time. The family always argue and we end up watching TV, [8] ______ I think is boring.

But in [9] ______ I love the weekend – I often get a bit depressed on Sunday afternoon when I know that the weekend is nearly over.

b Read the article again. Now cover it and, from memory, mark the sentences T (true) or F (false).

1 She works outside.
2 She has to get up early during the week.
3 She enjoys shopping on Saturdays.
4 Her husband always makes lunch on Sundays.
5 She doesn't like watching TV.

What do you think of the weekend? **WRITE** two paragraphs.

Paragraph 1 **The good side**
For me the best thing about the weekend is…

Paragraph 2 **The bad side**
However, there are some things I don't like. For example,…

Final paragraph Do you love it or hate it?
But in general,…

CHECK your article for mistakes (grammar , punctuation , and spelling).

8 What do you remember?

GRAMMAR

Circle the correct answer, a, b, or c.

What's ______ name?

a yours ⓑ your c you

1 **A** What did you do this weekend?
B ______
a Nothing.
b Nobody.
c Anything.

2 We didn't go ______ on Sunday.
a somewhere
b anywhere
c nowhere

3 She spoke to ______ in the office.
a anybody
b somebody
c nobody

4 He eats ______ crisps and chips.
a too
b too much
c too many

5 I can't go. I'm ______ busy.
a enough
b too
c too much

6 You don't drink ______.
a water enough
b enough water
c a few water

7 Here are your shoes. Put ______.
a on them
b them on
c it on

8 I can't find my keys. Can you help me ______?
a look them for
b look for them
c for them look

9 **A** My father loves jazz.
B ______
a So I do.
b So am I.
c So do I.

10 **A** I didn't go to university.
B ______
a Neither do I.
b Neither did I.
c Neither I did.

10

VOCABULARY

a adjectives ending *-ed* and *-ing*

Complete the sentences with an adjective.

The film was very e*xciting*.

1 We had a very r______ holiday – we just lay in the sun.
2 I only got three hours' sleep – I'm really t______.
3 I saw a really i______ TV programme last night.
4 She failed all her exams, so she feels a bit d______.
5 My job's very b______ – I have to do all the photocopying.

b health and lifestyle verbs

Complete the sentences with a verb.

She *drinks* a lot of coffee.

1 I don't ______ enough exercise.
2 You should ______ sunscreen if you're going to the beach.
3 He ______ too many biscuits.
4 I ______ my friends every weekend.
5 You should ______ smoking, it's a terrible habit.

c phrasal verbs

Complete the sentences with a verb.

I *get* up at 7.00.

~~get~~ look (x2) put turn wake

1 Please ______ off the TV when you go to bed.
2 You should ______ up new words in a dictionary.
3 ______ up. It's 7.00.
4 ______ on a coat. It's cold.
5 I have to ______ after my little brother today.

15

PRONUNCIATION

a Under<u>line</u> the word with a different sound.

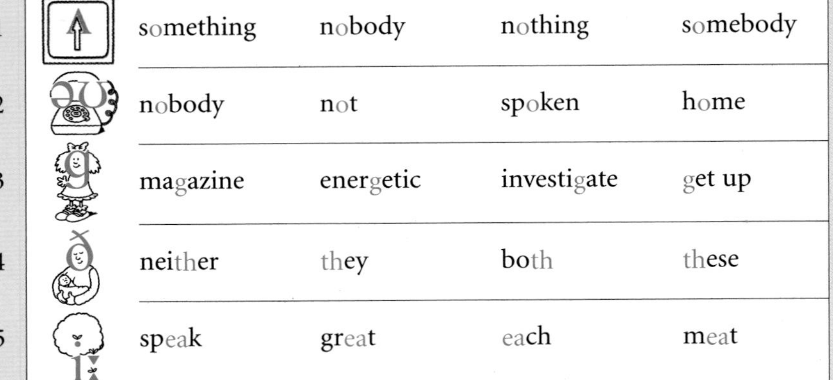

1	something	nobody	nothing	somebody
2	nobody	not	spoken	home
3	magazine	energetic	investigate	get up
4	neither	they	both	these
5	speak	great	each	meat

b Under<u>line</u> the stressed syllable.

infor<u>ma</u>tion

somebody relax diet enough identical

10

CAN YOU UNDERSTAND THIS TEXT?

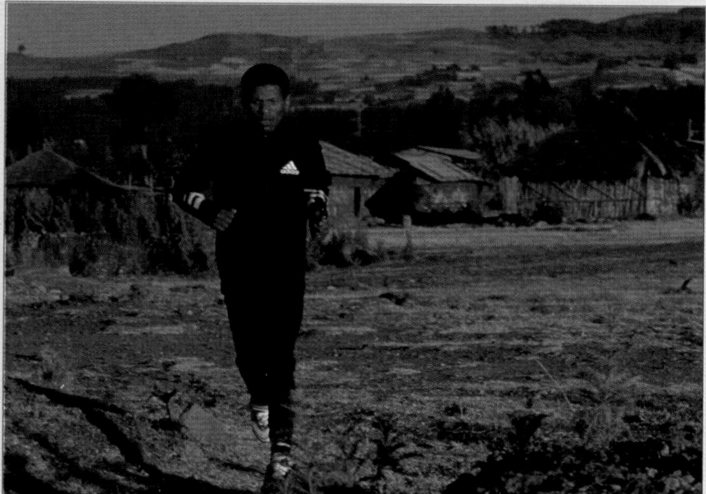

Born to run

The Ethiopian runner, Haile Gebreselassie, the 'Emperor', is probably the greatest athlete of all time. He has won two Olympic titles, seven world titles and has broken numerous world records at 5,000 and 10,000 metres. A Sunday Times journalist went to interview him at his home in Addis Ababa.

Haile's routine has not changed since he became an athlete. Every morning he gets up at 5.45 and runs for two hours. He has a nap after lunch and then goes out running again.

Haile was brought up in a very poor family. Although today he is a multi-millionaire he has never been comfortable with being a rich man in such a poor country. 'The thing that really offends me,' he says, 'is that the most important value in the 21st century is how much money you have.'

In the future, when he retires from athletics, Haile may go into politics. 'I want to do something to help the people of Ethiopia. I have travelled to many countries. I have experience and I want to share that experience.' What Haile can't understand is why Europe is so rich and Ethiopia so poor. 'I was in Germany a week ago and it was freezing! Minus five. We have a much better climate. But we don't have enough water and so we don't have enough food and there are too many people.'

As we drive through the city in his ten-year-old Mercedes everybody recognizes him and shouts his name. A lorry carrying soldiers waits to let us pass. 'Even the army are your fans,' I say. 'No,' replies Haile. 'That was because there is a white man sitting in the front seat of the car with me.'

Adapted from a British newspaper

a Read the article and mark the sentences T (true), F (false), or DS (doesn't say).

1. Haile Gebreselassie is a long-distance runner.
2. He runs twice a day.
3. He enjoys being rich.
4. His family are also very rich.
5. He can't understand why Europe is richer than his country.
6. The soldiers stop because Haile is famous.

b Find a word or phrase in the article which means:

1. a short sleep (paragraph 1)
2. looked after when he was young (paragraph 2)
3. give something you have to other people too (paragraph 3)
4. very cold (paragraph 3)
5. calls in a loud voice (paragraph 4)

CAN YOU UNDERSTAND THESE PEOPLE?

a 8.18 Listen and circle the correct answer, a, b, or c.

1. Where did the woman go at the weekend?
   a to the cinema b nowhere c to the beach
2. The man doesn't eat enough ______.
   a fruit b fish c vegetables
3. How often does the woman go to the gym?
   a only on Friday b twice a week c every day
4. What time does the woman get up?
   a 7.00 b 7.15 c 7.30
5. What do the men have in common?
   a They drink coffee. b They used to be married. c They're teachers.

b 8.19 Listen and write M (the man), W (the woman), or B (both).

Who…?

1. went to bed late ___
2. is good in the mornings ___
3. went to Liverpool University ___
4. studied Economics ___
5. knows Fiona ___

CAN YOU SAY THIS IN ENGLISH?

a Can you…? Yes (✓)

- [ ] talk about why you like / don't like the weekend
- [ ] talk about your lifestyle (food, exercise, etc.)
- [ ] talk about your typical morning

b Tell your partner about food you like / don't like. Find three things you have in common.

9 A

G past perfect
V adverbs: *suddenly*, *immediately*, etc.
P revision of vowel sounds, sentence stress

She had left the door open so the man went into her house.

What a week!

Fact is always stranger than fiction.

Here is a selection of true stories from around the world last week.

Prize of the week.

1 James Bolton, who is unemployed, was very excited when he won first prize in a raffle last week. The prize was a weekend for two at a hotel in Bournemouth on the south coast of England. Unfortunately, he was less excited when he saw the name of the hotel. ☐

Mistake of the week

2 A 33-year-old Norwegian man came home one night from the pub and got into bed next to his wife. The woman immediately woke up, screamed, and jumped out of bed. 'Who are you?' asked the man. 'You aren't my wife.' ☐

Helpful advice of the week

3 An Italian was driving along the motorway when his cousin phoned him on his mobile. He told him to drive more slowly, because the police were waiting a few kilometres ahead to catch drivers who were going too fast. The driver slowed down, but two kilometres later the police stopped him and gave him a fine. ☐

Animal story of the week

4 Nurse Katie Parfitt from Manchester couldn't understand why her cat was behaving so strangely. The cat came home, attacked her bed, and then jumped on her plate while she was having her dinner. Then it fell asleep and began snoring. The next day when she spoke to her neighbour the mystery was solved. ☐

Honest citizen of the week

5 A man in Baltimore was arrested last week when he tried to become a policeman. When he filled in his application form for the job, he answered 'yes' to the question, 'Have you ever committed a crime?' ☐

Romantic hero of the week

6 The passengers on a German bus were amazed when their driver suddenly stopped the bus, got out, and began hitting a man who was making a phone call in a public phone box. First, the bus driver hit the man twice. Then the other man hit the bus driver very hard with the phone. The passengers were left sitting in the bus, and the bus driver was taken to hospital. ☐

Adapted from a British newspaper

1 SPEAKING & READING

a Look at the pictures 1–6 on p.100. In which picture can you see...?

somebody **screaming** ☐
someone getting a **fine** ☐
somebody winning a **raffle** ☐
something **snoring** ☐
somebody being **arrested** ☐
some passengers looking **amazed** ☐

b Read the stories and look at the pictures. Then in pairs, match them with their endings A–F.

A They had seen him using his mobile phone while he was driving.

B He had discovered the day before that his wife was having an affair with the man in the phone box.

C When they questioned him, the man admitted he had stolen a car a few months before and had robbed five people in Texas.

D The neighbour had seen it earlier that evening in the local pub. One of the customers had given it a drink of rum. Luckily, it has not become an alcoholic!

E It was the hotel where he had worked as a porter the previous month. He had lost his job there.

F The man had accidentally gone into his neighbour's house. The neighbour had left the back door open as she was waiting for her husband to come home.

c Read the stories again. Look at the pictures. Can you remember the stories?

2 GRAMMAR past perfect

a Look at these sentences from story 3. Answer the questions.

a The police stopped the Italian driver.
b They had seen him using his mobile phone.

1 Which action happened first, **a** or **b**?
2 What's the form of the verb in sentence **b**?

b Read the endings of the other five stories again and underline examples of *had* + past participle. Did these actions happen *before* or *after* the main part of the story?

c **p.142 Grammar Bank 9A.** Read the rules and do the exercises.

3 PRONUNCIATION vowel sounds, sentence stress

a What sound do the pink letters make in each sentence? Match the sentences with the sound pictures.

A B C D E F

1 He suddenly understood why his brother hadn't come. ☐
2 I didn't know Linda hadn't written since the spring. ☐
3 The police had seen me in the street. ☐
4 Paul thought the train had left at four forty. ☐
5 We hadn't heard a word about the third murder. ☐
6 We'd waited for ages to see the famous painting. ☐

b 9.1 Now listen and repeat the sentences. Copy the rhythm, and practise making the sounds.

4 VOCABULARY adverbs

a Circle the adverbs in these five sentences from the stories in **1**. Underline the stressed syllable. Which two are opposites?

The man had accidentally gone into his neighbour's house.

Unfortunately, he was less excited when he saw the name of the hotel.

The passengers were amazed when their driver suddenly stopped the bus.

Luckily, it has not become an alcoholic!

The woman immediately woke up, screamed, and jumped out of bed.

b Complete the sentences with one of the adverbs.

1 I _______ took the office keys home with me.
2 They were having a relaxed dinner when _______ the baby started to cry.
3 The boss left, and _______ everyone started talking again.
4 _______, the weather was terrible when we were on holiday.
5 Last week I had a car crash. _______, nobody was hurt.

c In pairs, invent completions of these sentences.

1 She got to work very late. Luckily...
2 I was watching a good film on TV when suddenly...
3 When we got out of the car it was raining. Unfortunately, we...
4 I got home, had a shower, and immediately...
5 I'm really sorry about the book you lent me. I accidentally...

5 SPEAKING

Communication *What had happened? A p.111 B p.115.*
Try to say your partner's sentences.

G reported speech
V *say*, *tell*, or *ask*?
P rhyming verbs

He said that he loved me.

Then he kissed me

1 SPEAKING & LISTENING

a Number the pictures A–H in a logical order.

b Complete the song with the verbs in the past simple. Use the glossary to help you.

c 9.2 Listen and check. Were your pictures in the right order?

Then he kissed me

ask	dance	say	walk (x2)	want

Well, he [1] *walked* up to me and he [2]______ me if I [3]______ to dance.
He looked kind of nice and so I [4]______ I might take a chance.
When he [5]______ he held me tight
And when he [6]______ me home that night
All the stars were shining bright
And then he kissed me.

can't	don't know	is	say	see

Each time I [7]______ him I [8]______ wait to see him again.
I wanted to let him know that he [9]______ more than a friend.
I [10]______ just what to do
So I whispered 'I love you'
And he [11]______ that he loved me too
And then he kissed me.
He kissed me in a way that I've never been kissed before,
He kissed me in a way that I wanna be kissed forever more.

ask	feel	give	know	take

I [12]______ that he was mine so I [13]______ him all the love that I had
And one day he [14]______ me home to meet his mum and his dad.
Then he [15]______ me to be his bride
And always be right by his side
I [16]______ so happy I almost cried
And then he kissed me.

Glossary

L.2 He looked kind of nice	He looked like a nice boy.
L.2 take a chance	try something to see if you are lucky
L.3 hold somebody tight	put your arms around somebody strongly
L.5 shining bright	with a very strong light
L.14 wanna	want to

2 GRAMMAR reported speech

A 'I love you too.'

B 'Do you want to dance?'

C He said he loved me too.

D He asked me if I wanted to dance.

a Look at the sentences. In pairs, answer the questions.

1 Which sentences are the speaker's exact words (direct speech)? ☐ ☐
2 Which sentences describe what the speaker said (reported speech)? ☐ ☐
3 What tense are the verbs in direct speech? p______ simple
4 What tense are the verbs in reported speech? p______ simple

b ➲ **p.142 Grammar Bank 9B.** Read the rules and do the exercises.

c Change these sentences from direct speech to reported speech.

1 'My name's Dean.' He said that *his name was Dean*.
2 'Do you want a drink?' He asked her if ______.
3 'I'm not thirsty.' She said ______.
4 'Will you go out with me?' He asked ______.
5 'Can I walk you home?' He asked ______.
6 'Where do you live?' He asked ______.
7 'I live quite near.' She said ______.
8 'I fell in love at first sight.' He told Millie ______.

3 VOCABULARY *say*, *tell*, or *ask*?

Complete the sentences with *said*, *told*, or *asked*.

1 Jane ______ me if I could lend her some money.
2 I ______ him that I couldn't meet him tonight.
3 I ______ that I was too busy to go out.
4 We ______ the man if he could help us.
5 Annie ______: 'I have a problem.'
6 Annie ______ us that she had a problem.
7 She ______ her husband that she was leaving him.
8 He ______ the teacher that he had forgotten his homework.

4 PRONUNCIATION rhyming verbs

a Match a verb in the past tense from A with a rhyming one in B.

b 9.3 Listen and check.

A	B
said	crossed
paid	read
caught	wore
lost	stood
spent	meant
told	played
saw	sold
heard	bought
could	preferred

5 SPEAKING

a Choose and tick (✓) five questions below to ask your partner. Ask your questions and write down his / her answers.

Do you like flying?

What's your favourite colour? ☐

Can you play a musical instrument? ☐

Do you like flying? ☐

Where are your parents from? ☐

How long have you lived here? ☐

What languages do you speak? ☐

What kind of computer do you have? ☐

Do you have any phobias? ☐

Where do you buy your clothes? ☐

b Change partners. Tell partner 2 what you asked partner 1 and what his / her answers were.

I asked him what his favourite colour was and he told me that it was blue.

9 Grammar

FILE 1 Grammar Bank p.126

In pairs or small groups, circle a, b, or c.

1 Where ______?
a is from your sister b your sister is from
c is your sister from

2 **A** What ______?
B He's a doctor.
a does Richard do b is Richard do c does Richard

3 My father never ______ TV.
a watch b watchs c watches

4 In the painting two women ______ at a table.
a are sitting b sit c are sit

5 **A** What's that?
B It's the thing ______ connects my camera to the computer.
a who b which c where

FILE 2 Grammar Bank p.128

In pairs or small groups, circle a, b, or c.

1 Where ______ last summer?
a you went b did you went c did you go

2 The exercise was very difficult. We ______ do it.
a didn't can b didn't could c couldn't

3 When I opened the door I saw it ______.
a was raining b rained c were raining

4 Who ______ this song? I like it.
a write b wrote c did write

5 ______ it was dark, I could read the map.
a Because b But c Although

FILE 3 Grammar Bank p.130

In pairs or small groups, circle a, b, or c.

1 ______ have a holiday this year.
a I don't going to b I'm not going to
c I'm not going

2 **A** What ______ this evening?
B Nothing special.
a do you do b are you doing c are you going

3 **A** My exam is tomorrow.
B You ______.
a won't pass b don't pass c aren't passing

4 **A** It's hot in here.
B ______ open the window?
a I'll b Will I c Shall I

5 In my dream I saw a man. He ______ the violin.
a was played b played c was playing

FILE 4 Grammar Bank p.132

In pairs or small groups, circle a, b, or c.

1 ______ any of his films?
a Have you ever saw b Did you ever seen
c Have you ever seen

2 **A** Do you want a coffee?
B No thanks, ______ one.
a I've just had b I've had just c I just have

3 **A** Is your brother here?
B No, he ______.
a hasn't already arrived b hasn't yet arrived
c hasn't arrived yet

4 She doesn't work ______ me.
a as hard as b as hard than c as hard

5 This is ______ city I've ever been to.
a the nicest b the nicer c the most nice

FILE 5 Grammar Bank p.134

In pairs or small groups, circle a, b, or c.

1 He went to the supermarket ______ some milk.
a for to get b for get c to get

2 We're thinking of ______ a new office.
a opening b to open c open

3

Tomorrow's a holiday. We ______ work.

a don't must to b mustn't c don't have to

4 You ______ remember to bring your book tomorrow.
a must to b must c have

5 He ______ the stairs and opened the door.
a ran b up c ran up

FILE 6 Grammar Bank p.136

In pairs or small groups, circle a, b, or c.

1 What will you do if you ______ the exam?
a won't pass b don't pass c will pass

2 If we had a garden, I ______ a dog.
a would buy b bought c 'll buy

3 I wouldn't camp near a river if I ______ there were crocodiles there.
a would thought b thought c think

4 **A** What are you going to do this weekend?
B I don't know. I ______.
a might to go away b might go away
c may to go away

5 You ______ coffee late at night.
a shouldn't to drink b don't should drink
c shouldn't drink

FILE 7 Grammar Bank p.138

In pairs or small groups, circle a, b, or c.

1 I've known my best friend ______.
a since ten years b for ten years c for 1995

2 How long ______ your car?
a do you have b have you c have you had

3 He's divorced now, but he ______ for 20 years.
a has been married b was married
c is married

4 He ______ have a lot of friends at school. He wasn't very popular.
a didn't used to b didn't use to
c doesn't use to

5 The radio ______ by Marconi.
a invented b is invented c was invented

FILE 8 Grammar Bank p.140

In pairs or small groups, circle a, b, or c.

1 When I'm tired I don't want to see ______.
a anybody b nobody c somebody

2

a too many b too much c too

3 I don't eat ______. I should eat more.
a fruit enough b some fruit c enough fruit

4 There's a towel on the floor. Please ______.
a pick up b pick it up c pick up it

5 **A** I hate football.
B ______
a So am I. b So do I. c Neither do I.

FILE 9 Grammar Bank p.142

In pairs or small groups, circle a, b, or c.

1 We were too late. When we arrived the match ______.
a had finished b has finished c finished

2 They couldn't open the door because they ______ the key.
a didn't brought b hadn't brought c haven't brought

3 'I love you.' She said she ______ me.
a love b loved c is loving

4 I asked her if ______ to dance.
a he wanted b she wants c she wanted

5 She asked the boy what ______.
a was his name b is his name c his name was

9 Vocabulary

Do the exercises in pairs or small groups.

a Circle the word that is different.

	car	train	(station)	bus
1	funny	friendly	lazy	generous
2	eye	mouth	nose	toe
3	feet	legs	knees	fingers
4	see	hear	ear	smell
5	foggy	windy	sunny	cloudy
6	dress	cap	skirt	blouse
7	socks	trainers	pyjamas	boots
8	get an e-mail	get a message	get home	get a present
9	duck	chicken	butterfly	swan
10	dolphin	whale	eagle	shark

b Complete the phrases.

carry do get go know make
meet spend sunbathe wear

1 __________ on the beach
2 __________ a coat
3 __________ a bag
4 __________ a noise
5 __________ yoga
6 __________ somebody for a long time
7 __________ somebody for the first time
8 __________ swimming
9 __________ angry
10 __________ time (with your friends)

c Complete with *on*, *up*, etc.

1 I was born ______ 2nd April.
2 What are you doing ______ the weekend?
3 We always go on holiday ______ July.
4 I don't agree ______ you.
5 Wait ______ me. I'm nearly ready.
6 Don't throw ______ those papers.
7 I always try ______ clothes before I buy them.
8 Hurry ______. We're late.
9 I have to look ______ my little sister today.
10 I'll pay you ______ the money tomorrow.

d Write the opposite verb or adjective.

1 friendly __________
2 talkative __________
3 crowded __________
4 rude __________
5 patient __________
6 lend money __________
7 pass an exam __________
8 push the door __________
9 find your keys __________
10 buy clothes __________

e Label the pictures.

Pronunciation

Do the exercises in pairs or small groups.

a Underline the word with a different sound.

1	ʌ	nothing	enough	mouse	mustn't
2	uː	shoes	trousers	through	few
3	aɪ	since	tidy	might	neither
4	e	many	already	friends	secret
5	əʊ	although	clothes	come	most
6	ɒ	won't	want	borrow	body
7	ɜː	worn	shirt	dirty	worst
8	aʊ	mouth	how	slowly	round
9	ɔː	awful	ball	story	work
10	ɑː	fast	pass	ask	walk
11	h	who	hour	holiday	hate
12	dʒ	age	just	enjoy	glasses
13	g	gym	argue	forget	goal
14	j	used	yet	years	eyes
15	w	which	where	twin	two

b Underline the stressed syllable.

information

1 biography
2 exercise
3 university
4 divorced
5 borrow
6 decision
7 always
8 promise
9 dangerous
10 polite
11 towards
12 afraid
13 education
14 interesting
15 along
16 important
17 anything
18 depressing
19 language
20 unfortunately

c Write the words.

1 /ʃʊd/ ____________
2 /kwaɪt/ ____________
3 /luːz/ ____________
4 /ɔːl'ðəʊ/ ____________
5 /'tiːtʃə/ ____________
6 /'nʌθɪŋ/ ____________
7 /'rɪəli/ ____________
8 /'haʊswɜːk/ ____________
9 /ɪn'dʒɔɪ/ ____________
10 /lɑːf/ ____________

1B Claire and Nina **Student A**

a Ask **B** questions and complete the chart for Nina.

Name	**Claire**	**Nina**
Age?	25	
From?	Scotland	
Lives in?	Bristol	
Job?	Journalist	
Smokes?	No	
Likes?	comedy films, cats	
Doesn't like?	men who smoke	

b Answer B's questions about Claire.

c In pairs, decide who is the best partner for Richard. Why?

1C Describe and draw **Student A**

a Look at your painting for a minute. Then describe it for **B** to draw.

b Listen to **B** describing his / her painting. Try to draw it. **Don't look at it.** Ask **B** questions to help you.

c Now compare your drawings with the original paintings!

1D Crossword **Student A**

a Ask **B** for the definitions of your missing words. Guess the words and complete your crossword.

What's 1 across?
What's 3 down?

b Give definitions of the words **B** asks for.

1	2 I											3		
	C									4 S	H	O	R	T
5	E						6 S							
	C						A			7				
	R						N							
	E		8 B				D				9			
	A		I				W							
	10 M	A	T	C	11 H		I							
			E				12 C	I	N	E	M	A		
							H							
13														14 B
								15 K						E
		16						I						D
					17 F	O	O	T	B	A	L	L	E	R
18								C						O
								H						O
		19 E	X	T	R	O	V	E	R	T				M
								N						

2B Famous photos **Student A**

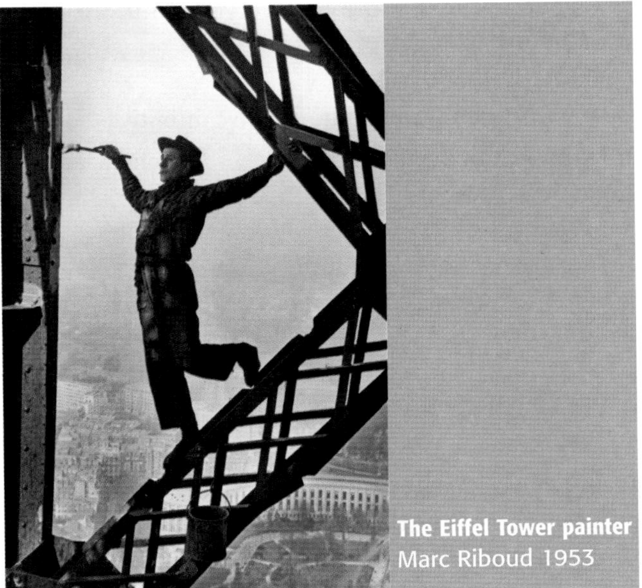

The Eiffel Tower painter
Marc Riboud 1953

IT WAS 1953. The photographer was living in Paris. He didn't have much money, and was living in a small room, and taking photos of the city every day. One day he saw that some people were painting the Eiffel Tower, and he decided to take some photographs. He went up the tower and suddenly he saw the man in the photo. The man was painting. The photographer was very nervous because he was sure that the painter was going to fall. He took his photo and a few weeks later the photo was in *Life* magazine. The photo became very famous and they made postcards and a poster with it. Later the company that paints the Eiffel Tower phoned him and invited him to lunch. They told him that the painter was an acrobat. His name was Zazou.

Leaving for Newfoundland
Willy Ronis 1949

a Look at the photos and read the text about *The Eiffel Tower painter*. Try to remember the information.

b Tell B the story of *The Eiffel Tower painter*. Try to tell it from memory.

c Now B will tell you about *Leaving for Newfoundland*.

2C Music quiz **Student A**

a Write your questions.

1 **Which singer (PLAY) football for Real Madrid?**
Which singer played football for Real Madrid ?
a Julio Iglesias b Enrique Iglesias c Placido Domingo

2 **Which group Beyoncé (SING) in?**
________________?
a Destiny's Child b The Spice Girls c Atomic Kitten

3 **Who (SING) *Philadelphia* in the film of the same name?**
________________?
a Phil Collins b George Michael c Bruce Springsteen

4 **What kind of music the Sex Pistols (INVENT)?**
________________?
a Reggae b Punk c Hip Hop

5 **When MTV (BEGIN)?**
________________?
a 1971 b 1981 c 1991

6 **Which of these groups (NOT HAVE) brothers or sisters in it?**
________________?
a Oasis b The Corrs c Red Hot Chilli Peppers

7 **Whose daughter Michael Jackson (MARRY) in 1994?**
________________?
a Elvis Presley's b Frank Sinatra's c Paul McCartney's

8 **Who (SAY) 'Eminem is the biggest danger to young Americans since polio'?**
________________?
a Clint Eastwood b Arnold Schwarzenegger c George W. Bush

9 **Which group (SING) *Losing my Religion*?**
________________?
a Blur b REM c Oasis

10 **Which instrument Sting (PLAY) on the song *Every Breath you Take*?**
________________?
a piano b guitar c double bass

b Ask B your questions. Give your partner one mark for each correct answer. Answer B's questions. Who got the most right answers?

3D Dreams **Student A**

a Last night you dreamt about these things. Prepare to tell **B** about your dream.

b **B** is a psychoanalyst. Tell him / her about your dream. He / she will tell you what it means.

> Last night I dreamt about a river...

c Swap roles. Now you are a psychoanalyst. Listen to **B**'s dream. Number the things below in the order he / she talks about them.

- ☐ **Ice cream** – You will get some money (from the lottery or from a relative).
- ☐ **Long hair** – You want to be free. Perhaps you have problems with your family or a partner.
- ☐ **A key** – You have a problem and you are looking for a solution.
- ☐ **People speaking other languages** – You think your life is boring – you would like to have a more exciting life.
- ☐ **Travelling by bus** – You are worried about a person who is controlling your life.

d Now use the information in **c** to interpret **B**'s dream.

> First you dreamt about... This means...

4D The best and the worst **Student A**

a Write names in at least **SIX** of the ovals on p.47.

In **1**, one of the best books you've ever read.
In **2**, the coldest place you've ever been to.
In **3**, the most generous person you know.
In **4**, the most beautiful modern building you've ever seen.
In **5**, the worst programme on TV at the moment.
In **6**, the most frightening film you've ever seen.
In **7**, the best restaurant you've ever been to.
In **8**, the most untidy person in your family.

b Go back to p.47.

5A Guess the infinitive **Student A**

a Look at sentences 1–6. What do you think the missing infinitives are?
Don't write anything yet!

[+] = positive infinitive [−] = negative infinitive

1 I don't like my job. I've decided ________ another one. [+]
2 Oh dear! I forgot ________ the lights. [+]
3 I promise ________ anybody your secret. [−]
4 Your sister's really friendly. It was very nice ________ her. [+]
5 I was sorry ________ you when you were here last week. [−]
6 You don't need ________ an umbrella. It's not going to rain. [+]

b Read your sentence 1 to **B**. If it's not right, guess another verb until **B** says 'That's right'. Then write in the infinitive. Continue with 2–6.

c Listen to **B**'s sentence 7. If it's the same as 7 below, say 'That's right'. If not, say 'Try again' until **B** gets it right. Continue with 8–12.

7 Remember **to phone** your father on his birthday.
8 It's often difficult **to understand** films in English.
9 It's a very formal dinner, so it's important **not to be** late.
10 I'm going to Australia **to visit** some friends.
11 The jacket was really expensive so I decided **not to buy** it.
12 My mobile number is very easy **to remember**.

6C Decisions, decisions **Student A**

a Imagine that you are a very indecisive person. **B** is going to ask you some questions. Answer **B**'s questions. Give two possibilities each time using *I may* or *I might*. Then **B** will help you to make a decision.

> I don't know. / I'm not sure. I might... or I may...

b Swap roles. Now **B** is indecisive. Ask **B** question 1 below. Help **B** to make a decision using *If I were you, I'd ...* Say why. Continue with the other questions.

1 Where are you going to go on holiday next summer?
2 What are you going to do after class?
3 What are you going to wear tomorrow?
4 What are you going to buy when you next go shopping?
5 Where are you going to have lunch on Sunday?

7D Passives quiz **Student A**

a Complete your sentences with the verb in the passive and the right answer.

1 **Until 1800 New York __________ (call) __________.**
a New Amsterdam b New Hampshire c New Liberty

2 **Chess __________ (invent) by __________.**
a the Egyptians b the Indians c the Chinese

3 **The Italian flag __________ (design) by __________.**
a Garibaldi b Mussolini c Napoleon

4 **The first Levi jeans __________ (wear) by __________.**
a miners b farmers c cowboys

5 **The first credit card __________ (use) in __________.**
a 1960 b 1970 c 1980

6 **The Indiana Jones films __________ (direct) by __________.**
a Steven Spielberg b George Lucas c Stanley Kubrick

7 **Penguins __________ (find) __________.**
a at the South Pole b at the North Pole c in Alaska

8 **In the world 15,000 babies __________ (be born) __________.**
a every second b every hour c every day

b Read your sentences to **B**. **B** will tell you if you are right.

c Now listen to B's sentences. Tell him / her if he / she is right.

B's answers
1 The CD player was invented by Philips.
2 The *Star Wars* films were directed by George Lucas.
3 The politician Winston Churchill was born in a toilet.
4 The book which is stolen most often from libraries is *The Guinness Book of Records.*
5 The electric chair was invented by a dentist.
6 Football was first played by the British.
7 In 1962 the original London Bridge was bought by a rich American.
8 The noun which is used most frequently in conversation is *time.*

9A What had happened? **Student A**

a Look at sentences 1–6 and think of the missing verb (+ = positive verb, − = negative verb). **Don't write anything yet!**

1 Diana was very angry because her husband __________ the dinner. −
2 He couldn't catch his plane because he __________ his passport at home. +
3 We went back to the hotel where we __________ on our honeymoon. +
4 The telephone wasn't working because they __________ the bill. −
5 Miriam was surprised to hear that she __________ the exam. +
6 The shop assistant agreed to change the sweater, because I __________ it. −

b Read your sentence 1 to **B**. If it's not right, try again until **B** tells you 'That's right'. Then write in the verb. Continue with 2–6.

c Listen to **B** say sentence 7. If it's the same as 7 below, say 'That's right'. If not say 'Try again' until **B** gets it right. Continue with 8–12.

7 We went back to see the house where we **had lived** when we were children.
8 The flat was very dirty because nobody **had cleaned** it for a long time.
9 The crocodile was hungry because it **hadn't eaten** anything for a long time.
10 I ran to the station, but the last train **had gone.**
11 I didn't want to lend him the book because I **hadn't read** it.
12 They got to the cinema late and the film **had started.**

8B Body age **Students A+B**

a Start with your calendar age. Add + or subtract − years according to your answers.

	a	b	c	d
1	**a** −2	**b** −1	**c** 0	**d** +1
2	**a** −2	**b** −1	**c** 0	**d** +2
3	**a** +2	**b** +1	**c** 0	**d** −1
4	**a** +1	**b** −1	**c** −2	
5	**a** −2	**b** −1	**c** +1	
6	**a** +1	**b** +1	**c** +2	**d** 0
7	**a** −3	**b** +1	**c** +5	
8	**a** −3	**b** +1	**c** +2	
9	**a** + 3	**b** 0	**c** −2	
10	**a** −2	**b** 0	**c** −1	
11	**a** −2	**b** −1	**c** 0	**d** +2
12	**a** +2	**b** +1	**c** −1	

Communication

1B Claire and Nina **Student B**

a Answer A's questions about Nina.

Name	Claire	Nina
Age?		23
From?		Hungary
Lives in?		London
Job?		Painter
Smokes?		Yes (but only one or two a day)
Likes?		good food, music
Doesn't like?		sport

b Ask A questions and complete the chart for Claire.

c In pairs, decide who is the best partner for Richard. Why?

1D Crossword **Student B**

a Ask A for the definitions of your missing words. Guess the words and complete your crossword.

What's 2 down?

What's 4 across?

b Give definitions of the words A asks for.

1 D	2 I	C	T	I	O	N	A	R	Y			3 P		
										4		O		
5 G	E	N	E	R	O	U	6 S					L		
										7 S	M	I	L	E
												T		
			8								9 K	I	C	K
												C		
	10				11 H							I		
					O		12					A		
					U							N		
					S									
13 P	A	I	N	T	E	R								14
					W			15 K	I	S	S			
		16 M			I									
		A			17 F									
18 D	A	R	K		E									
		K												
		19 E												
		T												

1C Describe and draw **Student B**

a Look at your painting for a minute.

b Listen to A describing his / her painting. Try to draw it. **Don't look at it.** Ask questions to help you.

c Now describe your painting for A to draw.

d Now compare your drawings with the original paintings!

2B Famous photos **Student B**

Leaving for Newfoundland
Willy Ronis 1949

HE TOOK THIS PHOTO in 1949 in France. He was working for a magazine. They wanted photos of fishermen. The people in the photo were a fisherman called Marcel, his wife, and their little baby boy. Marcel was leaving to go to Canada and the photographer wanted to take a photo of him and his wife in front of the boat. He said, 'Kiss your wife goodbye. I need a photo with a kiss.' But Marcel was very shy and he gave his wife a very cold kiss. So the photographer said, 'Is that how you kiss your wife?' So he kissed her again, very naturally. This time he forgot about the photographer. The photo became quite famous. Many years later Marcel saw his photo in my book and he wrote to the photographer. He said that his son (the baby in the photo) was now 30 years old and was a fisherman too.

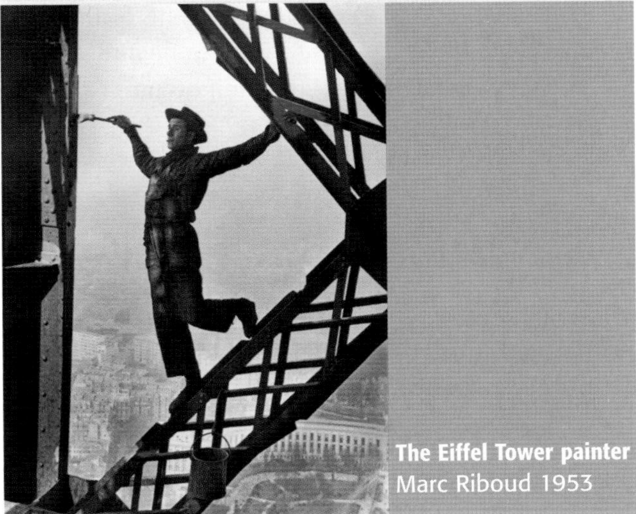

The Eiffel Tower painter
Marc Riboud 1953

a Look at the photos and read about *Leaving for Newfoundland.*

b A will tell you about *The Eiffel Tower painter.*

c Now tell A about *Leaving for Newfoundland.* Try to tell it from memory.

2C Music quiz **Student B**

a Write your questions.

1 **Which song Celine Dion (SING) in the film *Titanic*?**
Which song did Celine Dion sing in the film Titanic ____________?
a *I will always love you* **b** *My heart will go on* **c** *Love is in the air*

2 **Who (SEND) *A Message in a Bottle* in 1979?**
____________?
a The Beach Boys **b** Dire Straits **c** The Police

3 **Who (WRITE) the song *Nothing compares 2U*?**
____________?
a Prince **b** Sinead O'Connor **c** Bono

4 **Which 'boy band' Robbie Williams (SING) with?**
____________?
a Take That **b** Westlife **c** New Kids on the Block

5 **Which Beatle (DIE) in 2001?**
____________?
a Ringo Starr **b** John Lennon **c** George Harrison

6 **Who (BE) a *Material Girl*?**
____________?
a Mariah Carey **b** Madonna **c** Christina Aguilera

7 **Which heavy metal band Ozzy Osbourne (SING) with in the 1970s?**
____________?
a Black Sabbath **b** Deep Purple **c** Led Zeppelin

8 **Which Spice Girl David Beckham (MARRY) in 2000?**
____________?
a Posh Spice **b** Sporty Spice **c** Ginger Spice

9 **How the reggae singer Bob Marley (DIE)?**
____________?
a he took a drugs overdose **b** in a car accident **c** he had cancer

10 **Which song Elton John (REWRITE) for the funeral of Princess Diana in 1997?**
____________?
a *Sacrifice* **b** *Candle in the Wind* **c** *Your Song*

b Answer A's questions. Then ask A your questions. Give your partner one mark for each correct answer. Who got the most right answers?

3D Dreams **Student B**

a Last night you dreamt about these things. Prepare to tell A about your dream.

b You are a pyschoanalyst. Listen to A's dream. Number the things below in the order he / she talks about them.

- ☐ **Having a bath** – you have a secret which nobody knows about.
- ☐ **Dogs** – you are looking for friends.
- ☐ **Losing hair** – you are going to lose some money.
- ☐ **Lost luggage** – a problem you have will soon get better.
- ☐ **A river** – you are going to be very lucky.

c Now use the information in **b** to interpret A's dream.

> Well, first you dreamt about… This means…

d Swap roles. Now **A** is a psychoanalyst. Tell him / her about your dream. **A** will tell you what it means.

> Last night I dreamt that I had long hair…

4B Has he done it yet? **Students A+B**

a Work individually. Look at the list of things Max always does every morning. Has he already done them? Try to remember what was in the picture. Write sentences.

He's already made the bed. OR *He hasn't made the bed yet.*

make the bed	turn off computer
wash up his coffee cups	put his clothes in the cupboard
tidy his desk	have a shower
pick up towels	have breakfast
take the dog for a walk	

b Work in pairs. Compare your sentences with your partner. Are they the same? Then go back to p.116 and compare your sentences with the picture. Were you right?

4D The best and the worst **Student B**

a Write the names in at least **SIX** of the ovals on p.47.

In **1**, the healthiest person you know.
In **2**, the best concert you've ever been to.
In **3**, the most dangerous sport or activity you've ever done.
In **4**, the meanest person you know.
In **5**, the most boring sport you've ever watched.
In **6**, the most beautiful old building you've seen.
In **7**, the hottest place you've ever been to.
In **8**, the worst film you've seen this year.

b Go back to p.47.

5A Guess the infinitive **Student B**

a Listen to **A** say sentence 1. If it's the same as 1 below, say 'That's right'. If not, say 'Try again' until **A** gets it right. Continue with 2–6.

1 I don't like my job. I've decided **to look for** another one.
2 Oh dear! I forgot **to turn off** the lights.
3 I promise **not to tell** anybody your secret.
4 Your sister's really friendly. It was very nice **to meet** her.
5 I was sorry **not to see** you when you were here last week.
6 You don't need **to take** an umbrella. It's not going to rain.

b Look at sentences 7–12. What do you think the missing infinitives are? **Don't write anything yet!**

[+] = positive infinitive [–] = negative infinitive

7 Remember ________ your father on his birthday. [+]
8 It's often difficult ________ films in English. [+]
9 It's a very formal dinner, so it's important ________ late. [–]
10 I'm going to Australia ________ some friends. [+]
11 The jacket was really expensive, so I decided ________ it. [–]
12 My mobile number is very easy ________. [+]

c Read your sentence 7 to **A**. If it's not right, guess another verb until **A** says 'That's right'. Then write in the infinitive. Continue with 8–12.

6C Decisions, decisions **Student B**

a A is a very indecisive person. You are going to help him / her make some decisions. Ask **A** question 1 below. Help **A** to make a decision using *If I were you, I'd …* Say why. Continue with the other questions.

1 What's the next film you're going to see?
2 What are you going to cook for dinner tonight?
3 What are you going to do on Saturday night?
4 What car are you going to buy next?
5 How are you going to celebrate your next birthday?

b Swap roles. Now imagine that you are a very indecisive person. Answer A's questions. Give two possibilities each time using *I may* or *I might …* A will help you to make decisions.

I don't know. / I'm not sure. I might… or I may…

7D Passives quiz **Student B**

a Complete your sentences with the verb in the passive and the right answer.

1 The CD player ________ (invent) by ________.
a Sanyo **b** Sony **c** Philips

2 The *Star Wars* films ________ (direct) by ________.
a George Lucas **b** Steven Spielberg **c** Stanley Kubrick

3 The politician Winston Churchill ________ (be born) ________.
a on a train **b** in a toilet **c** under a bridge

4 The book which ________ (steal) most often from libraries is ________.
a The Bible **b** *The Guinness Book of Records* **c** *The Lord of the Rings*

5 The electric chair ________ (invent) by ________.
a a teacher **b** a dentist **c** a politician

6 Football ________ first ________ (play) by ________.
a the British **b** the Romans **c** the Greeks

7 In 1962 the original London Bridge ________ (buy) by ________.
a a rich American **b** a museum **c** the Royal family

8 The noun which ________ (use) most frequently in conversation is ________.
a *money* **b** *time* **c** *work*

b Now listen to A's sentences. Tell him / her if they are right.

A's answers
1 Until 1800 New York was called New Amsterdam.
2 Chess was invented by the Chinese.
3 The Italian flag was designed by Napoleon.
4 The first Levi jeans were worn by miners.
5 The first credit card was used in 1970.
6 The Indiana Jones films were directed by Steven Spielberg.
7 Penguins are found at the South Pole.
8 In the world 15,000 babies are born every hour.

c Read your sentences to A. A will tell you if you are right.

9A What had happened? **Student B**

a Listen to **A** say sentence 1. If it's the same as 1 below, say 'That's right.' If not say, 'Try again' until **B** gets it right. Continue with 2–6.

1 Diana was very angry because her husband **hadn't cooked** the dinner.
2 He couldn't catch his plane because he **had left** his passport at home.
3 We went back to the hotel where we **had stayed** on our honeymoon.
4 The telephone wasn't working because they **hadn't paid** the bill.
5 Miriam was surprised to hear that she **had failed** the exam.
6 The shop assistant agreed to change the sweater because I **hadn't worn** it.

b Look at sentences 7–12 and think of the missing verb (+ = positive verb, − = negative verb). **Don't write anything yet!**

7 We went back to see the house where we ________ when we were children. +
8 The flat was very dirty because nobody ________ it for a long time. +
9 The crocodile was hungry because it ________ anything for a long time. −
10 I ran to the station, but the last train ________. +
11 I didn't want to lend him the book because I ________ it. −
12 They got to the cinema late and the film ________. +

c Read your sentence 7 to A. If it's not right, try again until A tells you 'That's right'. Then write in the verb. Continue with 8–12.

3A Where are you going on holiday? **Students A+B**

FIJI

Spend two or four weeks in the South Pacific with tropical beaches, sun, water sports, etc. An unforgettable experience.

Departure 1st June

Return 15th or 30th June

Fly British Airways (via London) or Air France (via Paris)

Hotels Blue Lagoon (small beach hotel)
Tropics (modern luxury hotel)

KENYA

Go on a two- or four-week safari for the experience of a lifetime. In a 4x4 you will see lions, zebras, and elephants in their natural habitat.

Departure 1st June

Return 15th or 30th June

Fly British Airways (via London)
or KLM (via Amsterdam)

Accommodation in luxury campsites or in hotels

a Read the adverts and choose a holiday. Decide:

Where are you going? ________________

How are you getting there? ________________

When are you leaving? ________________

Where are you staying? ________________

When are you coming back? ________________

b Now find a partner who has planned exactly the same holiday as you:

A *Where are you going?*

B *To Fiji.*

A *Me too. How are you getting there?*

B *I'm flying with Air France.*

A *I'm flying with British Airways, so we can't go together.*

4B Has he done it yet? **Students A+B**

Look at the picture for one minute and try to remember what's in it. ➲ **p.114**

3C *I'll / Shall I?* game

Play the game.

5D Cross country **Students A+B**

a You are the organizer of a cross-country race. You have to plan the race for the runners. Draw a route on the map marked **MY RACE**, beginning at **START** and finishing at the **FINISH** line. Your route must include all the things in the picture but you can choose the order.

b Take turns. A describe your route to your partner. B must draw it on your map marked **MY PARTNER'S RACE**.

> You have to go down the hill, round the lake...

c Swap roles.

d Compare the two routes. Which is the most difficult?

1.2

1 **A** When's the exam?
B Next week.
A Yeah, I know, but what day? Is it Wednesday or Thursday?
B No, it's Tuesday.

2 **A** The weekend goes so quickly.
B I know. I can't believe that it's Monday tomorrow.

3 **A** Excuse me! Do you have the right time?
B Yes, it's twenty-five to nine.
A Thanks.

4 **A** We're going to be late for class.
B Relax. It doesn't start until quarter past ten. It's only five past.

5 **A** When was she born?
B Let's see. She was born on the 23rd August 1947.
A Where?
B In Germany.

6 **A** Do you have any tickets left for the 5th of June?
B Let's see…Yes, we do. How many would you like?
A Two please.
B OK, that's 27 euros please.

7 **A** Hello?
B Hi it's me. I'm in your street but I can't remember the number of your house. Is it 117?
A No, it's 170.

8 **A** How much are those flowers?
B 50 euros.
A 50? That's not cheap.

1.3

Richard

I was very optimistic when I went to meet Claire. My first impression was that she was very friendly and very extrovert. Physically she was my type – she was quite slim and not very tall with long dark hair – *very* pretty. And she was very funny too. She had a great sense of humour. We laughed a lot. But the only problem was that Claire was very talkative. She talked all the time and I just listened. She wasn't very interested in me. At the end of the evening I knew everything about her and she knew nothing about me. Claire was the kind of woman I could have as a friend but not as a girlfriend.

1.4

When I first saw Nina I couldn't believe it. I thought 'Wow! Thanks mum'. She's very attractive – she's got short dark hair – and she's quite tall. She's Hungarian, from Budapest but her English was fantastic.

At first she was a bit shy but when we started chatting we found we had a lot of things in common – we both like music, food, and travelling. We got on really well – we didn't stop talking for the whole evening. When it was time to go I knew I really wanted to see Nina again and I asked her for her phone number. But – she just smiled at me and said in her beautiful Hungarian accent. 'Richard, you're really sweet but I'm sorry, you're not my type.'

1.8

OK, now the painting we are looking at now is by the French painter Toulouse-Lautrec.

The painting is called *At the Moulin Rouge*. As you probably know The Moulin Rouge is a nightclub in Paris. Maybe some of you remember the film *Moulin Rouge?* In the 19th century, the nightclub was very famous for its beautiful dancers and singers.

Toulouse-Lautrec did a lot of paintings and posters of the Moulin Rouge. He especially loved painting the dancers. And in these paintings he sometimes included his friends too.

In the middle of the picture there are five people who are sitting at a table having a drink. The woman who's wearing a hat is a dancer – her name is la Macarona – and the man sitting next to her on the left is a friend of Toulouse-Lautrec. He was a photographer. On the right, here, there's a woman with fair hair, blue eyes, and very red lips. Her face looks very white. That's another famous dancer called Jane Avril. At the back of the picture, on the right, there are two women who are standing together. One of them is touching her hair. That's La Goulue and she was one of the most famous singers at the Moulin Rouge at that time.

Now this is very interesting. If you look carefully to the left of the two women, there are two men walking out of the nightclub. One of them is very tall and the other one is very short. The very tall man is Toulouse-Lautrec's cousin Gabriel, and the other man is Toulouse-Lautrec himself. Toulouse-Lautrec was only 1 metre 50 centimetres tall. He had very short legs and couldn't walk very well. Some people think that this is why he loved painting the dancers of the Moulin Rouge… because they all had beautiful, long legs.

1.10

Presenter Good evening, ladies and gentlemen and welcome to *What's the word?* And our first contestant tonight is Adam. Hello Adam. Are you nervous?
Adam Just a bit.
Presenter Well try and relax Adam and play *What's the word?* with us. In case you're watching the show for the first time here's how we play the game. I have six cards with things, people, or places written on them. I'm going to give Adam definitions and he's going to try and guess the words on my six cards. But of course, I can't use any of the words on the cards in my definitions. So, for example, if I have a card with *taxi driver*, I can't use *taxi* or *driver* in my definition. Are you ready Adam?
Adam Yes.
Presenter OK, you have two minutes to guess what's on the six cards starting now!

1.11

Presenter OK, Adam. Card number 1. It's a person. It's somebody who works in a restaurant.
Adam A cook.
Presenter No, no, no it's the person who takes the food from the kitchen to the tables.
Adam Oh a ______.
Presenter That's right. Card number 2. It's a place. It's a place where you go when you want to buy something.
Adam A shop.
Presenter Yes, but it's a very big shop where you can buy anything.
Adam Is it a ______?
Presenter Yes, well done. OK card number 3. It's a thing… mmm. It's a thing which you use to talk to people.
Adam Your mouth?
Presenter No, no. It's a kind of machine. It's very small. Nearly everybody has one nowadays.
Adam ______?
Presenter That's it! Card number 4. It's an adjective. It's the opposite of fat.
Adam Thin?
Presenter It's like thin, but it means thin and attractive.
Adam ______?
Presenter Yes! Number 5. It's an adjective again. Er…It's how you feel when you have a lot of work.
Adam Worried?
Presenter No, but it's similar to worried. It's how you feel when you have a lot of things to do but you don't have time to do them.
Adam Busy?
Presenter No!
Adam ______?
Presenter Yes, brilliant. And card number six, the last one. OK. It's a verb. For example, you do this with the TV.
Adam Watch?
Presenter No…
Presenter It's what you do when you finish watching the TV.
Adam Er…go to bed?
Presenter No, you do it to the TV before you go to bed.
Adam Is it ______?
Presenter Yes!

1.14

Mark

Hi. My name's Mark Ryder. I'm American and I live in San Francisco. I work for a music company called MTC. I'm divorced and I have a daughter.

Last month I went to England on a work trip, and I met Allie. She's British, and she works for MTC in the UK. We had a great five days. We went out for coffee. We went shopping. It was my birthday, and she bought me a present. We went out for dinner. I really liked her, and I think she liked me too.

I invited her to a conference in San Francisco, and she said yes. And now I'm at the airport. I'm waiting for her to arrive.

1.17

Mark Allie, hi!
Allie Hi Mark.
Mark You look great!
Allie You too. How are you?
Mark I'm fine. How was the flight?
Allie Long! Eleven hours.
Mark You must be really tired.
Allie Yes. I couldn't sleep at all. The people next to me had a baby with them. What's the time here? I need to change my watch.
Mark It's seven in the evening.
Allie It's three in the morning for me.
Mark OK, I'm going to take you right to the hotel and you can rest.
Allie Fine. Sorry!
Mark You are going to love San Francisco! I'm so pleased you came!
Allie Me too. It's great to see you again.
Mark Come on. My car's in the parking lot. Let's go.

2.3

Presenter Hello and welcome to today's Holiday Programme. Today we've asked you to call in with your holiday horror stories – holidays where things went wrong. Our first caller today is Sean from Belfast. Hi Sean.
Sean Hello.
Presenter So where was this holiday?
Sean Well, this didn't happen to me, it happened to my aunt and uncle, last summer.
Presenter Where did they go?
Sean To Ibiza.
Presenter A fantastic place for a holiday.
Sean Yes, fantastic place if you're seventeen – but they're nearly seventy!
Presenter Oh…
Sean And they wanted a quiet holiday, a relaxing holiday – you know. They like walking in the countryside, sitting on quiet beaches – things like that. They don't go abroad very often, but they wanted to do something different.
Presenter So why did they choose Ibiza? It's the party island.
Sean Yes, it is now but they didn't know that. You see, they first went to Ibiza in the late sixties, when it was a beautiful, peaceful island with traditional cafés and restaurants, deserted beaches. And this was exactly what they wanted. So they looked on the Internet – my uncle loves his computer – and they booked a hotel for a week in the same part of the island where they'd been before. And they found some cheap flights. It all seemed so perfect.
Presenter So what happened?
Sean You can imagine. It was a complete disaster. Their hotel was in San Antonio, a resort that's full of bars and discos. There was music until 5.00 in the morning, noise of car doors opening, motorbikes, and people shouting. They couldn't sleep at all. They were too tired to do anything during the day. They tried to get some sleep, but they couldn't because it was too hot. When they came home they were in a state of shock.
Presenter Oh dear – What are their plans for this year?
Sean I don't know. I think they'll probably stay at home this year…and next year… and probably the year after that…
Presenter Thank you Sean. And now…

2.4

Marinette We didn't know that our picture was so famous until thirty years later. One day I was working in the café when the man from the bookshop next door came in. He was holding a new book which had a photo on the cover. Suddenly I said, 'I don't believe it! That's Henri and I when we were very young!'
I remember that afternoon at the Bastille very well. When the man took that photo we were arguing! Henri was standing very near me. I was saying, 'Henri, don't stand so near me, there is somebody behind us.'
Henri We didn't know that the photographer was taking a photo of us. We were arguing. I can't remember exactly what we were arguing about. I think I was trying to kiss Marinette and she didn't want to. Or I think maybe we were arguing about our wedding – we got married a few months after the man took the photo.
Marinette People who know this photo always think of us as the eternal lovers, like Romeo and Juliet. But life isn't like that. It's very difficult to stay in love when you see your husband every day at home *and* you see him every day at work too. And I'm very hard-working but Henri is still a dreamer. Ah, those were the days…

2.15

Two hours later a police car arrived at Hannah's house. A policewoman knocked at the door. 'Good evening, Madam,' she said. 'Are you Hannah Davis? I'd like to speak to you. Can I come in?'
The policewoman came in and sat down on the sofa.
'Are you a friend of Jamie Dixon?' she said.
'Yes,' said Hannah.
'I understand you were going to meet him this evening.'
'Yes, at 5.30, at a coffee bar. But he didn't come so I didn't see him.'
'Well I'm afraid I have some bad news for you,' said the policewoman.
'What? What's happened?'
'Jamie had an accident this evening.'
'Oh no. What kind of accident?'
'He was crossing the road and a car hit him.'
'Is he … Is he …OK?'
'Well, he's going to be in hospital for a long time.'
'Oh no.'
'But don't worry, He's going to be OK.'
'When did this happen?'
'This evening at twenty-five past five. He was crossing the road in the High Street.'
'And the driver of the car?'
'She didn't stop.'
'She?'
'Yes, it was a woman in a white car. Every police officer in the town is looking for her.'
'Can I go to the hospital to see Jamie?'
'Yes, I can take you there now.'
'I'll get my coat. OK I'm ready.'
'Is that your car, madam? The white one over there?'
'Yes it is.'
'Can I have a look at it? Did you know your front light is broken?'
'No, I didn't.'
'What exactly were *you* doing at 5.25 this evening, madam?

2.16

Receptionist Good evening, ma'am. How can I help you?
Allie Good evening. I have a reservation. My name's Alison Gray. I'm here for the MTC conference.
Receptionist Just a moment. Ah, here it is. Ms Gray. For six nights?
Allie That's right.
Receptionist OK, Ms Gray. Here's your key. You're in room 419 on the fourth floor.
Allie Thank you. What time's breakfast?
Receptionist From seven to nine, in the Pavilion Restaurant on the sixth floor.
Allie Thanks. Where's the lift?
Receptionist The *elevators* are over there.
Allie Thanks.
Receptionist Do you need any help with your bags?
Allie Yes, please.

2.19

Mark Here you go, Allie. A cappuccino – see, I remembered!
Allie Well done! Thanks.
Mark Did you sleep well?
Allie Yes, very well. How are things?
Mark They're fine.
Allie What are the plans for the week?
Mark Well, today we don't have any free time. But tomorrow I'm going to take you to this great little restaurant I know.
Allie That sounds good.
Mark And then on Wednesday night there's a cocktail party here at the hotel, and then a conference dinner on Thursday. Is there anything special you want to do?
Allie Well, I'd like to see the bay and the Golden Gate Bridge. And I'd like to go shopping if there's time.
Brad Hi Mark, how are you doing?
Mark Hi Brad. I'm fine, just fine.
Brad Aren't you going to introduce me?

Mark Oh sure. Allie, this is Brad Martin. Brad works in the Los Angeles office. Brad, this is Allie Gray from the London office.
Allie Hello.
Brad Hi Allie, great to meet you. Mark told me you were very nice but he didn't tell me you were so beautiful. So, is this your first time in San Francisco?
Allie Yes. Yes, it is.
Brad Has Mark shown you the sights?
Allie Well, not yet.
Brad Then maybe I can show you round. I love this city.
Mark Allie, it's time to go. Excuse us, Brad.
Brad Well, great to meet you, Allie. See you round.
Allie Yes. Nice to meet you too. Goodbye.
Brad Bye.

3.1

Interviewer So Rima, did you find a job as an au pair?
Rima Well, I found a job, but not looking after children. I'm working in a restaurant – an Italian restaurant. I'm a waitress. I work very long hours!
Interviewer Was it difficult to find a job?
Rima No. There are lots of jobs in restaurants, hotels, cleaning, things like that.
Interviewer Are you still living in your friend's flat?
Rima Yes, because it's very expensive here and I can't afford to rent my own flat. London is incredibly expensive!
Interviewer Your English is much better!
Rima Well, a bit better, but I don't go to classes, because I don't have time. As I said, I work very long hours in the restaurant. But I watch a lot of English TV, and I speak English at work.
Interviewer When are you going back to Lithuania?
Rima I don't know. My plans have changed a bit.
Interviewer Why?
Rima Well, I met someone in the restaurant. He's the chef. We're getting married next month.
Interviewer Congratulations! Is he from Lithuania too?
Rima No, he's Italian. From Naples. He's a fantastic cook.
Interviewer So, are you going to stay in London?
Rima Yes. I'm very happy here now. We both really like London – our dream is to open a restaurant together one day.
Interviewer Are your family coming to the wedding?
Rima No! They don't even know I'm getting married! You see, they want me to go back to Lithuania.
Interviewer Well, good luck with everything, Rima.

3.7

Presenter Today's topic is 'positive thinking'. We all know that people who are positive enjoy life more than people who are negative and pessimistic. But scientific studies show that positive people are also healthier, get better more quickly when they're ill, and live longer. A recent study shows that people who are optimistic and think positively live, on average, nine years longer than pessimistic people who think negatively. So, let's hear what you the listeners think. Do you have any tips to help us be more positive in our lives?

3.8

Presenter And our first caller this evening is Andy. Hi Andy. What's your tip for being positive?
Andy Hello. Well, I think it's very important to live in the present and not in the past. Don't think about mistakes you made in the past. You can't change the past. The important thing is to think about how you will do things better in the future.
Presenter Thank you Andy. And now we have another caller. What's your name, please?
Julie Hi, my name's Julie. My tip is think positive thoughts, not negative ones. We all have negative thoughts sometimes but when we start having them we need to stop and try to change them into positive ones. Like, if you have an exam tomorrow and you start thinking 'I'm sure I'll fail', then you'll fail the exam. So you need to change that negative thought to a positive thought. Just think to yourself 'I'll pass.' I do this and it usually works.
Presenter Thank you Julie. And our next caller is Giovanna. Hi Giovanna.
Giovanna Hi. My tip is don't spend a lot of time reading the papers or watching the news on TV. It's always bad news and it just makes you feel depressed. Read a book or listen to your favourite music instead.
Presenter Thanks Giovanna. And our next caller is Miriam. Miriam?
Miriam Hi.
Presenter Hi Miriam. What's your tip?
Miriam My tip is every week make a list of all the good things that happen to you. Then keep the list with you, in your bag or in a pocket, and if you're feeling a bit sad or depressed just take it out and read it. It'll make you feel better.
Presenter Thanks Miriam. And our last call is from Michael. Hi Michael. We're listening.
Michael Hi. My tip is to try to use positive language when you speak to other people. You know, if your friend has a problem don't say 'I'm sorry' or 'Oh poor you', say something positive like 'Don't worry! Everything will be OK.' That way you'll make the other person think more positively about their problem.
Presenter Thank you, Michael. Well that's all we've got time for. A big thank you to all our callers. Until next week then, goodbye.

3.13

Patient So what does it mean, doctor?
Dr Muller Well, first the party. A party is a group of people. This means that you're going to meet a lot of people. I think you're going to be very busy.
Patient At work?
Dr Muller Yes, at work…you work in an office, I think?
Patient Yes, that's right.
Dr Muller I think the party means you are going to have a lot of meetings.
Patient What about the champagne?
Dr Muller Let me look at my notes again. Ah yes, you were drinking champagne. Champagne means a celebration. It's a symbol of success. So we have a meeting or meetings and then a celebration. Maybe in the future you'll have a meeting with your boss, about a possible promotion?
Patient Well, it's possible. I hope so …What about the garden and the flowers? Do they mean anything?
Dr Muller Yes. Flowers are a positive symbol. So, the flowers mean that you are feeling positive about the future. So perhaps you already knew about this possible promotion?
Patient No, I didn't. But it's true, I am very happy at work and I feel very positive about my future. That's not where my problems are. My problems are with my love life. Does my dream tell you anything about that?
Dr Muller Mm, yes it does. You're single, aren't you?
Patient Yes, well, divorced.
Dr Muller Because the violin music tells me you want some romance in your life – you're looking for a partner perhaps?
Patient Yes, yes, I am. In fact I met a very nice woman last month – I really like her, … I think I'm in love with her. I'm meeting her tonight…
Dr Muller In your dream you saw an owl…in a tree?
Patient Yes, an owl…a big owl.
Dr Muller The owl represents an older person. I think you'll need to ask this older person for help. Maybe this 'older person' is me? Maybe you need my help?
Patient Well, yes, what I really want to know is… Does this person…this woman…love me?
Dr Muller You remember the end of your dream? You were feeling cold?
Patient Yes, my feet were very cold.
Dr Muller Well… I think perhaps you already know the answer to your question.
Patient You mean she doesn't love me.
Dr Muller No, I don't think so. I think you will need to find another woman. I'm sorry.

3.15

Waiter Are you ready to order?
Mark Yes, to start a tomato and mozzarella salad – is that right, Allie?
Allie Yes.
Mark And the mushroom soup for me.
Waiter And for your main course?
Allie I'll have the fried chicken.
Waiter With French fries or a baked potato?
Allie A baked potato, please.
Waiter And for you, sir?
Mark And I'd like the steak, with French fries.
Waiter How would you like your steak? Rare, medium, well done?
Mark Rare, please.
Waiter And to drink?
Mark Could you bring us the wine list, please?

3.18

Waiter Your check, sir.
Mark Thanks.
Waiter Thank you.
Allie Thank you, Mark. That was a lovely dinner.
Mark I'm glad you enjoyed it.
Allie How's your daughter?
Mark Jennifer? She's fine. She's with her mother in Los Angeles.
Allie Mark?
Mark Yeah.
Allie Can I ask you something? Something personal?
Mark Sure. What?
Allie How long were you married?
Mark Three years.
Allie Why did you break up?
Mark There were a lot of reasons. We were very young when we had Jennifer. We were both working very hard. We didn't spend much time together…the usual story. What about you, Allie?
Allie Well, there was someone. I met him when I was at university. We were together for two years. We broke up.
Mark Why?
Allie I don't know. Usual story!
Mark Thank you. Listen, it's early – it's only nine o'clock. Shall we go for a walk?
Allie Good idea. Where shall we go?
Mark There's a place called Fisherman's Wharf, it's right on the bay. There are a lot of cafés and bars. We could have another cup of coffee.
Allie Fine. Let's go.

4.2

1
Interviewer Excuse me sir, I'm doing a … sir? Excuse me madam, do you have a few minutes to answer…
Woman Sorry, I really don't have time.
Interviewer Excuse me. Could I ask you a few questions about *Zara*?
Woman 1 Yes, OK.
Interviewer Have you ever been to a *Zara* store?
Woman 1 Yes, many times.
Interviewer And when did you last go there?
Woman 1 About three weeks ago.
Interviewer Where was that?
Woman 1 Here in London. In Oxford Street.
Interviewer OK, thank you. What did you buy?
Woman 1 Er, a white jacket.
Interviewer And are you happy with it?
Woman 1 Quite happy. I like the jacket but the colour was a mistake. It's already dirty.
Interviewer Thank you very much for your time.
2
Interviewer Hello. Do you mind if I ask you a few questions about *Zara*?
Woman 2 How long will it take?
Interviewer Only a few minutes.
Woman 2 Yes, all right then.
Interviewer Have you ever been to a *Zara* store?
Woman 2 Yes.
Interviewer When did you last go there?
Woman 2 Last Saturday.
Interviewer Where?
Woman 2 In Paris.
Interviewer What did you buy?
Woman 2 Just a scarf. I tried some trousers on but I didn't buy them.
Interviewer Are you happy with the scarf?
Woman 2 Yes. I like it a lot.
3
Interviewer Have you ever been to a *Zara* store?
Man Yes, once.
Interviewer When did you go there?
Man In August.
Interviewer Where?
Man At Barcelona airport.
Interviewer What did you buy?
Man I *nearly* bought lots of things, but in the end I didn't buy anything. But my girlfriend bought some shoes.

4.9

1 Definitely more. My daughter got married last year and she and her husband live quite far away. She rings me almost every day to tell me how everything is going, and we usually chat for hours. My phone bill is now double what it was when she was living at home.
2 I spend a lot less time than before. My youngest child has just started school, and I've gone back to work, so I never make lunch now during the week – I just have a sandwich. And in the evenings we often get take-away pizzas or Chinese food, or we heat something up in the microwave. I only really spend time in the kitchen at weekends.
3 Well I'd say less – though I'm not sure if my parents would agree. I get so much homework now that I never go to bed before 11 or 12, but I still get up at seven in the morning. It's true I get up later at weekends, but that's only two days out of seven.
4 More, much more. Before it only used to take me fifteen minutes to get to work, and now it takes me twenty-five, or even half an hour. It's mainly because there are just more cars on the road. Sometimes I think I should use public transport, but it's quite complicated from where I live.

4.10

Tim
First I did the photo test. I was near Charing Cross station. I stopped a man who was walking quite slowly down the road and I said, 'Excuse me, could you take my photo?' The man said, 'No, no, no time for that,' and just continued walking. Then I asked a businessman in a grey suit who was walking towards the station. He took one photo, but when I asked him to take another one he walked away quickly.

Next, it was the shopping test. I went to a tourist shop in Oxford Street and I bought a key ring and a red bus. The red bus was very expensive. The total price was forty pounds. I gave the man a hundred pounds – two fifty pound notes. He gave me sixty pounds back.

Finally it was time for the accident test. For this test I went down into the Tube (the London Underground). As I went down the stairs I fell over and sat on the floor. A man immediately stopped and looked down at me. I thought he was going to help me but he didn't – he just said, 'Why don't you look where you are going?'

4.12

Receptionist Good morning, ma'am. How can I help you?
Allie I want to go shopping. Where's the best place to go?
Receptionist Well, all the big department stores are around Union Square.
Allie Can you tell me how to get there?
Receptionist Yes, of course. Go out of the hotel and turn left. Go straight ahead, down Sutter Street. Turn left at Stockton – it's the third street on the left. Union Square will be right in front of you. You can't miss it.
Allie Thanks.

4.15

Allie Oh, where is it? Excuse me. Can you tell me the way to Union Square?
Brad Hey – don't I know you?
Allie I don't think so.
Brad Allie, I'm Brad! Brad Martin from the Los Angeles office. I'm Mark's friend, remember? We met yesterday at the hotel.
Allie Oh yes, that's right. Brad. I'm so sorry.
Brad No problem. What are you doing here?
Allie I want to go shopping. I'm looking for Union Square. But I'm lost.
Brad Where's Mark?
Allie He's at the hotel – he had a meeting, I think.
Brad Listen, Allie. I'm going to take you for a cup of coffee at Del Monico's – they have

the best coffee in San Francisco, and amazing cookies. And then I'll walk with you to Union Square.
Allie That's really kind of you. Are you sure?
Brad Absolutely. It's my pleasure.
Allie OK. Great. I'm awful with new cities. I always get lost.
Brad Oh, I love your British accent…

5.1

1
Harry Hello, you're one of Peter's friends aren't you?
Adrian That's right. I'm Adrian.
Harry Hi, I'm Harry. Are you enjoying the party?
Adrian Yes.
Harry So, what do you do for a living, Adrian?
Adrian I'm a doctor.
Harry A doctor? Oh that's good. Listen, I have a problem with my back. Could you have a look at it? I've got a pain just here…
Adrian Sorry, can you excuse me? I've just seen Peter over there and I want to wish him a Happy Birthday.
2
Man James, this is Sandra.
James Hi.
Sandra Nice to meet you.
Man Sandra's a teacher in secondary school.
James A teacher? Really? What a wonderful job! You're so lucky.
Sandra Why lucky?
James Well, you have really long summer holidays!
Sandra Yes, that's what people always say. Perhaps you would like to teach my class one day. When you teach teenagers all year you *need* a long summer holiday.
3
Catherine Hello. We haven't met before, have we?
Luke No, I don't think so.
Catherine I'm Catherine, I'm Peter's sister.
Luke Oh, hi, I'm Luke. I went to school with Peter.
Catherine Ah, Luke! You're the travel agent, aren't you?
Luke Yes, I am.
Catherine Peter's told me all about you. Listen, can you recommend a cheap holiday? I'd like to go somewhere hot. And I want to go in August. But when I say cheap, I mean cheap. Oh and I can't fly…because I'm terrified of flying…
4
Woman Deborah, can I introduce you to an old friend of mine, Lucy?
Deborah Hi Lucy.
Lucy Nice to meet you.
Woman Lucy's my hairdresser.
Deborah Ah. You're just the person I want to talk to, Lucy. What do you think of my colour?
Lucy Well…
Deborah No, come on, tell me the truth. Is it too blonde?
Lucy Er… no. I think it's fine.
Deborah Are you sure?
Woman Lucy, what would you like to drink?
Lucy Oh, a Diet Coke please.
Deborah Do you think my hair would look better shorter?
Woman Deborah, Lucy's not at work now.
Deborah Oh sorry.
5
Andrea Hi. I'm Andrea. Nice to meet you.
Simon Hello. My name's Simon.
Andrea What do you do Simon? No, don't tell me! Let me guess your job! Let me see. You look like a … professional footballer.
Simon No… I'm a psychiatrist.
Andrea A psychiatrist! Ooh how fascinating! Simon…? Are you analysing me?
Simon Er, no, I'm not. Excuse me, er, Andrea. I need to go to the bathroom.

5.5

Interviewer Good evening and welcome. In today's programme we're going to talk about singing. In the studio we have Martin, the director of a singing school in London and Gemma a student at Martin's school. Good morning to both of you.
Martin & Gemma Good morning.
Interviewer First Martin, can you tell us, why is it a good idea for people to learn to sing?
Martin First, because singing makes you feel good. And secondly because singing is very good for your health.
Interviewer Really? In what way?
Martin Well, when you learn to sing you need to learn to breathe correctly. That's very important. And you also learn to stand and sit correctly. As a result, people who sing are often fitter and healthier than people who don't.
Interviewer Are your courses only for professional singers?
Martin No, not at all. They're for everybody. You don't need to have any experience of singing. And you don't need to be able to read music.
Interviewer So how do your students learn to sing?
Martin They learn by listening and repeating. Singing well is really 95% listening.
Interviewer OK, Gemma. Tell us about the course. How long did it last?
Gemma Only one day. From ten in the morning to six in the evening.
Interviewer Could you already sing well before you started?
Gemma No, not well. But I have always liked singing. But I can't read music and I never thought I sang very well.
Interviewer So what happened on the course?
Gemma Well, first we did a lot of listening and breathing exercises and we learnt some other interesting techniques.
Interviewer What sort of things?
Gemma Well, for example we learnt that it is easier to sing high notes if you sing with a surprised look on your face!
Interviewer Oh really? Could you show us?
Gemma Well, I'll try.
Interviewer For those of you at home, I can promise you that Gemma looked *very* surprised. Were you happy with your progress?
Gemma Absolutely. At the end of the day we were singing in almost perfect harmony. It was amazing. In just one day we really were much better.
Interviewer Could you two give us a little demonstration?
Martin & Gemma Oh, OK.

5.7

I arrived at Kraków airport with Kasia, my guide. Test number one. I had to get a taxi to the hotel. I said to the taxi driver, in Polish, 'To the Holiday Inn hotel, please,' – *Proszę do hotelu Holiday Inn*. No problem. The driver understood me. But then he started talking to me in perfect English. I felt a bit stupid.

We got to the hotel, checked in, and then we went to the hotel bar for test number two.

A waitress came up to us and I said '*Proszę piwo*,' that is, a beer please. Then the waitress said something in Polish and I understood her! She said 'a big or small beer?' 'Big,' I said. I was so happy that I could understand her. I really enjoyed that beer.

Next we went out into the street for test three: asking for directions. I decided to ask for directions to a chemist, because I knew the word for chemist, *apteka*. I stopped a woman who looked friendly and I said, in Polish, 'Excuse me please, is there a chemist's near here? No problem. But then she started talking really fast and pointing. I tried to listen for left or right or anything I could understand but no, I couldn't understand anything. I was sure that Kasia was going to give me zero for this test!

I was feeling less confident now. We went back to the hotel for test four: making a phone call. Kasia gave me a phone number and told me to ask to speak to her friend. His name was Adam. I dialled the number. A woman answered the phone. 'Is Adam there?', I said hopefully. '*Adama nie ma*,' she said. I understood that! Adam's not in. I wanted to say 'When will he be back?' but I could only say 'When home? *Kiedy domu*?' And I didn't understand her answer. So I said thank you and goodbye very politely. Kasia smiled, so I thought, well, not bad.

Finally, test five: asking the time. I *knew* this test was going to be very hard. Numbers in Polish are incredibly difficult and I've always found telling the time is impossible. But I had a brilliant idea. I stopped a man in the street and said, 'Excuse me, what's the time?' I couldn't understand the answer but I just said, 'Sorry, can I see your watch please?' He showed it to me. Twenty past seven. Perfect!

How well did I do in the tests? Well, Kasia gave me five out of ten for language and eight for imagination. So can you learn a language in a month? Not Polish, definitely!

5.12

SA Can I help you?
Allie Yes, I really like this sweater. Do you have it in a medium?
SA Let's see… we have it in red in a medium.
Allie No, I want it in black.
SA Just a minute, I'll go and check. Here you are. A black medium. Do you want to try it on?
Allie No, thanks. I'm sure it'll be fine. How much is it?
SA 43.38.
Allie It says 39.99.
SA Yes, but that doesn't include sales tax – that's 8.5% extra.
Allie Oh, OK. Do you take MasterCard?
SA Yes, of course.

5.15

Mark Allie! You look great, as usual. How was your morning?
Allie Really good. First I went shopping, and then I went to the Museum of Modern Art.
Mark What did you think of it?
Allie It was wonderful. But I didn't have enough time to see it all. Never mind.
Mark Maybe next time.
Allie What a lovely evening!
Brad Hi, Allie. How was the shopping?
Allie Great, thanks.
Brad Hi Mark. And did you like the museum? I hope you didn't get lost again!
Mark Hey, I didn't know you two were friends already.
Allie We met this morning. I got lost. I was trying to find Union Square – and suddenly Brad appeared.
Brad So I took her to my favourite coffee shop.
Mark Allie, what would you like to drink?
Allie I'd like a cocktail please. A margarita.
Brad What a good idea. I'll have one too. Mark, could you get us a couple of margaritas?
Mark Oh, so now I'm the waiter, am I?
Brad So tell me about the museum, Allie. What was your favourite painting?

6.4

Interviewer OK, Michael, can you tell us what to do in these three situations? First what about the crocodile attack?
Michael Well, once a crocodile has seen you it will attack you, so doing nothing is not really an option. And a crocodile attacks so quickly that people never have time to swim to safety. The crocodile will try to get you in its mouth and take you under the water. Your only hope is to try to hit it in the eye or on the nose. If you did this and you were very lucky the crocodile would open its mouth and give you time to escape. But I have to say that it's very difficult, although not impossible, to survive a crocodile attack.
Interviewer What about the bear attack?
Michael When a bear attacks someone, their natural reaction is always to try to run away or to climb up a tree. But these are both bad ideas. Bears can run much faster than we can and they're also much better and faster at climbing trees.
The best thing to do in this situation would be to pretend to be dead. A bear usually stops attacking when it thinks that its enemy is dead and so, if you were lucky it would lose interest in you and go away.
Interviewer And finally, the bull attack?
Michael Well, if you were in the middle of a field, forget about running. Bulls can run incredibly fast. And don't shout or wave your arms because bulls react to movement and this will just make the bull come in your direction. The best thing to do is to try not to move, and just stay where you are, and then at the last moment to throw something, a hat or your shirt, away from you. If you were lucky, the bull would change direction to follow the hat or shirt and you'd be able to escape. By the way, it doesn't matter what colour the shirt is. It isn't true that bulls like red. They don't see colour, they only see movement.

6.11

Presenter Welcome to this morning's edition of *What's the problem?*. Today we're talking about friends, so if you have a problem with one of your friends, call us now. And if you're listening to the programme and you think you can help with any of the problems then just send an e-mail to our website. Our e-mail address is what.problem@radiotalk.com. Our first caller today is Barbara. Hello Barbara.
Barbara Hello.
Presenter What's the problem?
Barbara Well, I have a problem with a friend called Jonathan (that's not his real name). Well, Jonathan often goes out with me and my friends. The problem is that he's really mean.
Presenter Mean?
Barbara Yes, he never pays for anything. When we have a drink he always says he doesn't have any money or that he's forgotten his money. So in the end one of us always pays for him. At first we thought, 'Poor Jonathan, he doesn't have much money'. But it's not true. His parents work, and he works on Saturdays in a shop – so he must have some money. Do you think we should say something to him?
Presenter Thanks Barbara. I'm sure you'll soon get some e-mails with good advice. OK, our next caller is Kevin from Birmingham. Hello Kevin.
Kevin Hi.
Presenter What's the problem?
Kevin Yes. My problem is with my best friend. Well, the thing is, he's always flirting with my girlfriend.
Presenter Your best friend flirts with your girlfriend?
Kevin Yes, when the three of us are together he always says things to my girlfriend like, 'Wow! You look fantastic today,' or 'I love your dress, Suzanna,' things like that. And when we're at parties he often asks her to dance.
Presenter Do you think he's in love with your girlfriend?
Kevin I don't know, but I'm really angry about it. What can I do?
Presenter Well, let's see if one of our listeners can help, Kevin. And our last caller is Catherine. OK Catherine, over to you. What's the problem?
Catherine Hello. I'm at university and I live on the university campus. I live in a flat and I share a room with this girl. She's really nice. I get on very well with her, but there's one big problem.
Presenter What's that?
Catherine She always borrows things from me without telling me.
Presenter What does she borrow?
Catherine Well, first it was CDs and books, but now she's started taking my clothes as well, sweaters, jackets, and things. Yesterday she took a white sweater of mine and she didn't tell me. So when I wanted to wear it this afternoon it was dirty. I don't want to lose her as a friend but what should I do?
Presenter Thank you Catherine. So… if you can help Barbara, Kevin, or Catherine, e-mail us at…

6.14

Receptionist Hi. How can I help you?
Allie Do you have any painkillers? I have a headache.
Receptionist I'm sorry. We can't give our guests medicine. But we can call a doctor for you if you like.
Allie No, it's OK. I don't need a doctor. It's just a cold. But is there a chemist's near the hotel?
Receptionist Do you mean a pharmacy?
Allie Sorry, that's right, a pharmacy.
Receptionist Sure. There's one right across the street.
Allie Thank you.
Receptionist You're welcome.

6.17

Mark Bless you! Are you OK?
Allie It's just a cold. I had a bad headache this morning, but I feel better now.
Mark Listen. I'm really sorry about last night.
Allie What do you mean?
Mark At the party. I got kind of angry at Brad. He was really annoying me.
Allie Oh, I think he's very nice.
Mark Yeah, women always think so.
Allie Don't worry, Mark. Brad's not my type.
Mark So what is your type, Allie?
Allie You know what my type is. Dark hair, 34 years old, lives in San Francisco…
Mark Listen, tomorrow's your last day. I want to do something special. What would you like to do?

Allie I don't mind. You choose.
Mark How about a boat trip around the bay? We could do that in the morning, and then have a nice dinner in the evening.
Allie That sounds fantastic.
Mark It's too bad you can't stay longer.
Allie Yes, it's a pity – this week has gone so quickly. I feel I've just arrived and now I'm going home.
Mark Well, I'm going to make sure tomorrow is a really special day.

7.1

Interviewer What exactly is your phobia, Scott?
Scott Well, the medical name is Felinophobia or Gatophobia.
Interviewer And what does that mean exactly?
Scott It means I'm afraid of cats.
Interviewer Cats?
Scott Yes.
Interviewer How long have you had this phobia?
Scott Since I was a child.
Interviewer And how did it start?
Scott When I was five or six years old, I remember going to a friend's house and I saw a cat on the stairs. And the cat was looking at me, well staring at me. I went to touch it, and it bit me. And since then I've always been afraid of cats.
Interviewer What happens if you see a cat?
Scott Well, I start to feel very nervous, my hearts beats quickly. And I have to go away very quickly from where the cat is. For example, if I see a cat in the street, I always cross to the other side.
Interviewer What do you do?
Scott I'm a doctor.
Interviewer Is your phobia a problem for you in your work?
Scott Yes, sometimes. For example, if I go to a house and there is a cat I have to ask the people to put the cat in another room. I can't be in the same room as a cat.
Interviewer Have you ever had any treatment for your phobia?
Scott Yes, I've just started going to a therapist. I've had three sessions.
Interviewer How's it going?
Scott Well, now I can look at a photo of a cat without feeling nervous or afraid. And I can touch a toy cat. The next step will be to be in a room with a real cat.
Interviewer Do you think you will ever lose your phobia of cats?
Scott I hope so. I'm optimistic. Who knows, maybe one day I'll have a cat as a pet.

7.5

Presenter Good evening and welcome to *Film of the week*. Tonight we are going to see Sofia Coppola's film *Lost in Translation*. This film came out in 2003, and it gave the young film director her first Oscar nomination. Before it starts, Anthony, can you tell us a bit about her?
Anthony Well, of course as you know, Sofia Coppola is the daughter of Francis Ford Coppola, so you could say that she was born with a camera in her hand. She was born in New York in 1971 while her father was making the film *The Godfather*, and in fact she actually appeared in the film – she was the little baby in the baptism scene.

After she left school she decided to become an actress, but her career as an actress didn't last long. When her father made *The Godfather part III*, he gave his daughter a part in the film. She played Mary Corleone, the Godfather's daughter. But it was a disaster and the film critics wrote terrible things about her. So she stopped being an actress and she went to the California Institute of Art where she studied fine arts and photography. Then she decided to become a film director.

1999 was a really big year for her. She directed her first film, *The Virgin Suicides*, and this time the critics thought she was great. She also got married, to the film director Spike Jonze – but they separated after a few years.

And then in 2003 she made her next film, which is the one we're going to see now called *Lost in Translation*. *Lost in Translation* was the film which made Sofia Coppola famous. For this film she became the first American woman to be nominated for an Oscar for best director, although she didn't win it.
Presenter Thank you very much Anthony. And now, let's watch *Lost in Translation*.

7.6

Interviewer How old are you in the photograph, Melissa?
Melissa Twelve or thirteen, I think.
Interviewer Did you like school?
Melissa Not really.
Interviewer Why not?
Melissa Because I didn't like any of the subjects. Well, that's not quite true, I liked English, but that was the only lesson I used to look forward to. I didn't like maths, didn't like science at all, and I *hated* PE. I used to argue with the PE teacher all the time. She used to make us do impossible things, things we couldn't do, like climbing ropes and jumping over the horse. I think she just wanted to humiliate us.
Interviewer Were you a 'good girl' at school?
Melissa It depends what you mean by 'good'. I didn't smoke, I didn't use to write graffiti on the walls or anything like that. But I was a bit of a rebel. I used to break rules all the time, and of course the teachers didn't like that.
Interviewer What sort of rules did you break?
Melissa Well, for example the school was very strict about the school uniform – we had to wear a blue skirt, and the skirt had to cover our knees. I used to make the skirt shorter. And then I sometimes used to wear blue socks and a black sweater, like in the photograph instead of a grey sweater, and grey socks. The teachers used to get really angry; I just thought it was silly.
Interviewer What did you want to be when you were at school?
Melissa I wanted to be a lawyer.
Interviewer Why?
Melissa Well, there were a lot of American TV programmes and films about lawyers at the time, and I used to think it would be fun to argue with people all day.
Interviewer So why did you become a primary school teacher?
Melissa Lots of reasons. But I think the main reason is that both my parents were teachers and they both used to tell me, when you grow up and get a job *don't* be a teacher. So as I was a rebel, I did exactly the opposite.

7.11

Presenter Good afternoon, and welcome to another edition of *Science Today*. In today's programme we are going to hear about women inventors. When we think of famous inventors we usually think of men, people like Alexander Graham Bell, Guglielmo Marconi, Thomas Edison. But as Sally will tell us, many of the things which make our lives easier today were invented by women.
Sally That's absolutely right. Let's take the dishwasher for example. This was invented by a woman called Josephine Cochrane in 1886. She was a rich American who gave a lot of dinner parties. But she was annoyed that her servants used to break plates and glasses when they were washing them after the party. So, Josephine decided to try and invent a machine which could wash a lot of plates and glasses safely. Today the dishwasher is used by millions of people all over the world.

The car was invented by a man, but it was a woman, Mary Anderson, who in 1903 solved one of the biggest problems of driving. Until her invention, it was impossible for drivers to see where they were going when it was raining or snowing. The name of her invention? Windscreen wipers.

A fantastic invention that definitely improved the lives of millions of people was disposable nappies. They were invented by a woman called Marion Donovan in 1950. Anybody who has a small baby will know what a big difference disposable nappies make to our lives. Today more than 55 million nappies are used every day in the world.

A few years later in 1956, Bette Nesmith Graham was working as a secretary. She used to get very frustrated and angry when she made typing mistakes. In those days if you made a mistake you had to get a new sheet of paper and start again from the beginning. She had a brilliant idea, which was to use a white liquid to paint over mistakes. Her invention is called Tipp-Ex today. Mrs Graham was a divorced mother and her invention made her a very rich woman.

And finally… policemen, soldiers, and politicians all over the world are protected by something which was invented by a woman. In 1966 Stephanie Kwolek invented kevlar, a special material which was very light but incredibly strong, much stronger than metal. This material is used to make the bullet-proof vest. Her invention has probably saved thousands of lives.

Presenter Thanks very much Sally. So… if you thought that everything was invented by men, think again.

7.14

Mark Hi, Allie. How are you feeling today?
Allie Much better.
Mark Good. Are you going to be warm enough with just that sweater? It might be a little cold on the boat.
Allie I'll be fine. Are we going to walk to the bay?
Mark No, it's too far. It's better if we get a cab.
Allie How long does it take by cab?
Mark About ten minutes.
Allie And how long's the boat trip?
Mark I'm not sure. I think it's an hour. Why?
Allie Well, I have to be back here by 1.00 – I'm expecting an important phone call.
Mark Not from Brad, I hope?
Allie Well, actually… No, of course not! From the New York office.
Mark OK. Let's go.

7.17

Mark So, what do you think of San Francisco?
Allie It's beautiful, Mark. I love it.
Mark Better than London?
Allie Not better. Different.
Mark Do you think you could live here?
Allie No, I don't think so.
Mark Oh. Why?
Allie Well, it's a long way from London. I think I'd miss all my family and friends.
Mark Could you live somewhere else – but in *Europe*?
Allie Maybe. Why do you ask?
Mark Oh, no reason. I just wondered.
Tannoy *On your left you can see the island of Alcatraz.*
Mark Look, can you see that building? That used to be the prison, but it was closed in 1963. It's a museum now.
Allie Where are we going for dinner tonight?
Mark It's a surprise.
Allie I'm really looking forward to it.
Mark Me too.
Allie Brr. I'm cold.
Mark Do you want to borrow my coat?
Allie No. It's OK. I'm going to miss you, Mark.
Mark Hey, excuse me! Could you take a photo of us, please?
Man Sure. Are you ready?
Allie Ready.
Man Say cheese!

8.3

Newsreader Last Friday Sven, a company lawyer from Stockholm was looking forward to a relaxing two days in the mountains. He and his wife had booked a skiing weekend in a luxury hotel. But the weekend didn't work out exactly as they had planned. Sven worked until late on Friday evening. His office was on the 12th floor. When he finished, at 8 o'clock, he locked his office and got into the lift…and he didn't get out again until Monday morning!
Sven I pressed the button for the ground floor and the lift started going down but then stopped. I pressed the button again but nothing happened. I pressed the alarm and shouted but nobody heard me. Most people had already gone home. I tried to phone my wife but my mobile didn't work in the lift… I couldn't do anything. I just sat on the floor and hoped maybe somebody would realize what had happened. But on Saturday and Sunday I knew nobody would be there. I slept most of the time to forget how hungry I was.
Newsreader Meanwhile Sven's wife, Silvia was waiting for her husband to come home.
Silvia I was very worried when he didn't come home on Friday evening and I couldn't understand why his mobile wasn't going. I phoned the police and they looked for him but they couldn't find him anywhere. I thought maybe he was with another woman.
Newsreader So Sven was in the lift the whole weekend from Friday evening until Monday morning. At eight o'clock, when the office workers arrived, they phoned the emergency number and somebody came and repaired the lift.
Sven I was very happy to get out. I hadn't eaten since Friday afternoon and I was very hungry. It's lucky that I am not claustrophobic because the lift was very small. The first thing I did was to phone my wife to say that I was OK.
Newsreader Sven will soon be the fittest man in his office – from now on he's going to take the stairs every day – even though it's 12 floors.

8.6

Interviewer Hello. Could I ask you a few questions? We're doing some research.
David Sure. What's it about?
Interviewer Well, we want to find out if you are a morning or an evening person.
David OK, fine.
Interviewer OK and what's your name?
David David Cope.
Interviewer And, what do you do, David?
David I'm a magazine editor.
Interviewer OK, and when do you work?
David Monday to Friday, eight till four.
Interviewer What time do you get up in the morning?
David 5.45. I have to get up early because I start work at 8 and it takes me an hour to get to work.
Interviewer What time do you go to bed?
David Probably around 10.00.
Interviewer If you have an exam, do you study best in the morning, afternoon, or at night?
David Let me think, I haven't done an exam for a long time but when I was a student I used to study better in the morning.
Interviewer And…if you do exercise when do you prefer to do it?
David In the morning, definitely. I love going for a long walk or cycling. It's great early in the morning because you feel that you're the only person in the world who's awake at that time.
Interviewer Do you like your working hours?
David I don't mind them. Finishing work early means I can pick up my daughter from school, and look after her in the afternoons. It's true that I can't really have a social life during the week, because I go to bed at ten, but that's OK.
Interviewer Right, and the last question. Would you like to change your working hours?
David Yes, I would. I'd like to work four days a week, maybe working more hours in the day and have a three-day weekend. Then I could spend three full days a week with my family.
Interviewer That's great. Thank you very much for your time.

8.13

Receptionist Good afternoon. How can I help you?
Allie Hi. I'm leaving tomorrow morning very early. Could you prepare my bill so I can pay this evening?
Receptionist Of course.
Allie And could you order me a cab?
Receptionist For what time?
Allie My flight's at 9.15, so I have to be at the airport at 7.15.
Receptionist Then you'll need a cab at six o'clock. I'll order one for you.
Allie Thanks. Oh, and has there been a phone call for me?
Receptionist Oh yes. There's a message for you. Can you call this number in New York?
Allie Right. Thanks.
Receptionist You're welcome.

1

1A word order in questions

Questions with *do / does / did* in present and past simple

Question word	Auxiliary	Subject	Infinitive (= verb)
	Do	you	live with your parents?
	Does	Jenny	like Chinese food?
Where	do	you	live?
What food	does	Jenny	like?

- In the present simple use the auxiliary verb *do / does* to make questions.
- In the past simple use the auxiliary verb *did* to make questions.
- In these questions the subject goes after the auxiliary verb.
- Remember **ASI** (auxiliary, subject, infinitive) or **QUASI** (question word, auxiliary, subject, infinitive) to help you with word order in present or past simple questions.

Questions with *be*, present continuous, and *going to*

Question word	*be*	Subject	(adjective, noun, verb + *ing*, etc.)
	Is	Ana	a student?
What	are	they	doing?
	are	you	talking about?
Where	is	he	going to live?

- In questions with *be*, make questions by inverting the verb and the subject.

⚠ If a verb is followed by a preposition (*listen to, talk about*), the preposition goes at the end of the question.
What are you talking ***about****?*
NOT ~~About what are you talking~~.

1B present simple

	I / you / we / they	**he / she / it**
+	I usually **work** at home.	Danny **knows** me very well.
−	They **don't live** near here.	It **doesn't** often **rain** here.
?	**Do** you **smoke**?	**Does** Nina **like** music?
✔ ✘	Yes, I **do**. / No, I **don't**.	Yes, she **does**. No she **doesn't**.

- Use the present simple for things you do every day, week, year, or which are always true.
- Remember the spelling rules for 3rd person singular *s*:
  work>work**s** add *s*
  study>stud**ies** consonant + y: *y* and add *ies*
  finish>finish**es** *sh, s, ch, x*: add *es*
  go>go**es** do>do**es** have>ha**s**
- Remember the word order in questions (**ASI** and **QUASI** – see 1A above).

adverbs and expressions of frequency

- We often use the present simple with adverbs of frequency (*always, often, sometimes, usually, hardly ever, never*).
- Adverbs of frequency go before the main verb, but after *be*.
  He ***often*** *goes out.* NOT ~~He goes often out.~~
  She's ***always*** *late.* NOT ~~She's late always~~.
- Expressions of frequency (*every day, once a week*, etc.) usually go at the end of a sentence.
  I have English classes ***twice a week****.*

1C present continuous: *be* + verb + *ing*

	I	**you / we / they**	**he / she / it**
+	I'**m working**	You / We / They '**re working**	He / She / It '**s working**
−	I'**m not working**	You / We / They **aren't working**	He / She / It **isn't working**
? ✔ ✘	**Are** you **working**?	**Yes**, I **am**.	**No**, I'm **not**.
	Is he **working**?	**Yes**, he **is**.	**No**, he **isn't**.

- Use the present continuous for things happening now, at this moment.
  My brother is working in Germany.
  A *What are you doing?*
  B *I'm sending a text message to Sarah.*
- Remember the spelling rules for the *-ing* form.
  cook>cook**ing** study>study**ing**
  live>liv**ing** run>runn**ing**

⚠ Some verbs are not normally used in the present continuous, for example *like, want, have* (= possess), *need*.
I need to talk to you now.
NOT ~~I'm needing to talk to you now~~.

1D defining relative clauses with *who, which, where*

A cook is a person **who** works in a restaurant.
A clock is a thing **which** tells the time.
A post office is a place **where** you can buy stamps.

- Use relative clauses to explain what a place, thing, or person is or does.
  That's the woman who won the lottery last year.
  This is the restaurant where we had dinner last week.
- Use *who* for a person, *which* for a thing, and *where* for a place.

⚠ You can use *that* instead of *who* or *which*.
She's the girl ***who*** */* ***that*** *works with my brother.*
It's a thing ***which*** */* ***that*** *connects two computers.*

1A

a Put the word or phrase in the right place in the question.

How old are you? (old)
1 you going to go out this evening? (are)
2 Where does your work? (sister)
3 What music are you listening? (to)
4 Does finish at 8.00? (the class)
5 Why you write to me? (didn't)
6 Do you often to the cinema? (go)
7 What this word mean? (does)
8 What time did arrive? (your friends)

b Put the words in the right order to make questions.

you live where do? *Where do you live?*
1 you a do have car?
2 older is brother your you than?
3 often he how to write does you?
4 this time start does what class?
5 last go where you summer did?
6 languages how you many do speak?
7 see you are going to evening her this?
8 for waiting who you are?

1B

a Write sentences and questions with the present simple.

he / usually get up late [+] *He usually gets up late.*
1 Anna / like music [?] ______?
2 she / have a lot of hobbies [+] ______
3 I / get on very well with my sister [−] ______
4 my brother / know me very well [−] ______
5 they / have any children [?] ______?
6 the film / finish late [?] ______?
7 he / go out twice a week [+] ______
8 we / often talk about politics [−] ______

b Complete with a verb in the present simple.

get on | not have | listen | ~~live~~ | open | not talk | not work

He *lives* in a flat.
1 ______ the banks ______ in the afternoon?
2 My sister ______ many friends.
3 We usually ______ to the news in the car.
4 She's quite shy. She ______ much.
5 ______ Jane ______ well with her boss?
6 My cooker's new, but it ______ very well.

1C

a Write sentences with the present continuous.

It / rain. [−] *It isn't raining.*
1 Hey! you / stand on my foot! [+]
2 they / play very well today [−]
3 what / you study at the moment [?]
4 we / think of you [+]
5 she / wear make-up [?]
6 they / make / a big mistake [+]
7 your brother / work in London now [?]
8 she / talk to her father at the moment [−]

b Complete the sentences with the present simple or present continuous.

The girl in the painting *is playing* the guitar. (play)
1 My dog's not dangerous. He ______. (not bite)
2 Why ______ you ______ sunglasses? It ______! (wear, rain)
3 You can turn off the radio. I ______ to it. (not listen)
4 I ______ to go to the bank. I ______ any money. (need, not have)
5 Be careful! The baby ______ that pencil in her mouth! (put)
6 **A** ______ you usually ______ at weekends? (cook, eat)
B No, we normally ______ out.
7 **A** What ______ you ______ here? (do, meet)
B I ______ Emma. Look, there she is.

1D

a Complete the definitions with *who*, *which*, or *where*.

It's the person *who* serves you in a café.
1 They're people ______ make you laugh.
2 It's a machine ______ cuts the grass.
3 It's an animal ______ lives in the sea and has eight legs.
4 It's a room ______ people try on clothes.
5 He's the person ______ helps you with your luggage.
6 It's a kind of food ______ keeps vampires away.

A B C D E F

b Match the definitions and the pictures.

c Write sentences with *who*, *which*, or *where*.

that / the dog / always barks at night
That's the dog which always barks at night.
1 she / the woman / lives next door to me
2 that / the shop / I bought my dress
3 he / the actor / was in *Friends*
4 they / the children / broke my window
5 this / the restaurant / they do great pasta
6 that / the switch / controls the central heating
7 he / the teacher / teaches my sister
8 that / the room / we have our meetings

2A past simple regular and irregular

	+	−
I You He She It We They	**stayed** in a hotel. **went** on holiday.	**didn't stay** in a hotel. **didn't go** on holiday.
✔ ✘ ?	**Did** you **stay** in a hotel? **Did** you **go** on holiday?	Yes I **did**. No, I **didn't**.

- Use the past simple to talk about finished actions in the past.
- The past simple is the same for all persons.
- Use the infinitive after *Did…?* and *didn't* for negatives and questions.

infinitive	past
work	work**ed**
stay	stay**ed**
like	like**d** (just add *d* if verb finishes in *e*)
study	stud**ied** (*y*>*i* after a consonant)
stop	stop**ped** (if verb finishes in consonant–vowel–consonant, double the final consonant)

- To make the past simple + of regular verbs add *-ed*. Remember the spelling rules.
- Many common verbs are irregular in + past simple, for example *go*>*went*. See the **Irregular verb list** on p.155.

2B past continuous: *was* / *were* + verb + *ing*

+	I He **was working** She It	You We **were working** They
−	I He **wasn't working** She It	You We **weren't working** They
? ✔ ✘	**Was** he **working?** **Yes,** he **was.** **No,** he **wasn't.** **Were** they **working?** **Yes,** they **were.** **No,** they **weren't.**	

- Use the past continuous to describe an action in progress at a specific moment in the past.
  At six o'clock last night I was driving home.
  On April 1st I was staying with some friends in the country.

past simple or past continuous?

When I **took** the photo, they **were writing** a song.
I **was sitting** at home when I **saw** the news on TV.

- Use the past simple for a completed action.
  I took the photo. / I saw the news.
- Use the past continuous for an action in progress.
  They were writing a song. / I was sitting at home.

2C questions with and without auxiliaries

Questions with an auxiliary

Question	Auxiliary	Subject	Infinitive
What music	do	you	like?
Which CD	did	he	buy?
Who	did	you	go with?

- To make questions in the past and present simple, we normally use the auxiliary verbs *do / does / did* + the infinitive.
  What music do you like? NOT ~~What music you like~~?
- The normal order for questions in the present and past is **QUASI** (See p.126 1A).

Questions without an auxiliary

Subject	Verb	
What	happened	after the concert?
Which country	won	the Eurovision Song Contest?
Who	writes	their songs?

- When the question word (*Who? What? Which? How many?*) is the subject of the verb in the question, we do not use an auxiliary (*do, does, did*) and the verb is in the third person.
  Who writes their songs? NOT ~~Who does write their songs~~?

2D *so, because, but, although*

because and *so*

She was driving fast **because** she was in a hurry. (reason)
She was in a hurry **so** she was driving fast. (result)

Hannah spoke to the DJ **because** they didn't like the music. (reason)
They didn't like the music **so** Hannah spoke to the DJ. (result)

- Use *because* to express a reason.
- Use *so* to express a result.

but and *although*

She tried to stop **but** she hit the man.
Although she tried to stop, she hit the man.

It was late **but** she couldn't sleep.
She couldn't sleep **although** it was late.

- Use *but* and *although* to show a contrast.
- *Although* can go at the beginning or in the middle of the sentence.

2A

a Put the verbs in brackets in the past simple.

Two summers ago we *had* (have) a holiday in Scotland. We [1] ______ (drive) there from London, but our car [2] ______ (break) down on the motorway and we [3] ______ (spend) the first night in Birmingham. When we [4] ______ (get) to Edinburgh we [5] ______ (not can) find a good hotel – they [6] ______ (be) all full. We [7] ______ (not know) what to do but in the end we [8] ______ (find) a bed and breakfast and we [9] ______ (stay) there for the week. We [10] ______ (see) the castle, [11] ______ (go) to the Arts Festival, and we [12] ______ (buy) a lot of souvenirs. We [13] ______ (want) to go to Loch Ness but we [14] ______ (not have) much time and it [15] ______ (be) quite far away. The weather [16] ______ (be) good, but it [17] ______ (start) raining the day we [18] ______ (leave).

b Re-order the words to make questions.

Where did you go on holiday? go where holiday you on did?
Vancouver

1 ______________? time did have you good a?
Yes, it was great.
2 ______________? with did who go you?
With some friends.
3 ______________? stay where did you?
In a hotel.
4 ______________? you it why didn't like?
Because it was very modern and quite expensive.
5 ______________? how did cost plane much the ticket?
£500.

2B

a Complete with a verb in the past continuous.

1 He met his wife when he ______ in Japan. (work)
2 They ______ for us when we arrived. (wait)
3 ______ she ______ a coat when she went out? (wear)
4 What ______ you ______ at 7.30 last night? (do)
5 I ______ when you gave the instructions. (not listen)
6 I ______ when you phoned me. (drive)
7 It ______ when I woke up this morning. (not rain)

b Put the verbs into the past simple or past continuous.

She *arrived* when we *were having* dinner. (arrive, have)
1 I ______ my arm when I ______ football. (break, play)
2 ______ you ______ fast when the police ______ you? (drive, stop)
3 It ______ when we ______ the pub. (snow, leave)
4 I ______ the match because I ______. (not see, work)
5 When you ______ me, I ______ to my boss. (call, talk)

2C

a Cross out the wrong question.

What ~~**you did**~~ / **did you** do last night?
1 What **happened / did happen** to you?
2 What **means this word / does this word mean**?
3 How many people **came / did come** to this class?
4 Which bus **goes / does go** to the airport?
5 Which actor **won / did win** the Oscar this year?
6 What **said the teacher / did the teacher say**?

b Write the questions. Do you know the answers?

Who *said* 'Hasta la vista, baby'? (say)
1 How many Formula 1 world championships ______________? (Ayrton Senna / win)
2 Which US president ______________ the Nobel Peace Prize in 2002? (win)
3 Who ______________ the film *Reservoir Dogs*? (direct)
4 When ______________ president of South Africa? (Nelson Mandela / become)
5 Who ______________ *The Lord of the Rings*? (write)
6 What ______________ before he became a singer? (Sting / do)

2D

a Complete with *so*, *because*, *but*, or *although*.

We couldn't find a taxi *so* we walked home.
1 ______ it was very cold, she wasn't wearing a coat.
2 I woke up in the night ______ there was a noise.
3 I called him ______ his mobile was turned off.
4 ______ she's very nice, she doesn't have many friends.
5 There was nothing on TV ______ I went to bed.
6 All the cafés were full ______ it was a public holiday.
7 She wanted to be a doctor ______ she failed her exams.

b Match the sentence halves and complete with *so*, *because*, *but*, or *although*.

1 I was tired last night *so* [E]
2 She drove quite fast ______ [ ]
3 His English isn't very good ______ [ ]
4 I phoned him at his office ______ [ ]
5 She's not feeling very well ______ [ ]
6 I didn't write to you ______ [ ]
7 He called the hotel ______ [ ]
8 I took her to a restaurant ______ [ ]

A I lost your e-mail address.
B it was her birthday.
C they didn't have any rooms.
D he lived in the UK for two years.
E ~~I went to bed early.~~
F she was in a hurry.
G he was in a meeting.
H she can't go to class tonight.

3

3A *going to*

+	**I'm going to** work in a restaurant. She**'s going to** meet me at the airport.
–	We **aren't going to** stay very long. He **isn't going to** like the weather there.
?	**Are** you **going to** find a job? When **is** your brother **going to** visit you?

- Use (*be*) *going to* + infinitive to talk about future plans and predictions.
  *I'm **going to work** in the UK for six weeks.* (plan)
  *I think it's **going to rain** this afternoon.* (prediction)
- When you use *going to go*, you can omit *to go*.
  I'm going to go to university next year
  or *I'm going ~~to go~~ to university next year.*

present continuous for future arrangements

+	**I'm seeing** some friends tonight. We**'re having** dinner at their house tomorrow.
–	She **isn't leaving** until Friday. They **aren't coming** to the party.
?	What **are** you **doing** this evening? **Is** she **meeting** us at the cinema?

- You can also use the present continuous for future arrangements which we have planned for a fixed time or place.
- Don't use the present simple for this. NOT ~~I see some friends tonight.~~
- The present continuous is especially common with the expressions *tonight, tomorrow, this weekend*, etc. and with these verbs: *go, come, meet, see, leave*, and *arrive*.

3B *will, won't* + infinitive (predictions)

+		–	
I You He She It We They	**'ll be** late.	I You He She It We They	**won't be** late.

Contractions: 'll = will; won't = will not

?			✔			✘		
Will	I you he she it we they	**be** late?	**Yes,**	I you he she it we they	**will.**	**No,**	I you he she it we they	**won't.**

- Use *will / won't* + infinitive for future predictions. (You can also use *going to*. See 3A above.)
- The future of *there is / are* = *there will be*; the future of *I can* = *I'll be able to* NOT ~~I'll can~~.

- We often use *I think / I don't think …+ will… I think he'll fail the exam. I don't think he'll pass the exam.* NOT ~~I think he won't pass.~~

⚠ Sometimes in + sentences with *I* and *we*, people use *shall* (not *will*), but this is very formal (for example, in a business letter).
I shall write to you when I have studied your case.

3C *will* (promises, offers, and decisions)

Decisions	I **won't have** the fish, I'll have the steak. We'**ll take** the 6.30 train.
Offers	I'**ll help** you with your homework. **Shall I open** the window?
Promises	I'**ll** always **love** you. I **won't tell** anyone.

- Use *will / won't* + infinitive for making decisions, offering, and promising.
  I'll help you with those bags. NOT ~~I help you.~~
- Use *Shall I…?* or *Shall we …?* when an offer is a question.
  Shall I pay? Shall we call you tonight at 7.00?

3D review of tenses: present, past, and future

Tense	**Example**	**Use**
present simple	I **live** in the city centre. She **doesn't smoke.**	Things that happen always or usually.
present continuous	He**'s looking** for a new job. I**'m leaving** tomorrow.	Things that are happening now or in the near future.
past simple	We **saw** a good film last night. We **didn't do** anything yesterday.	Finished actions in the past.
past continuous	He **was working** in Paris. What **were you doing** at 7.00?	Actions that were in progress at a past time.
going to **+ infinitive**	I'm **going to see** Tom tonight. It's **going to rain.**	Future plans and predictions.
will / won't **+ infinitive**	You**'ll love** New York. I**'ll phone** her later. I**'ll help** you. I**'ll pay** you back tomorrow.	Predictions, instant decisions, offers, and promises.

3A

a Complete with *going to* + a verb.

be buy get married not go not pass ~~see~~ snow stay

What film *are* you *going to see* tonight?

1 He's very lazy. I'm sure he ______ his exams.
2 ______ your sister ______ a new flat?
3 You ______ in class 3 next year.
4 We ______ camping next summer. We ______ in a hotel.
5 **A** When ______ they ______? **B** In October.
6 It's very cold, but I don't think it ______ today.

b Cross out the wrong form. Tick (✔) if both forms are possible.

~~I see~~ / **I'm seeing** my boyfriend tonight.

1 What **are you doing** / **do you do** after class today?
2 Is it **going to rain** / **raining** tomorrow?
3 We're **going to go away** / **going away** this weekend.
4 **I'm meeting** / **I meet** Susan this evening.
5 Where are you **going to stay** / **staying** in Paris?
6 Hurry up! We're **going to be late** / **being late**.
7 She's **going to come** / **coming** tonight.

3B

a Write sentences and questions with *will* / *won't*. Use contractions where you can.

it / be difficult [+] *It'll be difficult.*

1 they / win [−]
2 the meeting / be long [?]
3 he / get the job [−]
4 you / see him at the party [?]
5 it / be impossible to park [+]
6 you / like the film [−]
7 she / love the chocolates we bought her [+]
8 there / be a lot of traffic at 6.00 [−]
9 you / can find a good job [+]

b Complete the predictions with *will* / *won't* + a verb.

be do ~~have~~ last make

'I don't think we*'ll have* another war. This one is probably the last.'
Richard Nixon, 1971 (talking about the Vietnam war)

1 'He ______ never ______ anything important in life.'
Albert Einstein's teacher (said to his father) 1895

2 'No film about the Civil War ______ ever ______ any money.'
An MGM executive 1945 (about the film *Gone With The Wind.*)

3 'It's a bad joke. It ______.'
Coco Chanel (about the miniskirt)

4 'I don't think there ______ a woman Prime Minister in my lifetime.'
Margaret Thatcher, 1973

3C

a Match the sentences.

It's cold in here.	G	A I'll help you to do it.
1 I'm thirsty.		B Shall I make you a sandwich?
2 I have a headache.		C Shall I carry one for you?
3 This exercise is hard.		D I'll lend you some money.
4 I'm hungry.		F I'll send it by e-mail now.
5 These bags are heavy.		~~G Shall I shut the window?~~
6 I left my wallet at home.		H Shall I turn off the music?
7 I need that photo urgently.		I I'll get you a glass of water.

b Complete the sentences with *will* / *won't* (or *shall*) + a verb.

call forget ~~have~~ help pay take tell

A What would you like? **B** I*'ll have* the pasta.

1 **A** I can't open this window. **B** ______ you?
2 **A** It's a secret. **B** I ______ anyone, I promise.
3 **A** When will I see you again? **B** I ______ you tonight.
4 Can I borrow €50? I ______ you back tomorrow.
5 **A** It's my birthday next week. **B** Don't worry. I ______.
6 **A** I don't feel very well. **B** ______ I ______ you home?

3D

a Complete the sentences with an auxiliary verb.

Where *did* you have lunch yesterday?

1 ______ you often remember your dreams?
2 When ______ your mother coming to stay?
3 ______ you see the match last night?
4 Who ______ you phoning last night?
5 Who ______ you think ______ win the elections?
6 ______ your brother like classical music?
7 What ______ you going to cook tonight?
8 ______ it raining when you left?

b Put the verb in the right form.

A What *are* we *doing* tonight? (do)
B We [1]______ dinner with my sister. (have)
A But we [2]______ dinner with her last week! (have)
B Yes, but she [3]______ to tell us some good news. (want)
A Oh, OK then. [4]______ I ______ some champagne? (buy)

B It's 7.00! What [5]______ to you (happen)?
A When I [6]______ home I [7]______ to buy the champagne. (come, stop). And then I [8]______ Jim in the shop… (meet)
B Well hurry up. We [9]______ late! (be)

4

4A present perfect (experience) + *ever*, *never*

+

I'**ve** (I **have**) You'**ve** (You **have**) He'**s** (He **has**) She'**s** (She **has**) It'**s** (It **has**) We'**ve** (We **have**) They'**ve** (They **have**)	**been** to London.

–

I **haven't** You **haven't** He **hasn't** She **hasn't** It **hasn't** We **haven't** They **haven't**	**worked** in a bank.

?	✔	✘
Have you **worked** in a bank?	Yes, I **have**.	No, I **haven't**.
Has he **been** to London?	Yes, he **has**.	No, he **hasn't**.

- Use the present perfect to talk about past experiences when you don't say exactly when they happened.
  I've been to London. NOT ~~I've been to London last year.~~
  My brother has worked abroad.
- For regular verbs the past participle is the same as the past simple (+ *ed*). For **Irregular verbs** see p.155.
- We often use the present perfect with *ever* (= in your life until now) and *never*.
  Have you ever been to London? No, I've never been there.

⚠ Compare the present perfect of *go* and *be*.
He's gone to Paris. = He's in Paris now.
He's been to Paris. = He went to Paris and came back.

present perfect or past simple?

A Have you ever been to Mexico?	**B** Yes, I have.
A When did you go there?	**B** I went last year.

- Conversations often begin in the present perfect (with a general question) and then change to the past simple (with questions asking for specific details, *when*, *where*, *who with*, etc.)
- Use the past simple to ask / say exactly when something happened.

4B present perfect + *yet*, *just*, *already*

yet

A Have you finished your homework **yet**?
B No, not **yet**. I haven't finished **yet**.

- Use *yet* + the present perfect in – and ? sentences to ask if something that you think is going to happen has happened or to say it hasn't happened.
- Put *yet* at the end of the sentence.

just

A Would you like a coffee?
B No thanks. I've **just** had one.
My sister's **just** started a new job.

- Use *just* in + sentences to say that something happened very recently.
- Put *just* before the main verb.

already

A Do you want to see this film?
B No, I've **already** seen it three times.
A Shall I buy a newspaper?
B No, I've **already** bought one.

- Use *already* in + sentences to say that something happened before now or earlier than expected.
- Put *already* before the main verb.

4C comparative adjectives

Adjective	Comparative	
short	short**er**	one syllable: + *er*
big	big**ger**	one vowel + one consonant: double final consonant
busy	bus**ier**	consonant + *y*: *y* + *ier*
relaxed	**more** relaxed	two or more syllables: *more* + adjective
good bad far	**better** **worse** **further**	Irregular

comparative adverbs

Adverb	Comparative	Adverb	Comparative
Regular		**Irregular**	
quickly	**more quickly**	hard	**harder**
slowly	**less slowly**	well	**better**
		badly	**worse**

- Use comparative adjectives to compare people and things.
  My brother's taller than me.
- Use comparative adverbs to compare actions.
  He drives more slowly than me.
- You can also use (*not*) *as* + (adjective / adverb) + *as*.
  I'm not as tall as my brother.
  He doesn't drive as fast as me.

4D superlatives (+ *ever* + present perfect)

Adjective	Comparative	Superlative
cold	cold**er**	**the** cold**est**
hot	hot**ter**	**the** hot**test**
pretty	prett**ier**	**the** prett**iest**
beautiful	**more** beautiful	**the most** beautiful
good	**better**	**the best**
bad	**worse**	**the worst**
far	**further**	**the furthest**

- Use *the* + superlative adjectives to say which is the biggest, etc. in a group.
  It's the highest mountain in Europe. She's the best in the class.
- We often use a superlative with the present perfect.
  Russia is the coldest place we've ever been to.
  It's the most beautiful church I've ever seen.

4A

a Write sentences or questions with the present perfect.

he / ever / be there ? *Has he ever been there?*

1 you / ever buy / clothes from that shop?
2 I / not read / the newspaper today.
3 We / never be / to the new shopping centre.
4 your brother / live abroad / all his life?
5 They / go / to live in South America.
6 She / never fly / before.
7 He / not meet / his wife's family.
8 you / eat / in this restaurant before?

b Right (✔) or wrong (✘)? Correct the wrong sentences.

He's got up late this morning. ✘ *He got up late this morning.*

1 We've been to Ireland last year. ______
2 Have you ever gone to Paris? ______
3 Jane's gone to the bank. She'll be back soon. ______
4 I like your shoes. Where did you buy them? ______
5 I've seen that film last week. ______
6 I spoke to him a minute ago. ______
7 My sister's a writer. She's written five novels. ______
8 World War II has ended in 1945. ______

4B

a Order the words to make sentences.

1 made have you yet your bed?
2 gone already to work she's.
3 just we've a cup of coffee had.
4 I found a job haven't yet.
5 sent me just an he's e-mail.
6 house already sold they've their.

b Write sentences or questions with *already*, *just*, or *yet*.

he / arrive (already) *He's already arrived.*

1 I / have / breakfast (just)
2 you / finish your homework? (yet)
3 the film / start (already)
4 I / not meet / his girlfriend (yet)
5 they / get married (just)
6 You're too late. He / go home (already)
7 you / speak to him? (yet)
8 I / not read his new book (yet)

4C

a Write comparative sentences.

London is / expensive / Manchester.
London is more expensive than Manchester.

1 my sister is / thin / me.
2 I'm / busy / this week / last week.
3 Cambridge is / far from London / Oxford.
4 I did the second exam / bad / the first.
5 Chelsea played / well / Arsenal.
6 the men in my office work / hard / the women.
7 my new job is / boring / my old one.

b Rewrite the sentences so they mean the same. Use *as… as*.

Mike is stronger than Jim. Jim isn't *as strong as Mike.*

1 Cindy is taller than Kelly. Kelly isn't ______.
2 Your case is heavier than mine. My case isn't ______.
3 Mexico City is bigger than London. London isn't ______.
4 Football is more popular than tennis. Tennis isn't ______.
5 Children learn languages faster than adults. Adults don't ______.
6 You work harder than me. I don't ______.
7 France played better than England. England didn't ______.

4D

a Complete the sentences with a superlative.

Is this *the noisiest* city in the world? (noisy)

1 Yesterday was ______ day of the year. (hot)
2 This is ______ time to drive through the city centre. (bad)
3 She's ______ person in the class. (friendly)
4 This is ______ part of the exam. (important)
5 The ______ month to visit is September. (good)
6 It's ______ city in the world. (polluted)
7 The ______ I've ever flown is to Australia. (far)

b Write sentences with *ever*.

it / hot country / I be to
It's the hottest country I've ever been to.

1 it / good film / I / see
2 he / unfriendly person / I / meet
3 it / hard exam / he / do
4 they / expensive shoes / she / buy
5 it / long book / I / read
6 she / beautiful girl / I / see
7 it / bad meal / I / have

5A uses of the infinitive (with *to*)

infinitive + *to*

I want **to go** to the party.
I need **to buy** some new clothes.
It'll be nice **to meet** some new people.
It's important **not to be** late.

- Use *to* + the infinitive after:
  – some verbs (*want, need, would like*, etc.) See **Verb Forms** p. 154.
  – adjectives
  It isn't easy to find a job. Nice to meet you.
- The negative infinitive is *not to* + verb.
  Try not to be late tomorrow.

infinitive of purpose

A Why did you go to the party? **B** **To meet** new people.
I went to the party **to meet** new people.

- Use *to* + the infinitive to say why you do something.
  I came to this school to learn English. NOT ~~for learn English~~.

5B verb + *-ing*

Eating outside in the summer makes me feel good.
I love **reading** in bed.
I'm thinking of **buying** a new car.

- Use verb + *ing*:
  – as the subject of a sentence
  Smoking is bad for you.
  – after some verbs, (*like, love, hate, enjoy*, etc.) See **Verb Forms** p. 154.
  I hate getting up early.
  – after prepositions
  He left without saying goodbye.
- Remember the spelling rules for the *-ing* form (See p. 126 1C)

5C *have to, don't have to, must, mustn't*

have to, don't have to

+	She **has to** get up at 7.00 every day. You **have to** drive on the left in the UK.
–	We **don't have to** wear a uniform at this school. He **doesn't have to** work on Saturdays.
?	**Do** I **have to** buy a grammar book? **Does** she **have to** study tonight?

Don't contract *have* or *has*.
I have to go. NOT ~~I've to go.~~

- Use *have to* + infinitive to talk about rules and obligations, or to say something is necessary.
- Use *don't have to* + infinitive to say there is no obligation, or something is not necessary.
- Use *do / does* to make questions and negatives.
  Do I have to go? NOT ~~Have I to go?~~

must / mustn't

+	You **must** do your homework tonight. She **must** tidy her room before she goes out.
–	You **mustn't** smoke in class. They **mustn't** leave their bags here.

Contraction: *mustn't* = must not

- Use *must* + infinitive to talk about rules and obligations.
  You must turn off your mobile phones before coming into class.
- *must / mustn't* are the same for all persons. It is not often used in questions (*have to* is more common).
- Use *mustn't* + infinitive to say something is prohibited.
  You mustn't smoke here.
- You can use *mustn't* or *can't* to talk about rules.
  You mustn't park here. You can't park here.

⚠ *Must* and *have to* are very similar, but there is a small difference. We normally use *have to* for a general obligation (a rule at work or a law). We normally use *must* when the speaker imposes the obligation (for example, a teacher to students or a parent to children). But often you can use either.

Mustn't and *don't have to* have completely different meanings. Compare:
You mustn't go = You can't go. It's prohibited.
You don't have to go = You can go if you want, but it's not obligatory/necessary.

5D expressing movement: *go*, etc. + preposition

The man **went up** the steps and **into** the church.
I **ran over** the bridge and **across** the park.
He **drove out of** the garage and **along** the street.

- To express movement use a verb of movement, for example, *go, come, run, walk*, etc. and a preposition of movement (*up, down*, etc.)
- Be careful with *in / into* and *out / out of*. Use *into / out of* + noun, but if there isn't a noun just use *in* or *out*.
  Come ***into*** *the living room. Come* ***in****.*
  He went ***out of*** *the house. He* ***went out****.*

5A

a Complete with *to* + a verb.

I'm planning *to have* a holiday next month.

do not drive go learn leave not make meet

1 **A** Hi, I'm Dagmara.
  B I'm Renata. Nice ________ you.
2 What do you want ________ this evening?
3 I need ________ to the bank. I don't have any money.
4 Try ________ a noise. Your father's asleep.
5 I'd really like ________ a new language.
6 Be careful ________ too fast on the way home.
7 She's decided ________ her husband.

b Match the sentence halves.

They want to go to Australia *D*
1 He's going to have a party
2 You'll need a visa
3 Don't forget to phone the restaurant
4 I stopped at the garage
5 She's gone to the supermarket
6 I went to the travel agent's
7 I'll send them a text message

A to celebrate getting the job.
B to get some petrol.
C to book our tickets.
~~D to visit their family there.~~
E to tell them where we are.
F to go to China.
G to book a table.
H to get some food for tonight.

5B

a Complete the sentences with a verb in the *-ing* form.

be ~~do~~ go learn remember study talk teach

I don't really enjoy *doing* exercise.
1 My mother's very bad at ________ names.
2 ________ teenagers is very hard work.
3 You can't sing well without ________ to breathe properly.
4 My sister spends hours on the phone ________ to her boyfriend.
5 I hate ________ the first to arrive at parties.
6 ________ by train is cheaper than by plane.
7 I'll go on ________ until dinner time.

b Put the verbs in the *-ing* form or infinitive.

I like *listening* to music. (listen)
1 ________ yoga is good for your health. (do)
2 We've decided ________ to the party. (not go)
3 We won't take the car. It's impossible ________. (park)
4 I'm not very good at ________ maps. (read)
5 You can borrow the car if you promise ________ slowly. (drive)
6 Have you finished ________ your homework? (do)
7 I don't mind ________ but I hate ________. (cook, wash up)

5C

a Write sentences with the right form of *have to*.

I / work on Saturday [–] *I don't have to work on Saturday.*
1 Jane / work very hard [+]
2 you / wear a uniform [?]
3 my sister / go to school [–]
4 I / finish this now [?]
5 we / get up early tomorrow [–]
6 Harry / work tomorrow [?]
7 we / hurry or we'll be late [+]

b Complete the sentences with *have to, don't have to*, or *mustn't*.

We *don't have to* work tomorrow. It's a holiday.
1 You ________ touch those animals. They're dangerous.
2 We ________ take the bus to school. It's too far to walk.
3 The concert is free. You ________ pay.
4 It's late. I ________ go now.
5 You ________ leave the door open – the cats will come in.
6 You ________ come if you don't want to. I can go on my own.
7 In Britain you ________ drive on the left.
8 You ________ be very tall to play football.

5D

a Cross out the wrong preposition.

My mobile stopped working when we went ~~**across**~~ / **through** a tunnel.
1 She ran **to** / **down** the lake, and jumped **into** / **out of** the water.
2 If you go **over** / **past** the church, you'll see my house on the left.
3 He walked **along** / **across** the street until he got to the chemist's.
4 The plane flew **on** / **over** the town and then landed.
5 The policeman walked **towards** / **to** me, but then he stopped.
6 We drove **over** / **out of** the bridge and **in** / **into** the city centre.
7 The cyclists went **round** / **under** the track three times.

b Complete the sentences with *in, into, out*, or *out of*.

He jumped *into* his car and drove away.
1 I like to go ________ on a Friday night.
2 Come ________. The door's open.
3 He took his passport ________ his jacket.
4 He walked ________ the café and ordered a coffee.

6

6A *if* + present, *will* + infinitive (first conditional)

If I **miss** the bus, **I'll** get a taxi.
She **won't be** angry **if** you **tell** her the truth.
What **will** you **do if** it **rains**?

⚠ You can also use the imperative or *can*.
If you miss the bus, get a taxi.
If you miss the bus, you can get a taxi.

- Use *if* + present, *will* + infinitive to talk about a possible future situation and its consequence.
- The *if* clause can come first or second.
  I'll come if you like. OR *If you like, I'll come.*

6B *if* + past, *would* + infinitive (second conditional)

If a bear **attacked** me, I**'d run** away.
If I **didn't have** children, I **wouldn't live** in the country.
Would you **take** the manager's job **if** they **offered** it to you?

- Use *if* + past, *would* + infinitive to talk about an improbable / impossible or hypothetical future situation and its consequence.
  If a bear attacked me, I'd run away. = I'm imagining this situation. It's very improbable.
- *would / wouldn't* is the same for all persons.
- The contraction of *would* is *'d* (*I'd, you'd, he'd*, etc.) and of *would not* is *wouldn't*.
- The *if* phrase can come first or second.
  If I saw a bear, I'd run. OR *I'd run if I saw a bear.*
- Remember with *can*, use *could* + infinitive, not ~~would can~~.
  If I had a car, we could drive there.

⚠ With the verb *be* you can use *were* (instead of *was*) after *I* and *he / she / it*.
If he was / were here, he'd help you.
Use *were* (not *was*) in the expression *If I were you…*
We often use this expression for advice.

First and second conditionals

Compare the first and second conditionals:
Use the **first conditional** for **possible** future situations.
If I have time tomorrow, I'll help you. (= maybe I will have time)
Use the **second conditional** for **improbable / impossible** or **hypothetical** situations.
If I had time tomorrow, I'd help you. (= I won't have time.)

6C *may / might* + infinitive (possibility)

We **might** have a picnic tomorrow, but it depends on the weather.
I **might not** go to the party. I haven't decided yet.
I **may** go to the party, but I'm not sure.
I **may not** have time to do everything today.
Might not and ***may not*** aren't usually contracted.

⚠ You can also use *May I… / May we…* to ask for permission.
May I use your phone? (= can I use your phone).

- Use *might / may* and *might not / may not* +infinitive to talk about a future possibility.
  It might / may rain. = It's possible that it will rain.
- *Might / May* (*not*) is the same for all persons, *I might / may, he might / may, we might / may*, etc.

6D *should / shouldn't* (advice)

I think you **should** change your job.
The government **should** do more for old people.

- Use *should / shouldn't* + infinitive to give somebody advice or say what you think is the right thing to do.
  You should cut your hair. = I think it would be a good idea.
- *should / shouldn't* + infinitive is the same for all persons.
- You can also use *ought to / ought not to* instead of *should / shouldn't*.
  You ought to change your job.

6A

a Match the sentence halves.

If you leave now	*C*	A if you don't start now.
1 It will be cheaper		B will you give it back to me?
2 If I don't see you later,		C ~~you'll catch the 8.00 train.~~
3 You'll learn more		D if you go by bus.
4 If you get the job,		E I'll see you on Friday.
5 You won't have time		F if you come to every class.
6 If I lend you this book,		G will you earn more money?

b Complete with the correct form of the verbs.

If you *tell* me your secret, I *won't tell* anybody. (tell, not tell)
1 If we ________ walking, the bus ________. (start, come)
2 He ________ angry if you ________ him. (be, not tell)
3 If I ________ it down, I ________ it. (not write, not remember)
4 ________ you ________ me if you ________ any news? (call, get)
5 If you ________ her nicely, she ________ you. (ask, help)
6 You ________ if you ________. (not pass, not study)

6B

a Match the sentence halves.

You'd feel much better	*C*	A we could go shopping.
1 I'd enjoy the weekend more		B I'd get a new job.
2 If you stayed for another day,		C if ~~you stopped smoking~~.
3 Would you wear it		D if I went to live in China?
4 If I were you,		E if I bought it for you?
5 I wouldn't work		F if I didn't need the money.
6 Would you come with me		G if I didn't have to work on Saturday.

b Complete with the correct form of the verbs.

If I *found* a good job, I *would move* to the USA. (find, move)
1 We ________ the house if it ________ a garden. (buy, have)
2 If I ________ his number, I ________ him. (know, phone)
3 You ________ more if you ________ harder. (learn, work)
4 If you ________ for a week, you ________ see everything. (stay, can)
5 We ________ our son more often if he ________ nearer. (see, live)
6 I ________ to the doctor's if I ________ you. (go, be)

6C

a Match the sentence halves.

Take your umbrella.	*D*	A You might fall.
1 Let's buy a lottery ticket.		B It might not be your size.
2 Phone the restaurant.		C We might get lost.
3 Don't stand on the wall.		D ~~It might rain.~~
4 Let's take a map.		E I might be late.
5 Try the shirt on.		F You might cut yourself.
6 Don't wait for me.		G It might be closed on Sundays.
7 Be careful with that knife.		H We might win.

b Complete the sentences with *may* / *might* + a verb.

be cold   be ill   be in a meeting   ~~go to the cinema~~
not have time   not like it   win

I'm not sure what to do tonight. I *might go to the cinema.*
1 Kate wasn't in class today. She ________
2 He isn't answering his phone. He ________
3 It's an unusual film. You ________
4 I don't know if I'll finish it. I ________
5 It's a difficult match but we ________
6 Take your coat. It ________

6D

a Complete with *should* or *shouldn't*.

You *should* stop smoking.
1 You ________ eat red meat.
2 You ________ work 12 hours a day.
3 You ________ lose a bit of weight.
4 You ________ eat more fruit.
5 You ________ drink a lot of coffee.
6 You ________ put salt on your food.
7 You ________ start doing some exercise.

b Complete the sentences with *should* or *shouldn't* + a verb.

drive   go   ~~leave~~   relax   study   walk   wear

We *should leave* early. There might be a lot of traffic later.
1 You ________ a jacket. It's quite cold today.
2 I ________ tonight. I have an exam tomorrow.
3 You ________ alone in that part of the city. Get a taxi.
4 She ________ more. She's very stressed.
5 People ________ so fast when it's raining.
6 You ________ to bed early tonight. You look really tired.

7

7A present perfect + *for* and *since*

A	Where do you live now?	B	In Manchester.
A	**How long have you lived** there?	B	**I've lived** there **since** 1990.
A	Where do you work?	B	In a primary school.
A	**How long have you worked** there?	B	**I've worked** there **for** five years.

⚠ You can't use the present simple here.
NOT ~~How long do you live here?~~
~~I live in Manchester since 1980.~~

- Use the present perfect + *for* or *since* to talk about actions and states which started in the past and are still true now.
  I've lived in Manchester since 1990. = I came to live in Manchester in 1990 and I live in Manchester now.
- Use *How long?* to ask questions about the duration of an action or a state.
- Use *since* with the beginning of a period of time, for example, *since 1980, since last June*, etc.
  I've been afraid of water since I was a child.
- Use *for* + a period of time, for example, *for two weeks, for ten years*, etc.
  I've had this car for three months.

7B present perfect or past simple (2) ?

How long **has** Tarantino **been** a director?	He'**s been** a director since the 1980s.
How many films **has** he **made**?	He'**s made** six films.
How long **was** Hitchcock a director?	He **was** a director for 50 years.
How many films **did** he **make**?	He **made** 52 films.

⚠ Don't use *since* with the past simple.
NOT ~~He was Prime Minister since 1999.~~
You have to use *from…to*.
He was Prime Minister from 1999 to 2003.

- Use the present perfect + *how long?, for*, and *since* to talk about a period of time from the past until now.
  How long have you been married? I've been married for 10 years. (= I'm married now.)
- Use the past simple + *how long?* and *for* to talk about a finished period of time in the past.
  How long was he married? He was married for two years. (= He's not married now.)

7C *used to / didn't use to*

+		−	
I You He She It We They	**used to** wear glasses.	I You He She It We They	**didn't use to** wear glasses.

?			✔			✘		
Did	I you he she we they	**use to** wear glasses?	**Yes,**	I you he she we they	**did.**	**No,**	I you he she we they	**didn't.**

- Use *used to / didn't use to* + infinitive for things that happened repeatedly or over a long period of time in the past, but are usually not true now, for example for things which happened when you were a child.
  I used to have long hair. I used to play in the street. I didn't use to have a TV.
- You can also use the past simple here. *I had long hair when I was a child.*

⚠ *used to* only exists in the past.
Don't use *use to* for present habits.
Use the present simple + *usually*.
I usually cook in the evenings.
NOT ~~I use to cook in the evenings.~~

7D passive: *be* + past participle

Present

+	−	?
Risotto **is made** with rice. These offices **are cleaned** every morning.	It **isn't made** with pasta. They **aren't cleaned** on Saturdays.	**Is** it **made** with meat? **Are** they **cleaned** on Sundays?

Past

+	−	?
Guernica **was painted** by Picasso. The pyramids **were built** by the Egyptians.	It **wasn't painted** by Dali. They **weren't built** by the Greeks.	When **was** it **painted**? Why **were** they **built**?

- You can often say things in two ways, in the active or in the passive.
  Picasso painted Guernica. (**active**) Guernica *was painted by Picasso.* (**passive**)
- In the active sentence, the focus is more on the person (e.g. Picasso).
- In the passive sentence the focus is more on the painting (e.g *Guernica*).
- You can also use the passive when it's not known or not important who does or did the action.
  My car was stolen last week. (I don't know who stole it.)
- Make the present passive with *am / is / are* + the past participle.
- Make the past passive with *was / were* + the past participle.
- Use *by* to say who did the action.
  The Lord of the Rings *was written by Tolkien.*

7A

a Write questions with *How long* and the present perfect.

you / be married _How long have you been married?_

1 he / have his car ______________________?
2 your parents / lived in this house ______________________?
3 you / be a teacher ______________________?
4 she / know her boyfriend ______________________?
5 Poland / be in the EU ______________________?
6 you / have your dog ______________________?
7 Tim / be frightened of water ______________________?

b Answer the questions in a. Use the present perfect + *for* or *since*.

I've been married since 1986.

1 He ______________________ three years.
2 They ______________________ a long time.
3 I ______________________ 1990.
4 She ______________________ May.
5 It ______________________ 2004.
6 We ______________________ about two years.
7 He ______________________ he was a child.

7B

a Right (✔) or wrong (✘)? Correct the wrong sentences.

She is married since 1990. ✘ *She's been married since 1990.*

1 He has left school last year. ☐
2 I lived in Brighton for two years, but then I moved to London. ☐
3 She lives in Hollywood since 2004. ☐
4 My sister has had her baby yesterday! ☐
5 I work in a bank. I work there for twenty years. ☐
6 The city has changed a lot since I was a child. ☐
7 They're divorced now. They have been married for a year. ☐

b Complete with the present perfect or past simple.

1 **A** Where does Joanna live now?
B In Washington.
A How long ____________ there? (she / live)
B For six months. She ____________ there in February. (move)

2 **A** When ____________? (Picasso / die)
B In 1977, in Paris I think.
A How long ____________ in France? (he / live).
B For a long time. He ____________ Spain when he was 25. (leave)

3 **A** My sister and her husband get on very well.
B How long ____________ married? (they / be)

7C

a Look at how James has changed. Write five sentences about how he was THEN.

THEN

He didn't use to be slim.

1 ______________________ short hair.
2 ______________________ quite fat.
3 ______________________ glasses.
4 ______________________ a uniform.
5 ______________________ wine.

NOW

b Make sentences with *used to*, *didn't use to*, or *did … use to*.

you / have long hair ?
Did you use to have long hair?

1 where / you / go to school ?
2 I / like vegetables when I was a child −
3 my sister / hate maths at school +
4 what / you / do in the summer ?
5 they / live near here −
6 this building / be a cinema +
7 your brother / study here ?

7D

a Complete with present or past passive.

The Eiffel Tower _was built_ in 1889. (build)

1 All the singer's clothes ____________ specially for her. (make)
2 The grass ____________ every month. (cut)
3 Australia ____________ by Captain Cook in 1770. (discover)
4 This morning I ____________ up by the neighbour's dog. (wake)
5 Cricket ____________ in the summer in the UK. (play)
6 These songs ____________ last year. (record)
7 Most children ____________ in state schools. (educate)

b Rewrite the sentences in the passive.

Shakespeare wrote Hamlet in 1603.
Hamlet _was written by Shakespeare in 1603._

1 Last night the police stopped us.
Last night we ______________________.
2 American teenagers eat a lot of fast food.
A lot of fast food ______________________.
3 Toulouse-Lautrec painted *At the Moulin Rouge.*
At the Moulin Rouge ______________________.
4 The marketing manager organizes weekly meetings.
Weekly meetings ______________________.
5 The Italians make Fiat cars.
Fiat cars ______________________.

8

8A something, anything, nothing, etc.

	+	? and − verb	✗ Short − answer
people	somebody someone	anybody anyone	nobody no one
things	something	anything	nothing
places	somewhere	anywhere	nowhere

Somebody's in the bathroom.

Is **anybody** in the bathroom?

There isn't **anybody** in the bathroom.

- Use *somebody, something, someone*, etc. when you don't say exactly who, what, or where.
  Somebody broke the window.
  I went somewhere nice at the weekend.
- Use *anything, anybody, anywhere* in questions or with a − verb.
  I didn't do anything last night. NOT ~~I didn't do nothing.~~
- Use *nobody, nothing, nowhere* in short − answers or in a sentence (with a + verb).
  Who's in the bathroom?
  Nobody. Nobody's in the bathroom.
  NOT ~~Anybody is in the bathroom.~~
- *Somebody, Nobody*, etc. are the same as *Someone, No one*, etc.

8B quantifiers

too, too much, too many

I'm stressed. I have **too much** work.
My diet is unhealthy. I eat **too many** cakes and sweets.
I don't want to go out. I'm **too** tired.

- Use *too, too much, too many* to say 'more than is good'.
- Use *too* + an adjective NOT ~~I'm too much tired.~~
- Use *too much* + uncountable nouns (e.g. coffee, time).
- Use *too many* + countable nouns (e.g. cakes, people).

enough

Do you eat **enough** vegetables?
I don't drink **enough** water.
This dress isn't big **enough**.

- Use *enough* before a noun to mean 'all that is necessary'.
- Use enough after an adjective.

a little, a few

A Do you take sugar? **B** Yes. Just **a little**.
A Do want some chips? **B** Yes, but **just a few**.
I eat **a little** meat.
I drink **very little** coffee.
Can you buy **a few** bananas?
He has **very few** friends.

- Use *a little / very little* and *a few / very few* to talk about small quantities.
- Use *a little / very little* with uncountable nouns and *a few / very few* with countable nouns.

8C word order of phrasal verbs

Every morning I **get up** at 8.00.
Then I **turn on** the radio.
I always have to **look for** my glasses.

- A phrasal verb = verb + particle (preposition or adverb) *get up, turn on, look for*.

1 **Some phrasal verbs don't have an object.**
__Come in__ and __sit down__.
What time do you __get up__?

2 **Some phrasal verbs have an object and are separable.**
__Put on__ your coat.
__Turn off__ the TV.

- With these verbs you can put the particle (*on, off*, etc.) before or after the object.
  ***Put on** your coat* OR ***Put** your coat **on**.*
  ***Turn off** the TV* OR ***Turn** the TV **off**.*
- When the object is a pronoun (*me, it, him*, etc.) it always goes between the verb and particle.
  Here's your coat. ***Put it on.*** NOT ~~Put on it.~~
  I don't want to watch TV. ***Turn it off.*** NOT ~~Turn off it.~~

3 **Some phrasal verbs have an object and are inseparable.**
I'm __looking for__ my keys.
I'm __looking for__ them.

With these phrasal verbs, the verb (*look*) and the particle (*for*) are never separated.
I looked after my little sister. NOT ~~I looked my little sister after.~~
I looked after her. NOT ~~I looked her after.~~

8D so, neither + auxiliaries

A I love football.
B So do I.
A I went to university.
B So did I.
A I'm not married.
B Neither am I.
A I don't smoke.
B Neither do I.

- Use *So do I / Neither do I*, etc. to say that you have something in common with somebody.
- Use *So* + auxiliary + *I* with positive sentences.
  A *I'm happy.* **B** *So am I.* NOT ~~So I am.~~
- Use *Neither* + auxiliary + *I* with negative sentences.
  A *I'm not hungry.* **B** *Neither am I.*
  NOT ~~Neither I am.~~
- The auxiliary you use depends on the tense.

I love football.	*So **do** I.*
I didn't like the film.	*Neither **did** I.*
I can swim.	*So **can** I.*
I wasn't very tired.	*Neither **was** I.*
I've been to Spain.	*So **have** I.*
I wouldn't like to go there.	*Neither **would** I.*

8A

a Complete with *something, anything, nothing,* etc.

Did you meet *anybody* last night?

1 Are you doing ______ tonight?
2 ______ phoned when you were out. He said he'd call back later.
3 I've seen your car keys ______ but I can't remember where.
4 Did ______ come while I was out?
5 Did you go ______ exciting last night?
6 I've bought you ______ for your birthday.
7 I knocked at the door but ______ answered.
8 We went shopping but we didn't buy ______.

b Answer with *Nobody, Nowhere,* or *Nothing.*

1 What did you do last night? ______
2 Where did you go yesterday? ______
3 Who did you see? ______

c Answer the questions in **b** with a full sentence.

1 I didn't do ______
2 ______
3 ______

8B

a Cross out the wrong form.

How **much** / ~~**many**~~ meat do you eat?

1 I drink **too** / **too much** coffee.
2 I eat **too much** / **too many** biscuits.
3 I don't drink **enough water** / **water enough**.
4 I can't go. I am **too** / **too much** busy.
5 You work **too much** / **too many**.
6 I only drink **a few** / **a little** coffee.
7 I don't have **enough time** / **time enough**.
8 He has **a few** / **a little** good friends.

b Complete the sentences with *too, too much, too many,* or *enough.*

You eat *too much* red meat. It isn't good for you.

1 My father's not very fit. He doesn't do ______ exercise.
2 I can't walk to work. It's ______ far.
3 There are ______ cars on the roads today.
4 I don't sleep ______ – only five or six hours, but I really need eight.
5 I was ______ tired to go out last night.
6 There were ______ people at the party, so it was impossible to dance.

8C

a Complete the sentences with a particle from the box.

after	away	back	down (x2)	for	~~off~~	on	up

Turn *off* your mobile before you come into class. ✔

1 Turn ______ the radio. It's too loud.
2 What time do you usually get ______ in the morning?
3 John phoned when you were out. He'll call ______ later.
4 My brother is looking ______ a new job.
5 I think you should throw ______ those old jeans.
6 I always try ______ new clothes before I buy them.
7 I have to look ______ my little sister tonight.
8 You should write ______ new words in your book.

b Tick the sentences in **a** where the particle (*on, off,* etc.) could also go after the object.

c Complete the sentences with *it* or *them* and a particle.

away	off (x2)	on	up (x3)

1 I can't hear the radio. Turn ______ ______.
2 Your clothes are all over the floor. Pick ______ ______.
3 Here's your coat. Put ______ ______.
4 What does this word mean? Look ______ ______.
5 Your shoes are wet. Take ______ ______.
6 I don't need those papers. Throw ______ ______.
7 Don't watch the TV now. Turn ______ ______.

8D

a Complete B's answers with an auxiliary verb.

A I like coffee — **B** So *do* I.

1 **A** I'm really hungry. — **B** So ______ I.
2 **A** I didn't go out last night. — **B** Neither ______ I.
3 **A** I was born in Liverpool. — **B** So ______ I.
4 **A** I don't smoke. — **B** Neither ______ I.
5 **A** I've been to Bangkok. — **B** So ______ I.
6 **A** I can't swim. — **B** Neither ______ I.
7 **A** I'd like to go to India. — **B** So ______ I.
8 **A** I saw a film last night. — **B** So ______ I.

b Respond to **A**. Say you are the same. Use *So…I* or *Neither…I*

A I don't like whisky. — *Neither do I.*

1 **A** I live near the school. ______
2 **A** I'm not afraid of snakes. ______
3 **A** I went to bed early. ______
4 **A** I haven't been to China. ______
5 **A** I don't have any children. ______
6 **A** I can speak three languages. ______
7 **A** I always have breakfast. ______

9A past perfect

+

I You He She **'d seen** the film before. It We They	I You He She **hadn't seen** the film before. It We They
contractions: I'd = I had	**I hadn't = I had not**

?	✔	✘
Had I / you / he / she / we / they **seen** it before?	**Yes,** I / you / he / she / we / they **had.**	**No** I / you / he / she / we / they **hadn't.**

Suddenly he remembered that he had seen the film before.

- Use the past perfect when you are already talking about the past, and want to talk about an earlier past action.
  When I woke up the garden was all white.
  It had snowed in the night.
  I arrived at the coffee bar twenty minutes late and my friends had already gone.
- Make the past perfect with *had* / *hadn't* + the past participle.
- The past perfect is the same for all persons.

⚠ Be careful: *I'd* can be *I had* or *I would.*

9B reported (or indirect) speech

reported sentences

Direct speech	Reported speech
'I love you.'	He said (that) he loved her.
'I want to see you again.'	He told her (that) he wanted to see her again.

- Use reported speech to say what another person said.
  I **love** you. → He said (that) he **loved** her.
- Other tenses change like this:

Direct speech	Reported speech
'I **can** help you.'	He said (that) he **could** help me.
'I**'ll** phone you.'	He told me (that) he **would** phone me.
'I **met** a girl.'	He told me (that) he **had met** a girl.
'I**'ve broken** my leg.'	He said (that) **he had broken** his leg.

- *that* is optional after *say* and *tell.*
- Pronouns also change in reported speech, for example *I* changes to *he* / *she*, etc.
  I'm coming. → She told me that **she** was coming.

⚠ You can use *said* or *told* in reported speech but they are used differently.
– You can't use *said* with an object or pronoun
NOT ~~He said her he loved her~~
– You must use *told* with an object,
He told her that he loved her NOT ~~he told that…~~

reported questions

Direct speech	Reported speech
'**Do you want** to dance?'	He asked her **if she wanted** to dance.
'**Where do you live**?'	He asked her **where she lived.**

- In reported questions:
  – the tenses change in exactly the same way as in sentences, eg present to past, etc.
  – we don't use *do* / *did.*
  What **do** you **want**?
  He asked me ***what I wanted.***
  NOT ~~He asked me what did I want.~~
  – if the question begins with *do, can,* etc. add *if.*
  Do you like the music? → *He asked her* ***if*** *she liked the music.*
  Can you sing? → *She asked him* ***if*** *he could sing.*
  – the word order is subject + verb.
  Are you a student? → *He asked her if* ***she was*** *a student.*
  Have you seen the film? → *She asked him if* ***he had seen*** *the film.*

9A

a Match the sentence halves.

I couldn't get into my flat because *D*
1 When our friends arrived ☐
2 I took the sweater back because ☐
3 Jack didn't come with us. ☐
4 I turned on the TV ☐
5 Jenny was nervous because ☐
6 When the film started ☐
7 At work I suddenly remembered that ☐

A He had made other plans.
B I realized that I'd seen it before.
C it was the first time she had flown.
D I'd forgotten my keys.
E I hadn't turned off the cooker.
F he had bought me the wrong size.
G we hadn't finished cooking the dinner.
H to see what had happened.

b Complete the sentences. Put the verbs in the past simple or past perfect.

We *didn't get* a table in the restaurant because we *hadn't booked*. (not get, not book)
1 I ________ Maria because she ________ her hair. (not recognize, cut)
2 My friend ________ to tell me I ________ my jacket in the car. (phone, leave)
3 When I ________ the TV, the match ________. (turn on, finish)
4 She ________ me the book because she ________ it yet. (not lend, finish)
5 He ________ all his exams because he ________ at all. (fail, not study)
6 When we ________ home we saw that somebody ________ the kitchen window. (get, break)

9B

a Write the sentences in reported speech.

He said, 'I love you.' He told her that *he loved her*.

1 'I'm tired.' She said that she ________.
2 'I don't like rock music.' He told her he ________.
3 'I'll book a table.' He said ________.
4 'I've bought a new car.' Paul told us that ________.
5 'I live in the city centre.' She said that she ________.
6 'We can do it.' They said that ________.
7 'I saw the film on TV.' Julie said that ________.

b Make reported questions.

Do you want to dance? He asked her if she *wanted to dance*.

1 'Do you like football?' Mike asked me if I ________.
2 'What music do you like?' I asked her what music ________.
3 'Are you tired?' She asked me ________.
4 'Have you been to New York?' I asked them ________.
5 'Where did you live before?' He asked me ________.
6 'Can you swim?' She asked him ________.
7 'Where are you from?' I asked him ________.

Classroom language

YOU HEAR

a Match the phrases and pictures.

- [ ] Ask and answer the questions.
- [ ] Don't write.
- [ ] Don't speak (*Italian*).
- [ ] Go to page 33.
- [ ] Write down the words.
- [ ] Sit down.
- [ ] Stand up.
- [ ] Look at the board.
- [ ] Turn off your mobile (phone).
- *1* Work in pairs.

b Cover the phrases. Look at the pictures and remember the phrases.

YOU SAY

a Match the phrases.

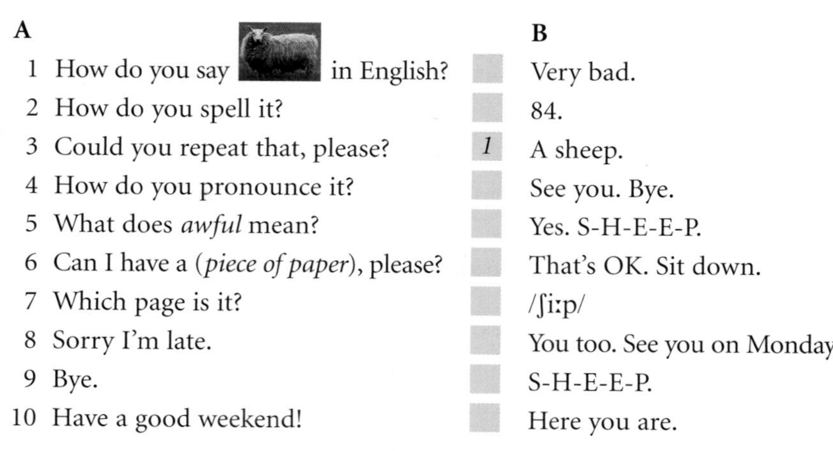

A		B
1 How do you say [picture] in English?		Very bad.
2 How do you spell it?		84.
3 Could you repeat that, please?	*1*	A sheep.
4 How do you pronounce it?		See you. Bye.
5 What does *awful* mean?		Yes. S-H-E-E-P.
6 Can I have a (*piece of paper*), please?		That's OK. Sit down.
7 Which page is it?		/ʃiːp/
8 Sorry I'm late.		You too. See you on Monday.
9 Bye.		S-H-E-E-P.
10 Have a good weekend!		Here you are.

b Cover column **B**. Remember the answers. Then cover column **A**. Remember the phrases.

YOU READ

a Match the instructions and pictures.

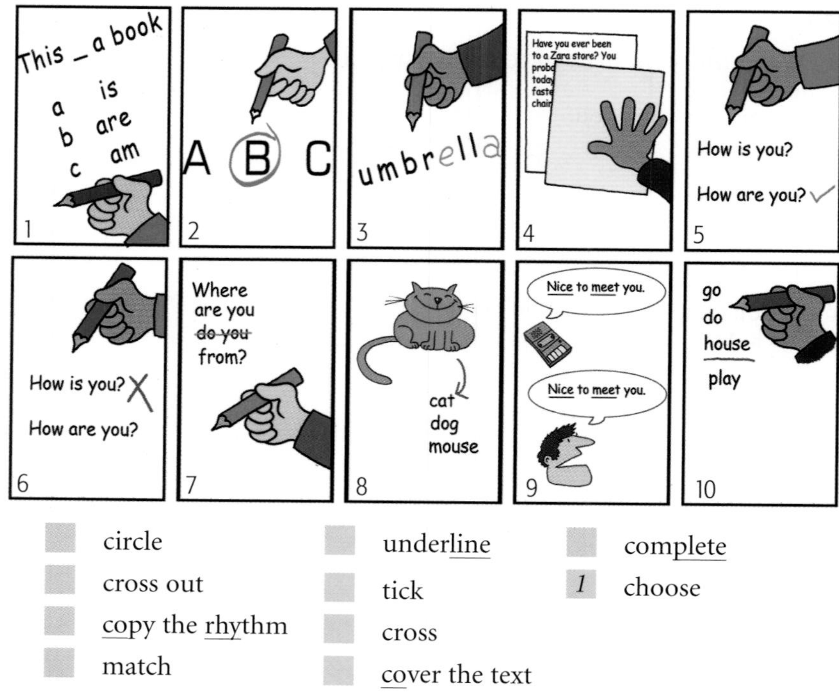

- [ ] circle
- [ ] cross out
- [ ] copy the rhythm
- [ ] match
- [ ] underline
- [ ] tick
- [ ] cross
- [ ] cover the text
- [ ] complete
- *1* choose

b Cover the instructions. Look at the pictures and remember them.

p.5

Adjectives

1 Personality adjectives

a Match the adjectives and definitions.

friendly /'frendli/   funny   generous   lazy   shy   ~~talkative~~

	Adjective	Opposite
A person who talks a lot is …	*talkative*	
A person who likes giving presents is …		
A person who never does any work is …		
A person who makes people laugh is …		
A person who is open and nice is …		
A person who is nervous and uncomfortable meeting new people is …		

b Complete the **Opposite** column.

extrovert   hard-working   mean   quiet /'kwaiət/   serious /'sɪəriəs/   unfriendly

c Cover the **Adjective** and **Opposite** columns. Look at the definitions and say the adjective and its opposite.

p.6

2 Opposite adjectives

a Match the words and pictures 1–8.

		Opposite
	boring	
	crowded /'kraʊdɪd/	
	dangerous /'deɪndʒərəs/	
1	far	*near*
	modern	
	noisy	
	polite /pə'lait/	
	polluted	

b Match these adjectives with their opposites in **a**.

clean   empty   exciting / interesting   near   old   quiet   rude   safe

c Cover the words and look at the pictures. Remember the adjectives and their opposites.

d Put the adjectives with the correct prefix to make opposites.

comfortable /'kʌmftəbl/   ~~happy~~
healthy /'helθi/   patient /'peɪʃənt/
polite   possible   tidy /'taɪdi/

un

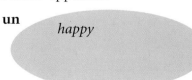

happy

im

e Test a partner. **A** say an adjective. **B** say the opposite.

p.47

The body

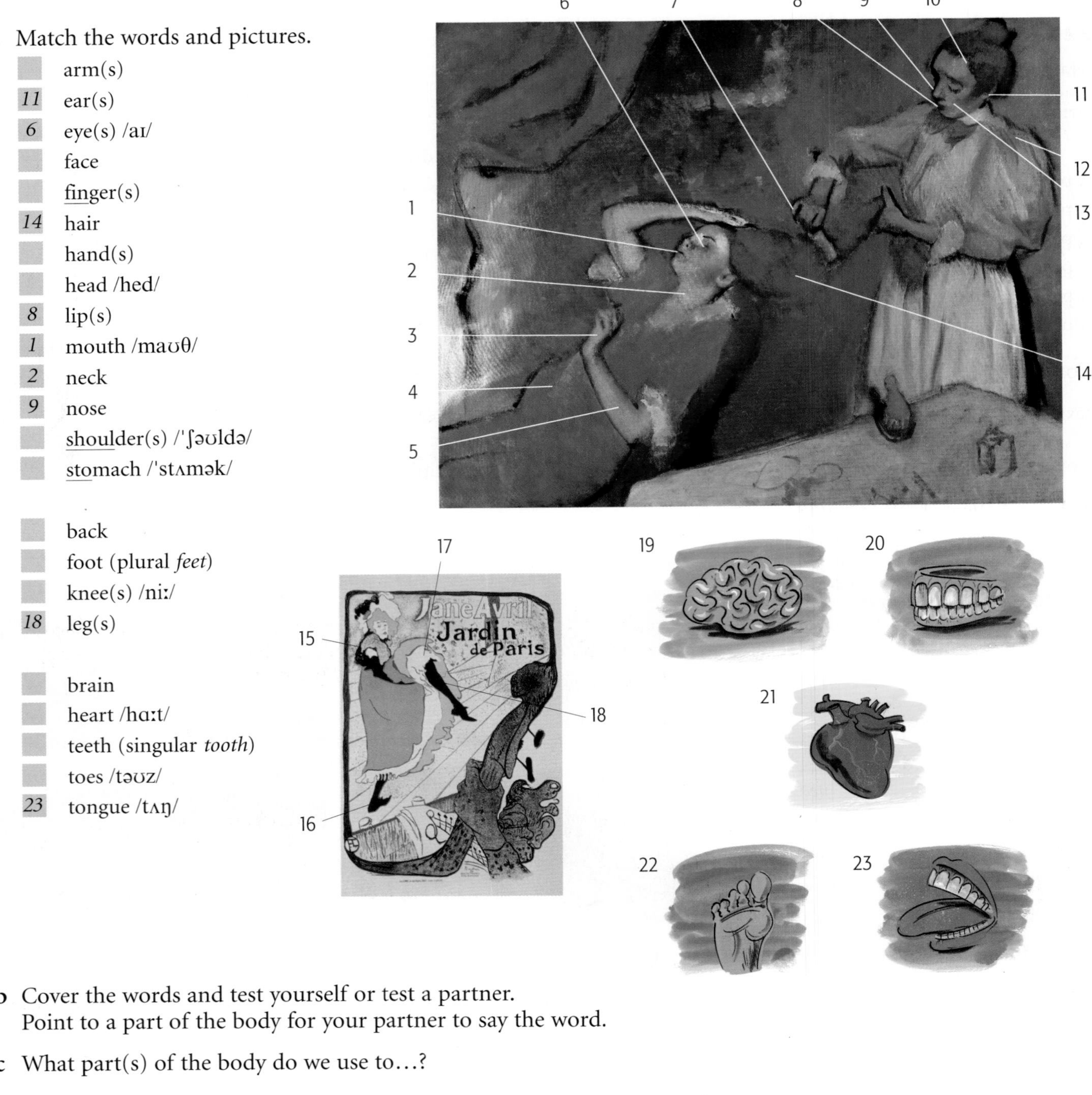

a Match the words and pictures.

- [ ] arm(s)
- [11] ear(s)
- [6] eye(s) /aɪ/
- [ ] face
- [ ] finger(s)
- [14] hair
- [ ] hand(s)
- [ ] head /hed/
- [8] lip(s)
- [1] mouth /maʊθ/
- [2] neck
- [9] nose
- [ ] shoulder(s) /ˈʃəʊldə/
- [ ] stomach /ˈstʌmək/

- [ ] back
- [ ] foot (plural *feet*)
- [ ] knee(s) /niː/
- [18] leg(s)

- [ ] brain
- [ ] heart /hɑːt/
- [ ] teeth (singular *tooth*)
- [ ] toes /təʊz/
- [23] tongue /tʌŋ/

b Cover the words and test yourself or test a partner.
Point to a part of the body for your partner to say the word.

c What part(s) of the body do we use to…?

see ________ hear ________ smell ________ kiss ________ bite ________
touch /tʌtʃ/ ________ think ________ feel ________ kick ________ smile ________

d Test a partner. Ask *What do you use to see?* etc.

> ⚠ In English we use possessive adjectives (*my*, *your*, etc.) with parts of the body, not *the*.
> *Give me your hand.* NOT ~~Give me the hand~~.

➲ **p.8**

1 Phrases with *go*

a Match the verbs and pictures.

- [ ] go abroad /əˈbrɔːd/
- *1* go swimming / sailing
- [ ] go sightseeing
- [ ] go camping
- [ ] go by car / bus / plane / train
- [ ] go to the beach
- [ ] go out at night
- [ ] go away for the weekend
- [ ] go for a walk

b Cover the phrases and look at the pictures. Test yourself or a partner.

2 Other holiday activities

a Complete the verb phrases.

buy have hire meet rent spend ~~stay~~ sunbathe /ˈsʌnbeɪð/ take walk

stay	in a hotel / campsite	______	on the beach	______	an apartment	______	friends
______	photos	______	a good time	______	in the mountains / around the town	______	a car
______	souvenirs	______	money / time				

b Test yourself. Cover the verbs. Remember the phrases.

3 The weather

a Match the words and pictures.

- [ ] sunny
- [ ] windy
- [ ] foggy
- [ ] cloudy /ˈklaʊdi/

- *1* rain
- [ ] snow

- [ ] hot
- [ ] cold
- [ ] boiling
- [ ] freezing

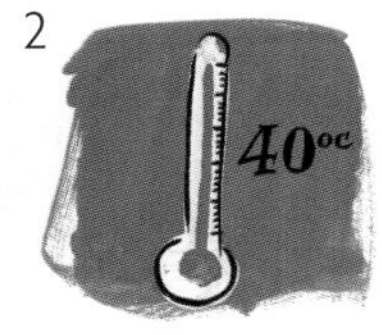

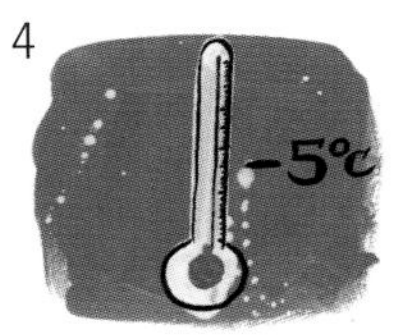

⚠ All these words are adjectives except *rain* and *snow*, which are nouns or verbs.
It's snowing. It snows every year. There's snow on the ground.
It rarely rains. It rained a lot this morning. There was a lot of rain last year.

b Test a partner. Imagine you were on holiday last week. Point to a picture.

A Say *What was the weather like?*
B Answer in the past simple.
It was sunny. / It rained.

p.16

Prepositions

1 *at / in / on*

Complete the chart with *at*, *in*, or *on*.

___	___	___
PLACE		
Countries and cities *France, Paris* **Rooms** *the kitchen* 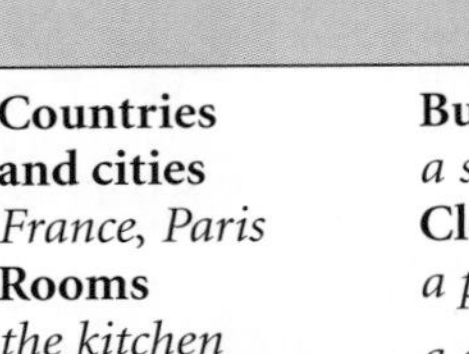 **Buildings** *a shop, a museum* **Closed spaces** *a park, a garden* *a car*	**Transport** *a bike, a bus, train, plane, a ship* (not *car*) **a surface** *the floor, a table, a shelf, the balcony, the roof, the wall*	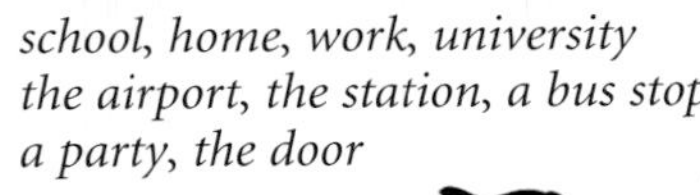 *school, home, work, university* *the airport, the station, a bus stop* *a party, the door* 
TIME		
Months *February, June* **Seasons** *winter* **Years** *2004* **Times of day** *morning, afternoon, evening* (not *night*)	**Dates** *March 1st* **Days** *Tuesday, New Year's Day, Valentine's Day*	**Times** *6 o'clock, half past two, 7.45* **Festival periods** *Christmas, Easter* *night* *the weekend*

b Look at the chart for a few minutes. Then test a partner:

A (book open) say a place or time word, e.g. *Paris, Tuesday*, etc.
B (book closed) say the preposition (*at*, *in*, or *on*).
Swap roles.

p.19

2 Prepositions of movement

Match the prepositions and pictures.

- [ ] under (the railway line)
- [ ] along (the street)
- [ ] round / around (the lake)
- [ ] through /θruː/ (the tunnel)
- [ ] into (the shop)
- [ ] across (the road)
- [ ] over (the bridge)
- [ ] up (the steps)
- [ ] past (the church)
- [ ] towards /təˈwɔːdz/ (the lake)
- *1* down (the steps)
- [ ] out of (the shop)

b Cover the prepositions. Where did the dog go? *It went down the steps...*

p.58

Verbs

1 Opposite verbs

a Match the verbs and pictures.

		Opposite
	buy (a house)	______
1	win (a match)	______
	lend (money to somebody)	______
	find (your keys)	______
	push (the door)	______
	pass (an exam)	______
	forget (a name)	______
	turn on (the TV)	______
	send (an e-mail)	______
	miss (a train)	______
	arrive (at the station)	______
	teach (a language)	______

1 

2 

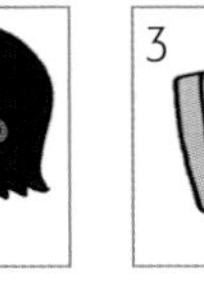

3 

4 

5 

6 

7 

8 

9 

10 

11 

12 

b Find the opposite verbs in the box. Write them in the **Opposite** column.

borrow (from somebody) catch fail get / receive
learn leave lose (x2) pull remember sell turn off

c Cover the verbs and look at the pictures. Remember the verbs and their opposites. p.31

2 Confusing verbs

a Match the verbs and pictures.

	wear *clothes*	**carry** *a bag*
	win *a prize* *a match*	**earn** *a salary*
	know *somebody* *something*	**meet** *somebody for the first time*
	make *a cake* *lunch, dinner* *a noise*	**do** *an exam, test, course* *housework, the washing up* *sport, yoga, aerobics*
	hope *that something good will happen*	**wait** *for a bus*
	watch *TV*	**look at** *a photo*
	look *happy*	**look like** *your mother*

p.64

b Cover the words and phrases and look at the pictures. Test yourself or a partner.

Clothes

a Match the words and pictures.

Singular clothes

- [ ] a dress
- [1] a top
- [ ] a skirt /skɜːt/
- [ ] a shirt
- [ ] a belt
- [ ] a T-shirt
- [ ] a sweater /ˈswetə/
- [ ] a suit /suːt/
- [ ] a coat /kəʊt/
- [ ] a tie /taɪ/
- [ ] a scarf
- [ ] a tracksuit
- [ ] a jacket
- [ ] a hat
- [ ] a cap
- [ ] a blouse

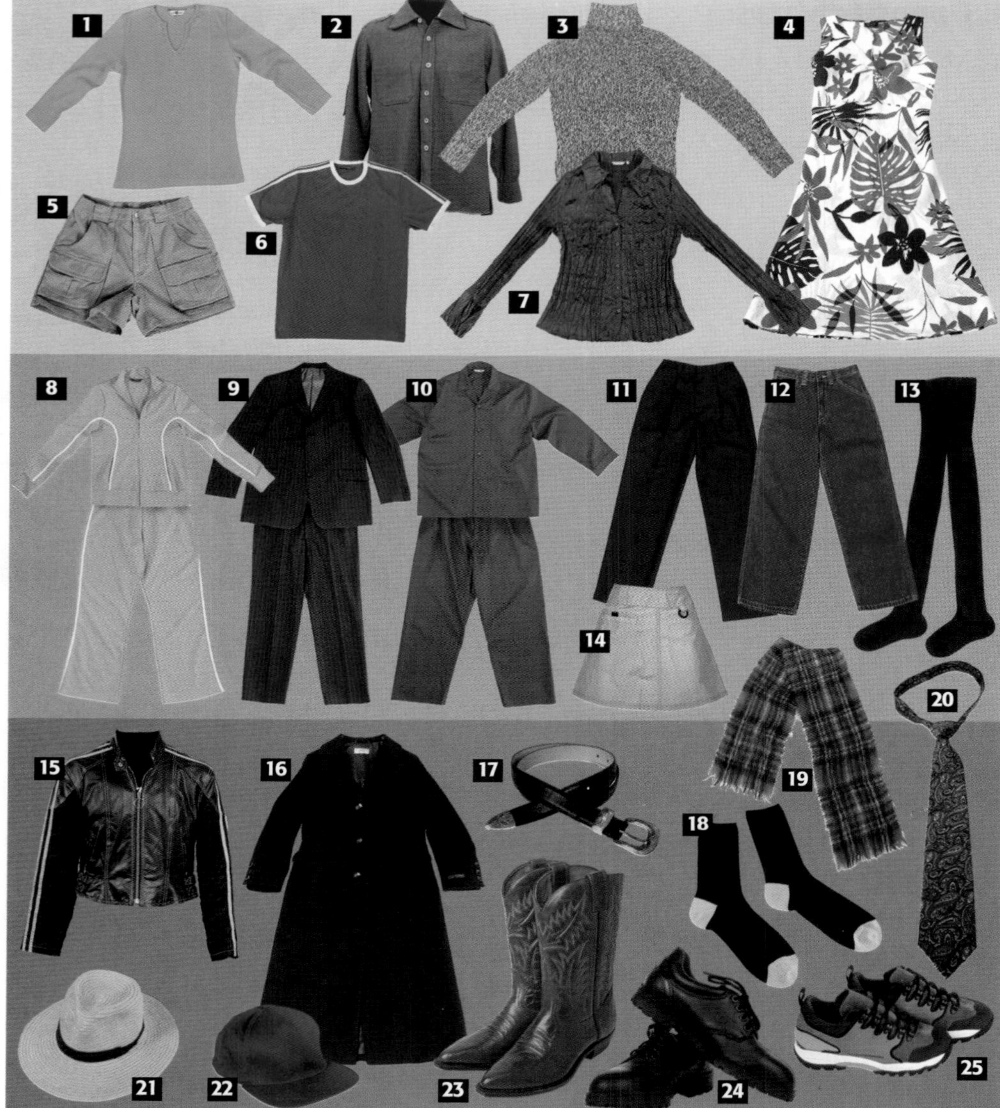

Plural clothes

- [ ] pyjamas /pəˈdʒɑːməz/
- [ ] trousers
- [ ] jeans
- [ ] shorts
- [ ] shoes /ʃuːz/
- [ ] boots
- [ ] trainers
- [ ] socks
- [ ] tights

b Cover the words and look at the pictures. Test yourself or a partner.

Verbs used with clothes

a Match the phrases and pictures.

- [ ] **get dressed**
- [ ] **wear** (a black hat)
- [ ] **take off** (her boots)
- [ ] **try on** (a dress)
- [ ] **put on** (her coat)

1

2

3

4

5

b Cover the phrases. What is she doing in each picture?

p.40

Animals

a Match the animals and the pictures.

insects

- ☐ bee
- ☐ butterfly
- ☐ fly
- ☐ mosquito
- ☐ spider
- *18* wasp /wɒsp/

farm animals

- ☐ bull
- ☐ chicken
- ☐ cow /kaʊ/
- ☐ goat /gəʊt/
- ☐ horse
- ☐ pig
- ☐ sheep

wild animals

- ☐ bear
- ☐ camel
- ☐ crocodile
- ☐ dolphin
- ☐ elephant
- ☐ giraffe
- ☐ gorilla
- ☐ kangaroo
- ☐ lion
- ☐ mouse (plural *mice*)
- ☐ rabbit
- ☐ shark
- ☐ tiger
- ☐ whale

birds

- ☐ duck
- ☐ eagle
- ☐ swan /swɒn/

b Cover the words and look at the pictures. Test yourself or a partner.

➲ p.67

get

a Match the phrases and the pictures.

get + adjective

- get divorced
- 1 get angry
- get fit
- get married
- get lost

get + comparative

- get older
- get worse
- get better

get = buy / obtain

- get a job
- get a ticket
- get a flat
- get a newspaper

get + preposition (phrasal verbs)

- get on (well) with
- get on (opposite *off*)
- get into (opposite *out of*)
- get up

get = arrive

- get to work
- get home
- get to school

get = receive

- get a salary
- get a letter
- get a present
- get an e-mail

b Cover the words and look at the pictures. Test yourself or a partner.

p.71

get

1 

2 

3 

4 

5 

6 

7 

8 

9 

10 

11 

12 

13 

14 

15 

16 

17 

18 

19 

20 

21 

22 

23 

Phrasal verbs

a Match the sentences and the pictures.

- [ ] We often stay up late at the weekend.
- [ ] The match will be over at about 5.30.
- [ ] I don't get on with my father.
- [ ] I need to give up smoking.
- [ ] Please put away your clothes.
- [ ] Don't throw away that letter!
- [ ] Turn down the music! It's very loud.
- [ ] Turn up the TV! I can't hear.
- *1* He looked up the words in a dictionary.
- [ ] Could you fill in this form?
- [ ] I want to find out about hotels in Madrid.
- [ ] Please pick up that towel.

1 
2 
3 
4 
5 
6 
7 
8 
9 
10 

11 
12 

b Cover the sentences and look at the pictures. Remember the phrasal verbs.

c Look at these other phrasal verb from Files 1–7. Can you remember what they mean?

get up	turn on (the TV)	look after (a child)
come back	turn off (the TV)	look for (something you've lost)
go back	put on (clothes)	look forward to (the holidays)
hurry up	take off (clothes)	
go away	try on (clothes)	
go out	give back (something you've borrowed)	
come in	take back (something to a shop)	
sit down	call back (later)	
stand up	pay back (money you've borrowed)	
run away	write down (the words)	

Green = no object. The verb and the particle (*on*, *up*, etc.) are **never separated**.

I get up at 7.30.

Blue = + object. The verb and the particle (*on*, *up*, etc.) are **never separated**.

Look for your keys. NOT ~~Look your keys for~~.

Red = + object. The verb and the particle (*on*, *up*, etc.) **can be separated**.

Turn the TV on. OR *Turn on the TV.*

p.92

Verb forms

A Verbs + infinitive

decide to	We decided to go to France.
forget to	Don't forget to turn off all the lights.
help to	He helped her to start the car.
hope to	We hope to see you again soon.
learn to	I'm learning to drive.
need to	I need to go the bank. I don't have any money.
offer to	He offered to take me to the airport.
plan to	They're planning to get married soon.
pretend	He pretended to be ill, but he wasn't really.
promise to	He promised to pay me back.
***remember to**	Remember to bring your dictionaries tomorrow.
start	She started to cry.
***try to**	I'm trying to find a job, but it's very hard.
want to	I want to go home.
would like to	I'd like to buy a new car.

p.53

B Verbs + *-ing*

enjoy	I enjoy reading in bed.
finish	Have you finished getting dressed?
go on (=continue)	I have to go on working until 9 o'clock.
hate	I hate getting up early.
like	I like having lunch in the garden.
love	I love waking up on a sunny morning.
(don't) mind	I don't mind cooking. It's OK.
spend (time)	She spends hours talking on the phone.
***start**	I started reading this book last week.
stop	Please stop talking.

p.55

⚠ *start* can be used with both the infinitive and verb + *-ing* with no real difference in meaning.
It started ***raining****.*
It started ***to rain****.*

start + *-ing* is more common when we talk about a habit or a longer activity.
I started ***working*** *here in 1998.*
When did you start ***playing*** *the piano?*

try and *remember* can also be used + *ing* but the meaning is different.
Why don't you try ***doing*** *yoga?* = experiment with something
Do you remember ***meeting*** *him last year?*
= remember something after it happened

After *make* and *let* use the infinitive without *to*.
Singing makes me ***feel*** *good.*
My parents don't let me ***go*** *out during the week.*

C Irregular verbs

Infinitive	Past simple	Past participle
be	was	been
become	became	become
begin	began	begun
break	broke	broken
bring	brought /brɔːt/	brought
build	built /bɪlt/	built
buy	bought /bɔːt/	bought
can	could /kʊd/	–
catch	caught /kɔːt/	caught
come	came	come
cost	cost	cost
choose	chose	chosen
cut	cut	cut
do	did	done /dʌn/
drink	drank	drunk
drive	drove	driven
eat	ate	eaten
fall	fell	fallen
feel	felt	felt
find	found	found
fly	flew /fluː/	flown /fləʊn/
forget	forgot	forgotten
get	got	got
give	gave	given
go	went	gone
grow	grew /gruː/	grown
have	had	had
hear	heard /hɜːd/	heard
hit	hit	hit
keep	kept	kept
know	knew /njuː/	known /nəʊn/
learn	learnt	learnt
leave	left	left
lend	lent	lent
let	let	let
lose	lost	lost
make	made	made
meet	met	met
pay	paid	paid
put	put /pʊt/	put
read	read /red/	read /red/
ring	rang	rung
run	ran	run
say	said /sed/	said
see	saw /sɔː/	seen
sell	sold	sold
send	sent	sent
sing	sang	sung
shut	shut	shut
sit	sat	sat
sleep	slept	slept
speak	spoke	spoken
spend	spent	spent
stand	stood /stʊd/	stood
steal	stole	stolen
swim	swam	swum
take	took /tʊk/	taken
teach	taught	taught
tell	told	told
think	thought /θɔːt/	thought
throw	threw /θru/	thrown /θrəʊn/
understand	understood	understood
wake	woke	woken
wear	wore	worn
win	won /wʌn/	won
write	wrote	written

Vowel sounds

- short vowels
- long vowels
- diphthongs

1	fish /fɪʃ/	2	tree /triː/	3	cat /kæt/	4	car /kɑː/
5	clock /klɒk/	6	horse /hɔːs/	7	bull /bʊl/	8	boot /buːt/
9	computer /kəmp'juːtə/	10	bird /bɜːd/	11	egg /eg/	12	up /ʌp/
13	train /treɪn/	14	phone /fəʊn/	15	bike /baɪk/	16	owl /aʊl/
17	boy /bɔɪ/	18	ear /ɪə/	19	chair /tʃeə/	20	tourist /'tʊərɪst/

Sounds and spelling

	usual spelling		but also
fish	i	thin lips history kiss if since	English women busy decide repeat gym
tree	ee ea e	feel teeth teach mean she we	people machine key niece
cat	a	hands hat back catch carry match	
car	ar a	far arms scarf fast pass after	aunt laugh heart
clock	o	top lost socks wrong hot box	what watch want because
horse	or al aw	boring more walk ball awful saw	water four bought thought abroad towards
bull	u oo	pull push foot book look room	would should woman
boot	oo u* ew	school choose rude use new knew	do suit juice shoe lose through
bird	er ir ur	person verb dirty shirt nurse turn	earn work world worse
computer	Many different spellings, always unstressed. further nervous arrive polite inventor agree		

* especially before consonant + **e**

	usual spelling		but also
egg	e	spell lend smell send very red	friendly head sweater any said
up	u	sunny mustn't funny run lucky cut	come does someone enough young touch
train	a* ai ay	face wake brain fail away pay	break steak great eight they grey
phone	o* oa	open hope won't so coat goal	snow throw although shoulders
bike	i* y igh	smile bite shy why might sights	buy eyes heights
owl	ou ow	trousers round mouth blouse towel down	
boy	oi oy	coin noisy boiling toy enjoy	
ear	eer ere ear	beer engineer here we're near fear	really idea serious
chair	air are	airport stairs fair hair square careful	their there wear bear
tourist	A very unusual sound. Europe furious sure plural		
/i/	A sound between /ɪ/ and /iː/. Consonant + **y** at the end of words is pronounced /i/. happy angry thirsty		
/u/	An unusual sound. education usually situation		

Consonant sounds

voiced

unvoiced

21 parrot /ˈpærət/	22 bag /bæg/	23 key /kiː/	24 girl /gɜːl/
25 flower /ˈflaʊə/	26 vase /vɑːz/	27 tie /taɪ/	28 dog /dɒg/
29 snake /sneɪk/	30 zebra /ˈzebrə/	31 shower /ˈʃaʊə/	32 television /ˈtelɪvɪʒn/
33 thumb /θʌm/	34 mother /ˈmʌðə/	35 chess /tʃes/	36 jazz /dʒæz/
37 leg /leg/	38 right /raɪt/	39 witch /wɪtʃ/	40 yacht /jɒt/
41 monkey /ˈmʌŋki/	42 nose /nəʊz/	43 singer /ˈsɪŋə/	44 house /haʊs/

Sounds and spelling

	usual spelling		but also
parrot	p pp	promise possible copy cap opposite appearance	
bag	b bb	belt body probably job cab rabbit rubbish	
keys	c k ck	camping across skirt kind neck kick	chemist's stomach
girl	g gg	grow goat forget begin foggy bigger	
flower	f ph ff	find afraid safe elephant nephew off different	enough laugh
vase	v	video visit lovely invent over river	of
tie	t tt	try tell start late better sitting	walked dressed
dog	d dd	did dead hard told address middle	loved tired
snake	s ss ce/ci	stops faster miss message place circle	science
zebra	z s	zoo lazy freezing reason lose has toes	
shower	sh ti (+ vowel)	shut shoes wash finish patient information	sugar sure machine
television	An unusual sound. revision decision confusion usually garage		

	usual spelling		but also
thumb	th	thing throw healthy tooth maths both	
mother	th	weather the clothes sunbathe that with	
chess	ch tch t (+ure)	chicken child beach catch match picture future	
jazz	j dge	jacket just journey enjoy bridge judge	generous teenager
leg	l ll	little less plan incredible will silly	
right	r rr	really rest practice trainers borrow married	written wrong
witch	w wh	wet twins worried win why which whale	one once
yacht	y before u	yet year young yoga useful uniform	
monkey	m mm	mountain modern remember smell summer swimming	
nose	n nn	need nephew none any funny dinner	knees knock
singer	ng	tongue fingers along thing bring going	think thank
house	h	hit hate ahead perhaps hard	who whose whole

OXFORD
UNIVERSITY PRESS

Great Clarendon Street, Oxford OX2 6DP

Oxford University Press is a department of the University of Oxford. It furthers the University's objective of excellence in research, scholarship, and education by publishing worldwide in

Oxford New York

Auckland Cape Town Dar es Salaam Hong Kong Karachi Kuala Lumpur Madrid Melbourne Mexico City Nairobi New Delhi Shanghai Taipei Toronto

With offices in

Argentina Austria Brazil Chile Czech Republic France Greece Guatemala Hungary Italy Japan Poland Portugal Singapore South Korea Switzerland Thailand Turkey Ukraine Vietnam

First published 2005
2009 2008
10

ISBN-13: 978 0 19 438433 9

Printed and bound in China

ACKNOWLEDGEMENTS

Design and composition by: Stephen Strong

The authors would like to thank all the teachers and students round the world whose feedback has helped us to shape New English File. We would also like to thank: Qarie and Victoria (Mark and Allie), Dominic and Barbara for the photos of Rima and Zanzibar, Krysia for *Then he kissed me* and other ideas, all our friends round the world who told us 'what made them feel good', and Melissa for her interview. The authors would also like to thank all those at Oxford University Press (both in Oxford and around the world), and the design team.

Finally, very special thanks from Clive to Maria Angeles and Lucia, and from Christina to Cristina for all their help and encouragement. Christina would also like to thank her children Joaquin, Marco, and Krysia for their constant inspiration.

The Publisher and Authors would like to thank the following for their invaluable feedback on the materials: Beatriz Martin, Michael O'Brien, Lester Vaughan, Wendy Armstrong, Javier Santos Asensi, Tim Banks, Brian Brennan, Susanna di Gravio, Jane Hudson, Graham Rumbelow, and Krzysztof Wierzba.

The authors and publisher are grateful to those who have given permission to reproduce the following extracts and adaptations of copyright material: p.18 'A moment in time' from *Harry Benson: 50 Years in Pictures* by Harry Benson. Reproduced by permission of Harry N. Abrams, Inc. p.19 'Where are These Lovers Now?' Appeared in *Marie Claire* February 1992 © Katie Breen/Marie Claire/IPC Syndication. Reproduced by permission of IPC Syndication. p.27 'Alpine climber is rescued after SOS text to London' by Patrick Barkham, *The Times* 7 October 2003. Reproduced by permission of NI Syndication. p.39 '2020: Woman the hunter, man the house husband' by David Charter, *The Times* 25 April 1998. Reproduced by permission of NI Syndication. p.43 'Spoilt teenagers? You could just evict them' by Elizabeth Nash, *The Independent* 18 October 1999. Reproduced by permission. p.46 'Wish you weren't here' by Tim Moore, *The Sunday Times* 6 July 2003. Reproduced by permission of NI Syndication. p.51 'Hepburn's dress made peasant film star for a day' by Richard Owen, *The Times* 4 October 2002. Reproduced by permission of NI Syndication. p.63 'Kournikova of chess makes her move' by Judith O'Reilly, *The Sunday Times* 31 March 2002. Reproduced by permission of NI Syndication. p. 87 'First accident for 100-year old motorist' by Gillian Harris, *The Times* 16 October 2001. Reproduced by permission of NI Syndication. p.99 'Haile the Chief' by Paul Kimmage, *The Sunday Times* 23 February 2003. Reproduced by permission of NI Syndication. p.100 Extracts from 'This Life' by Roland White, *The Sunday Times*, 16 December 2001, 25 November 2001, 9 September 2001 and 21 November 1999. Reproduced by permission of NI Syndication. p.102 *Then he kissed me* Words and Music by Phil Spector, Ellie Greenwich and Jeff Barry© 1963 by Trio Music Co Inc, Mother Bertha Music Inc and Abkco Music Inc – All Rights Reserved – Reproduced by kind permission of Carlin Music Corp., London NW1 8BD.

Although every effort has been made to trace and contact copyright holders before publication, this has not been possible in some cases. We apologize for any apparent infringement of copyright and if notified, the publisher will be pleased to rectify any errors or omissions at the earliest opportunity.

The Publisher would like to thank the following for their kind permission to reproduce photographs and other copyright material: Action Images p.59 (Bayern Munich), Alamy pp.13 (Photofusion/David Montford), 16 (Robert Harding Picture Library/Stockholm), p.40 (Foybles/Reuters/HO/Zara), 57 (RHPL/Sylvain Grandadam/girl on phone), 58 (Image State/Lee Atherton/tennis, Aflo Foto Agency/rugby and cycling, Ace Stock Ltd/basketball, Gai Wyn Williams/ aerobics), 66 (Nicholas Pill/Travelsnaps/crocodile) 70 (Photofusion/Pete Jones), 82 (Mark Wood/biro), 85 (CuboImages srl/Enzo Signorelli/Madonnina) Allstar p.55 (Cinetext/20th Century Fox), Art Institute of Chicago/Helen Birch Bartlett Memorial Collection p.9, Associated Press pp.21 (Paul Baker/Yoko Ono), 58 (volleyball), 73 (dancing), 79 (Kevork Djansezisn/Francis Coppola), 80 (Mick Jagger), Harry Benson p.18, Mark Boudillon p.46 (Tim Moore), Bridgeman Art Library p8 (Musee Picasso, Paris), Camera Press pp.10 (David Long/Kate Moss), 21 (Tom Hanley/John & Yoko Ono), 79 (Yousuf Karsh of Ottowa/Hitchcock, Phil Wilkinson/TSPL/Tarantino), Corbis Images pp.10 (Bierce), 16 (Owen Franken/seafood, 20 (Steve Azzara/Robbie Williams, Henry Diltz/Nirvana, Sygma/Touhig Sion/Spice Girls, 51 (Reuters), 57 (M,ou Me Desjeux Bernard/Kraków), 73 (Galen Rowell/mountains), 79 (Rufus F. Folkks/Sofia Coppola), El Mundo p.43, FLPA p.151 (Mammal Fund/ Earthviews/shark), Thomas England pp.94, 95, Getty Images pp.4 (Arthur Tilly/family, Image Bank/student,) 17 (Robert Harding Picture Library), 29 (Photo Assignments/couple), 59 (John Peters/Manchester United), 66 (Getty Images (Darrell Gulin/bear), 82 (Image Bank/dishwasher and windscreen wipers), 85 (RHPL/Tony Gervis/Duomo), 99 (Allsport), 116 (Photographers Choice/Fifi, Taxi/Kenya), 151 (fly, National Georgraphic/whale), PW Henry p.63, Images of Portugal p49 (João Paulo/bridge/plastic hammers/festival), Kobal Collection pp.76 (20th Century Fox/Winona Ryder), 78 (Universal/The Birds, A Band Apart/Miramax/Andrew Cooper/Kill Bill), Dominic Latham-Koenig pp.25, 28 (woman in sunglasses), 29 (woman in scarf), Magnum p.109 and 113 (Marc Riboud/Eiffel Tower), Museo Botero p.108, 112, National Gallery p.146 (Edgar Degas/La Coiffure), NHPA p.151 (Stephen Dalton/mouse, Ernie James/chicken, Kevin Schafer/goat, Harold Palo JR/mosquito, Ernie James/horse, Daniel Zupanc/crocodile, Mike Lane/camel, John Shaw/butterfly, wasp, Andy Rouse/cow and pig, duck, Martin Harvey/kangaroo, Patrick Fagot/ bull, rabbit, Oxford University Press pp.4 (windsurfing, baby), 7, 16, 28 (man), 47, 49 (fireworks), 58 (golf, judo), 67, 90, 106 (Hemera/jacket) 108, 112, 150 (Hemera/ skirt, shirt, belt, jacket, hat, cap shorts, shoes, boots trainers), 151 (Lion, sheep, gorilla, eagle, bear, spider, elephant, tiger swan), Photonica p.6 (Lottie Davies), 46 (Steve Marsel/Eiffel Tower), 61 (Ko Fujiwara/tennis), Private Eye p.44, Popperfoto p.82 (stockings), Punchstock pp.4 (Big Cheese Photo LLC/Café, MedioImages/Engineer), 16 (snorkelling), 37, 61(Thai food), 82 (Photodisc Red/Ryan McVay/nappies, tippex, Ingram Publishing/bullet proof vest, Photodisc Green/Kim Steele/washing machine), 97 (Comstock/ food), 146 (Photodisc green/Toulouse-Lautrec), Rapho pp.19 (Willy Ronis), 109 and 113 (Leaving for Newfoundland/Willy Ronis), Reuters p.40 (Amancio Ortega), Rex Features pp.20 (Mick Jagger), 58 (baseball, skiing, swimming), 66 (bull), 76 (Rupert Grint and Dennis Bergkamp), 80 (school photo), 82 (Dyson), 151 (dolphin and bee). *Portrait of Dora Maar* 1937 is copyright Succession Picasso/DACS 2005. The painting on page 108 is *Pareja Bailando* and 112 is *Concierto Campestre* both by Fernando Botero. The painting on page 146 top is *La Coiffure* by Hilaire-Germain-Edgar Degas.

Illustrations by: Nick Baker pp.71, 116, 129, 131, 137, 140, 142; Paul Dickinson p.102; Phil Disley 30, 52, 53, 64, 65, 67, 80, 88, 89, 92, 106, 146, 147; Mark Duffin pp.48; Ellis Nadler pronunciation symbols; Gary Kaye p.42, 68, 69; Jan McCafferty pp.83, 144, 145, 150; Nigel Paige p.39; Colin Shelbourn pp.58, 106, 117, 127, 144, 148, 149, 152, 153; Stephen Strong p.9; Colin Thompson pp.5, 15, 32, 33, 41, 45, 81, 87,100, 104, 105, 134, 139; Annabel Wright pp.22, 23, 34, 54, 76, 77, 110, 114

Commissioned photography by: Mark Mason pp.12, 24, 27, 36, 48, 60, 72, 84, 96, 97 (deckchair), 106 (t-shirt) 150 (dress, top, t-shirt, sweater, suit, coat, scarf, tracksuit pyjamas, trousers, jeans, socks, tights)

Picture research and illustrations commissioned by: Cathy Blackie